MOLTING TIME FOR ANTITRUST

Molting Time for Antitrust

MARKET REALITIES, ECONOMIC FALLACIES, AND EUROPEAN INNOVATIONS

Dudley H. Chapman

Foreword by Barry E. Hawk

PRAEGER

New York
Westport, Connecticut
London

Library of Congress Cataloging-in-Publication Data

Chapman, Dudley H.
Molting time for antitrust : market realities, economic fallacies, and European innovations / Dudley H. Chapman.
p. cm.
Includes bibliographical references.
ISBN 0-275-93478-0
1. Antitrust law—United States. 2. Antitrust law—United States—Economic aspects. 3. Competition—United States. 4. Antitrust law—Europe. I. Title.
KF1649.C38 1991
343.73'0721—dc20
[347.303721] 90-45199

British Library Cataloguing in Publication Data is available.

Library of Congress Catalog Card Number: 90-45199
ISBN: 0-275-93478-0

First published in 1991

Praeger Publishers, One Madison Avenue, New York, NY 10010
An imprint of Greenwood Publishing Group, Inc.

Printed in the United States of America

The paper used in this book complies with the Permanent Paper Standard issued by the National Information Standards Organization (Z39.48-1984).

10 9 8 7 6 5 4 3 2 1

Contents

Foreword

Antitrust law and policy, both in the United States and abroad, have undergone revolutionary changes in the last decade or so. United States antitrust has moved from the strict enforcement policies and strict case law of the 1970s to the more relaxed case law and enforcement of the Reagan years. Business practices that were condemned in the 1960s and 1970s are now treated with benign neglect or even encouraged, such as in restrictions on the distribution of goods and licensing of intellectual property rights. This revolution in U.S. antitrust law and policy was occasioned by shifts in both economic and political philosophies. The prevailing approach rejects populist political goals and purports to limit antitrust analysis to price-theory microeconomic considerations with primary (if not exclusive) emphasis on efficiencies.

A counterrevolution calling for tougher antitrust enforcement is now being urged by many lawyers, economists and public officials (particularly state officials). Traditionalists argue that the emphasis on allocative efficiency is an inappropriate political judgment. A new wave of economists is challenging many of the premises underlying the prevailing approach, notably its static nature, its undue assumption of information symmetries and its underestimation of the dynamic aspects of many business practices, particularly strategic behavior.

Outside the United States, there has been since the end of World War II an exponential increase in competition, or antitrust, enforcement. Today antitrust law is more strict in many foreign jurisdictions than it is in the United States—the most noteworthy examples probably being the European Economic Community and the Federal Republic of Germany. The shift toward more market-oriented economies in Eastern Europe and in Third World countries is also encouraging the enactment of antitrust laws and the formulation of antitrust policy throughout the world.

Given this background of domestic political and economic debate and the worldwide movement toward greater reliance on competition and antitrust law, a work that argues for a radical reexamination of antitrust law and economics is particularly timely and welcome.

Barry E. Hawk

Preface

For most nonspecialists, and especially politicians, the world "antitrust" evokes an ambivalent reaction. On the one hand, the idea of a competitively organized economy remains intuitively attractive, one of the motherhood values in the U.S. political tradition. On the other hand, antitrust policy is often associated with the doctrinaire and unrealistic. Businesspeople in general exhibit this schizophrenia: No one is against competition in principle; but when confronted with conflicting realities of the marketplace and seemingly rigid and unrealistic rules and, even worse, the outlandish proposals of adventurist bureaucrats and academics, many business people come to look upon the antitrust laws as just one of the many hazards of being in business—along with fire, flood, theft, or a general depression.

Both of these impressions have a legitimate basis in fact. Among professionals involved in antitrust law and policy, it is a rare individual who cannot cite a collection of anomalies, paradoxes, and aberrations in the way that the law has been applied—or failed to be applied.

It was an accumulation of such observations over a decade of private law practice and government service that led me to the present study. It was in private practice that the occasional aberrations of the law were first observed; and three years' service on the staff of the Antitrust Division following a tour with the staff of the 1969 Cabinet Task Force on Oil Import Control made the conflicts between the conventional wisdom of antitrust and reality increasingly obvious. It was in government, too, that the unreality of economic theory and its tendency to distort policy were observed at first hand.

The study took an uncommonly long time. The idea for it occurred shortly after my leaving the Antitrust Division for the Office of the Counsel to the President in the summer of 1973. The demands of government service put off the beginning of research for almost three years, but it was the unforeseen and unimagined fruitfulness of that research that delayed completion by many times the one year initially planned. For what had been only an intuition arising from a few observed contradictions proved to have deep roots in basic historical and doctrinal misperceptions, compounded by a degree of confusion difficult to exaggerate that has been injected by the influence of economic theory. (The author wishes to acknowledge the assistance of Heinz Diehlmann for research assistance with respect to the German law, Stedman Noble for general assistance with respect to the economic theory, and Sigmund Timberg for his advice generally.)

The conventional wisdom of antitrust policy, at its core (leaving aside the nuances of policy differences between recent enforcement regimes), views antitrust as a consumer protection measure primarily through price competition, and as a policy declaration in favor of the self-regulating mechanism of unfettered competition. The contrary view advanced here is that antitrust legislation is an outgrowth of market malfunction, that it represents a political choice to prefer a competitive context as an end in itself even at the cost of higher prices and regardless of whether monopoly is more efficient, and that the objective of the law is to preserve this competitive context artificially where unfettered competition may tend to break it down.

The conventional wisdom and its flaws are the cumulative result of several distinct sources of confusion. One is a major historical misperception of what led the Standard Oil Company to its quest for monopoly, which was rooted in a demonstrated failure of petroleum markets to be self-regulating. This misperception was compounded by the historically coincidental transition of U.S. agriculture from subsistence economy to the sale of cash crops and a further experience of market malfunction; and it was further compounded by the various market malfunctions associated with the nineteenth-century railroad industry.

Wholly independent of these problems, the mandate Congress handed to the judiciary by the Sherman Antitrust Act of 1890 was fumbled by the Supreme Court in 1897 and, due allowance being made for recent trends, has never been fully recovered. This has resulted in a mechanistic structure of rules fashioned more by the need of the judiciary for clear rules of decision than by considerations of economic policy.

Yet a third, and prolific, source of confusion has been the teaching of economic theory. It is wholly incompetent and yet parades under a false guise of expertise that has led policy down one blind alley after another.

A fourth area of misunderstanding is one that if properly understood provides a source of enlightenment rather than confusion. The conventional wisdom has always viewed the new "antitrust" legislation adopted in Europe in the aftermath of World War II as a pale imitation of the more rigorous U.S. law. In reality, the European laws, which were conceived free of most of the confusions that have influenced the U.S. law, are far more rationally conceived and realistic in their objectives than their rigid U.S. counterpart.

The U.S. antitrust literature is replete with descriptions of the law—quoted from a single Supreme Court decision—as having the generality and flexibility of a constitutional provision. Ironically, the decision that gave rise to that remark has proved to be one of a kind, now regarded as an aberration rather than a precedent (*Appalachian Coals*, 288 U.S. 344 (1933); Baker 1976 ("Mecca"): 913). In fact, the U.S. law is characterized by nothing so much as wooden-headed rigidity, both in what it prohibits and in what it lacks the resourcefulness to remedy.

There is much to be said for firmness in the law, and it may be conceded that the rigidity has had some positive effects. But just as a growing crustacean molts from one hard shell to another as it matures, U.S. antitrust law by now has reached a point where it would benefit from a similar process.

From what has already been said, it should be evident that what is proposed here is not simply a tinkering with the rules but a basic rethinking and redesign of the whole structure. Yet it is a conservative and pragmatic, not a radical or theoretical, redesign. It proceeds from the proposition that the basic political instincts that motivated antitrust legislation were then, and still are, sound—however much was lost in the translation. The problem is viewed here as one of practical government policy, not in terms of any theoretically ideal system.

Such an effort involves tearing down as well as building up; and because the misconceptions are both pervasive and firmly entrenched, a major part of the effort here is addressed to the first of these tasks.

On the affirmative side, the magnitude of the effort is greatly eased by the example of postwar European "antitrust" legislation. It will be viewed here in a different light than what is customary in U.S. antitrust literature, as a model for the displacement of the anachronistic concept of "antitrust" by a modern "competition policy."

Recent events call for a word of clarification. Antitrust policy under the Reagan administration has already undergone significant changes under the influence of that especially virulent strain of economic doctrine known as the "Chicago School." That viewpoint is sharply criticized here, but that criticism should not be construed as a call for a return to the "good old days" before the idealogues came to town. This study was conceived before that turn of events occurred, on the basis that antitrust policy was already off course. The argument here is, not that we should go back, but, rather, that we should turn in an entirely different direction.

MOLTING TIME FOR ANTITRUST

1

Introduction

OF STEEL AND ANTITRUST

The steel industry of the United States at the end of World War II was unparalleled in the world. It had performed a vital and successful role in the war and it would continue to play a key role in the economy. The steel industries of Europe and Japan had been reduced to rubble.

But this seeming disaster for the European and Japanese steel industries proved a blessing in disguise. Technology had advanced since the time that the older plants had been built; and starting from scratch, the Europeans and Japanese built new plants that were so much more efficient that those that survived in the United States that this once proud giant of an industry found itself a few decades removed from the world war engaged in a life-or-death struggle for survival.

In the realm of antitrust law the picture at the end of World War II was very much like that of the steel industry. The United States had an old and established law that had become a venerated institution; Europe and Japan had nothing. The U.S. government in the postwar period was messianic in its efforts to induce both its former allies and enemies to adopt antitrust legislation of their own. They did so; and just as with their steel industries, they did not copy the old models but devised original designs of their own. The result was a legislative design more accurately attuned to the needs of the present than the antiquated U.S.

model. Like the steel industry, antitrust had a vital and continuing role to perform in the United States, but its design was basically out of date. And just as the survival of its outdated plant was the biggest obstacle to the modernization of the steel industry, so an old and prestigious, but largely obsolete tradition of antitrust stands as the greatest barrier to the design of a modern competition policy.

THE OIL CRISIS OF 1973

On October 21, 1973, the Arab oil-exporting nations declared their second embargo within seven years. The first, in 1967, had caused no serious disruptions in the United States and Western Europe because the United States had ample spare production capacity to meet the shortfall. In the years following 1967, however, oil consumption increased more rapidly than predicted to the point that by 1971 spare production capacity no longer existed. The declaration of the second Arab oil embargo was a calamity without precedent.

There was, of course, a physical shortage, manifest in the unforgettable gas lines, heating oil shortfalls in the Northeast, and farmers lacking fuel to dry their crops. Prices, and the profits of the major oil companies, went off the charts. All of this was bad enough but there was yet another dimension to the crisis that prompted government intervention. The U.S. oil industry was not monopolized; though dominated by a handful of major integrated companies, there were also numerous, exquisitely misnamed "independents" who were anything but that (Goldschmid 1974: 401). These were refining and marketing companies that had grown up in an era of crude oil surplus. Largely by reason of the U.S. tax structure, crude oil production was disproportionally far more profitable than refining and marketing. The majors were therefore content to let others handle a portion of the bothersome marketing chore, while taking their profits from crude oil production.[1] The system had the incidental effect of providing an element of competitive flux in the industry: The independents were not large enough to seriously threaten the majors, who were for the most part willing to tolerate some price undercutting by the independents without resorting to the drastic response of price wars.

The embargo threatened a swift and brutal end to this more or less benign competitive balance. The majors no longer had enough crude to supply their own refining and marketing operations, let alone sell to the not exactly beloved independents, whose cries of anguish found a receptive ear on Capitol Hill.

The first response from Congress was to ask, Where are the antitrust laws in the face of this major competitive crisis? Yet 83 years after the passage of the Sherman Antitrust Act in 1890, 62 years after the Supreme

Court–ordered breakup of the Standard Oil Company in 1911, and 59 years after the passage of the Clayton and Federal Trade Commission (FTC) Acts in 1914, the antitrust laws had no answers. While the public, the media, and the politicians decried the shortage, high prices, and threat to the independents, one major oil company gleefully ran an ad displaying the logos of 72 such companies under the headline "What a Way to Run a 'Monopoly'!" (*Saturday Review* 6/12/76: 32–33).

And so, as early as November 27, 1973, a little over a month after the embargo was declared, Congress enacted the Emergency Petroleum Allocation Act of 1973.[2] In addition to allocating the physically short supplies of petroleum, the act provided for price controls and for a system of crude oil allocation designed to guarantee the survival of the "independents." The act spelled out more explicitly than ever before the congressional sense of priorities, listing at the fourth rank "to preserve the competitive viability of independent refiners, small refiners, nonbranded independent marketers, and branded independent marketers"; relegating to the ninth level of priority "economic efficiency," and to the tenth and last, "minimization of economic distortion, inflexibility, and unnecessary interference with market mechanisms."[3]

Neither the Department of Justice nor the Federal Trade Commission (FTC) was given any formal responsibilities under this legislation, nor was there any significant coordination or interchange of personnel with the older agencies. When questioned about this seeming oversight, an official of what was then the Federal Energy Administration (FEA) replied matter-of-factly that the older agencies did not yet understand "what we're trying to do."

Just what they were trying to do was not clear. But it is understandable why the antitrust agencies did not seem a promising source of counsel. During the height of the embargo crisis, in response to the political pressures, the Antitrust Division formed a special Energy Unit, armed with economists and other specialists to investigate the crisis. The only result of this unit's activity was a criminal indictment brought in 1976 against a group of independent and offbrand sellers—the very group the 1973 legislation was enacted to protect—who consistently undersold the majors, but who, in order to do so, had exchanged price information among themselves and indulged in a bit of cajolery to keep the price cutting within limits that would not provoke retaliation by the majors.[4]

The instant regulatory regime swiftly mushroomed into a nightmare of complex, wasteful, and at times wholly counterproductive interference in the industry. To reconcile the price control objective with incentives to find new sources of oil a distinction was made between "old oil" and "new"; the resulting price disparity—$5.80 a barrel versus $13.00—was great enough to prompt the drilling of new wells in old fields. To deter this, new restrictions were imposed, and new exceptions to the restrictions: The definition of "new oil" came to be elaborated in some 19,000 words, and a new subcategory of "new" "new oil" was created. The allocation program was biased so strongly in favor of small refiners that new, inefficiently small refineries were constructed simply to capture the subsidy; and in the process, by reason of the capacity they added, they deterred the construction of more efficient refineries.[5] Thus, to the madness of useless oil wells was added the folly of useless refineries.

In West Germany also the 1973 embargo raised concerns about price gouging and the survivability of smaller companies. But there, unlike the United States, "antitrust" legislation had answers to these problems; and Germany found no need to create its version of the FEA. The same principles of German law that provided these answers applied more broadly under the antitrust laws of the European Economic Community (EEC), where, again, they were deemed a sufficient answer. No dramatic actions were taken under either the German or the EEC law (and there were some modest administrative allocations), but the fact that it existed was regarded as sufficient to make unnecessary the kind of massive and wasteful regulation that was resorted to in the United States. As one American oilman lamented, "I do not think there exists in Europe a government or department offering a price regulation manual running 225 pages or an allocation regulations manual of some 375 pages with three sets of amendments each month.[6]

The United States, for all its proud tradition of antitrust, had found no solution to this crisis either in the marketplace or in that law; so it abandoned both for a drastic, inefficient, and costly new regulatory program.

Nowhere in antitrust legislation has Congress articulated its policy priorities as explicitly as in the legislation provoked by the oil crisis of 1973. The values expressed in that legislation, nevertheless, represent a fair approximation of the legislative policies reflected in antitrust legislation dating back to 1890. That expression of policy, however, conflicts in major respects with the tenants of conventional antitrust doctrine as reflected partly in the case law, but more particularly in the enforcement policies and even more in the policy views of both the Antitrust Division and the FTC. It was not oversight that led the administrators of the emergency oil crisis program to ignore the petroleum expertise of the two antitrust agencies. The crisis management officials of 1973 understood that their objectives and those of the antitrust agencies differed fundamentally.

Just as the oil industry was succumbing to this massive new regulation, increasing momentum was developing on other fronts for reform in the older systems of regulation, calling in some cases for their complete removal, a process that is still continuing. Yet the experience of the oil industry poses a substantial question about the adequacy of antitrust and the marketplace as an alternative to regulation. And if that question cannot be answered satisfactorily, one of the major premises of the argument for deregulation may be seriously undermined. There is merit to the arguments for deregulation as an alternative to the plainly inefficient former regulatory systems, but it does not follow that removal of the regulation in reliance on existing antitrust laws is an adequate alternative in industries that have a history of unsatisfactory competitive performance. If the experience with regulation has been unsatisfactory, and the policy preference is to rely on the antitrust laws, which have also proven inadequate, there is some point to improving the capacity of the antitrust laws to respond to such problems.

RECURRING QUESTIONS AND OPEN SECRETS

That antitrust policy ought to be rethought in depth has been a recurring theme in U.S. politics. The first such outbreak led to the Clayton and FTC Acts of 1914. Both represented a substantial conceptual departure from the Sherman Act, but for reasons that we shall examine further on, the shift was indecisive and never "took."

The questions again surfaced in the 1930s, culminating in President Franklin Roosevelt's formation of the Temporary National Economic Committee (TNEC), which took the testimony of 552 witnesses that filled 37 volumes and produced another 43 volumes of staff studies (Gressley 1977: 42, 48). The project, however, encountered two unforeseen complications. The first was the appointment of Thurman Arnold to head the Antitrust Division, just six months after Roosevelt's call for the study (ibid., 40, 43). Arnold was a vigorous prosecutor who thought that serious enforcement, not changes in the law, was what was needed; and he proceeded to do just that, taking no real interest in the study group (ibid., 48). The second complication was the outbreak of World War II, for this new emergency altered the administration's priorities. The TNEC report produced only an anticlimatic recommendation for vigorous enforcement of the existing antitrust laws (ibid.).

With the return to a peacetime economy, the questions surfaced again, under President Eisenhower, and resulted in the 1955 *Report of the Attorney General's National Committee to Study the Antitrust Laws*. The project was undertaken in response to Congressional pressure, but the Antitrust Division took control and the result was a treatise on the law that avoided troublesome questions about its basic purposes. This led Louis B. Schwartz "and some other members" to feel that this "narrow view of its function prevented the committee from giving any direct answer to the one question that warranted bringing the committee into existence, namely are the antitrust laws serving the purpose for which they were passed, and if not, what should be done about it?" (*Report* 1955: 4–5).

Passing some more recent studies that went nowhere—The Neal Report (Goldschmid 1974: 393–400) and the Ash Report (Nader et al. 1972: 425–426)—a recent former head of the Antitrust Division, Prof. Thomas E. Kauper, published a thoughtful article filled with probing questions about the existing governmental architecture of antitrust policy (Kauper 1978).

In addition to these public expressions of discontent, there are some major demonstrable flaws in the fabric of U.S. antitrust policy that no one talks about, what may be termed the "open secrets" of antitrust: open, because they are ascertainable from wholly public sources; but secret, because they remain unknown even to most specialists in the area. The three most prominent are (1) the actual, untold motive for the Standard Oil Company's drive for monopoly, which was rooted in market failures; (2) the Supreme Court's mishandling of the Sherman Act from the very beginning; and (3) the scandalous incompetence of academic economic theory that has come to dominate present-day antitrust policy.

ANTITRUST IN RETROSPECT

U.S. antitrust policy is not based on any single, coherent objective or rationale. There are two reasons for this. One is the diversity of its sources; the other stems from ideological confusions about competitive markets and the realities that provoked antitrust legislation.

The diverse sources include the policy's origins in the English common law, the Sherman Act of 1890 based on that common law, the legislation of 1914—the Clayton and FTC Acts—which recognized some tendencies for free competition to break down, the judicial gloss put on the legislation, which has taken on a life of its own, and most recently, the intrusion of economic theory that has come to dominate enforcement policy. This diversity of origins brings with it ideological conflicts between its legislative, judicial, bureaucratic, and academic authors.

The confluence of these diverse sources and conflicts has resulted in three distinct rationales for antitrust policy: (1) that it is a moral issue involving behavioral wrongdoing. This is reflected in the criminal penalties of the Sherman Act and the prosecutorial zeal of the Antitrust Division of the Department of Justice that sees its mission as putting "bad guys" in jail; (2) that antitrust is a consumer welfare measure. This viewpoint stems from two distinct, unrelated sources, though their ultimate conclusion is essentially the same. One is the perception of judges and legislators reacting against trade restrictions that in addition to the harm to the business interest, consumers are also disadvantaged. The second is a theoretical conception of economists thinking in terms of an idealistically efficient system, which benefits consumers through unfettered price competition. This second rationale may thus be characterized as the consumer welfare/efficiency theory. (3) Finally there is what may be characterized as the "game theory" rationale. The objective is to keep the game going, through governmental intervention, to preserve a competitive context as an end in itself—and this regardless of wrongdoing and even at some possible cost to consumers. This perspective is reflected in the Clayton and FTC Acts of 1914 and in the Sherman Act ban on monopolization.

On different occasions the courts have embraced all three of these rationales, though in recent years there has been an increasing tendency to emphasize the second, consumer welfare/efficiency. The prevailing tendencies in the law, however, have been significantly influenced by two institutional factors: the nature of the judicial process and the institutional separation of the Federal Trade Commission and the Department of Justice.

The judiciary's function is to decide cases, not make economic policy. The Sherman Act, however, carries a substantial economic policy content with wide latitude for judicial discretion. With notable exceptions, the Supreme Court has not welcomed this latitude, preferring clear rules that facilitate decision making. The Sherman Act did not provide such, so the Court proceeded to invent its own, in the form of per se rules. The Court's enthusiasm for this approach lasted for 50 years, from 1927 to 1977, when the Court itself acknowledged that it had been carried too far. Since then the policy vacuum has only worsened.

The second institutional factor is the separation of the Federal Trade Commission and the Department of Justice. The Justice Department's focus is primarily on the Sherman Act and only partly on the legislation of 1914. Because the Sherman Act contains no substantive rules that intervene in the conduct of business such as the Clayton Act's rules on price discrimination and tying agreements, it is logically consistent with the idea of faith in self-regulating free markets, and this is the way the Justice Department has always viewed it. Because of this the Division is institutionally justified in viewing the world though the limited perspective of the Sherman Act, unqualified by the market failure perceptions of the 1914 legislation.

Unlike the Sherman Act, both of the 1914 acts were permeated with perceptions of how various types of business practices could tend to break down the competitive process. This cannot be interpreted as a declaration of faith in self-regulating free markets.

The importance of this limited Sherman Act perspective of the Justice Department is enhanced by another institutional accident. The Justice Department is an integral part of the executive branch, with policy making vested in a single individual, the attorney general, advised by the chief of the Antitrust Division. The FTC is both outside the executive branch and a collegial body, which tends to dilute and limit its role in articulating antitrust policy.

The Antitrust Division has an expertise regarding questions of competitive policy on a broad range of issues that extend beyond its basic law enforcement role. Its role as spokesperson on such issues within the executive branch in this broader sense has long been recognized. The fact that it does so from a viewpoint conditioned by the tunnel vision of the Sherman Act has had a significant impact on policy.

Viewing these somewhat conflicting historical, conceptual, and institutional components of a century-old antitrust policy, it is a reasonable speculation that if the whole issue were to be rethought anew, a different design would emerge. Exactly that has happened, but not in the United States. Western Europe, which prior to World War II had no meaningful equivalent to the U.S. antitrust laws, was moved, largely at the urging of the U.S. government, to adopt such legislation. They did so, but drew some conclusions that political habit and inertia have thus far made impossible in the United States. Just as antitrust policy in the United States is deteriorating from its own inherent contradictions, the European policies are in a state of vibrant health.

A CONTRETEMPS ABROAD

The European laws were adopted both nationally and through the supranational institutions of the European Community. Although modeled in part on the U.S. law and experience, they were differently conceived and differently structured. The leading national systems are those of West Germany and Great Britain. The supranational rules of the EEC are of the greatest practical importance, but for purposes of this study, which looks to these laws as a source of alternative concepts, the national laws are equally useful.

The three principal differences between the European and U.S. approaches to antitrust are (1) the European perception that the problem is one of economic policy, not morality, reflected in a greater reliance on administrative agencies and a flexibility to make exceptions; (2) recognition that concentrations of private economic power are inevitable, and that the appropriate governmental response in most cases is not to break them up but to set limits to what they do with their power; and (3) that the problems reflect a diversity of flaws in market systems spanning the full range of government economic policy issues that in many cases require resolution at the highest levels of government.

PERSPECTIVE

Perspective is an important ingredient of antitrust policy. The judicial, the bureaucratic, and the economic theory perspectives are not viewed favorably here; the political perspective is treated more kindly. Politicians, though much disparaged, are practitioners of an art that requires great insight. They need technical help, which is what they seek from their professional staffs, and it is from that perspective that the present study is offered.

NOTES

1. Sherrill 1983: 169–71; "The Oil Majors Retreat from the Gas Pump," *Business Week* 8/7/78: 50; "Crude-poor Ashland: Prototype of the Future," ibid. 1/31/77: 98.
2. PL 93–159; 87 STAT. 627, 15 U.S.C.A. Secs. 751–56 (1973).
3. ibid., Sec. 4, 15 U.S.C.A. Sec. 753.
4. *United States v. Society of Independent Gasoline Marketers of America*, 624 F. 2d 461 (4th Cir. 1980), *cert. denied*; *Kayo Oil Co. v. U.S.*, 449 U.S. 1078; *Amerada Hess Corp. v. U.S.* (1981). Following a trial resulting in conviction, appeal, and a remand, the case was dismissed.
5. See, e.g., Copp, E. Anthony 1976: 72–73, 94–101; "Entitlements Trigger More Controversy," *Oil and Gas Journal* 6/2/75: 50; "Big Oil Howls That Rule 6 Is Catch 22," *Business Week* 4/19/76: 37; "How Little Oil Hit a Gusher on Capitol Hill," *Fortune* 8/14/78: 148; "Old Oil in a New Wonderland," *Forbes* 12/11/78: 80; "Major Oil Firms Decry Subsidies They Provide to Smaller Refineries," *Wall Street Journal* 1/30/80: 1; "Day of Reckoning for Oil Refiners," *Fortune* 1/12/81: 38; "Teakettle Refiners Scramble to Survive," *Fortune* 7/13/81: 47.
6. *Oil and Gas Journal* 12/8/75: 27.

2

Origins of the Sherman Act

THE POST-MEDIEVAL ECONOMY

> The day of combination is here to stay. Individualism has gone, never to return.
>
> John D. Rockefeller (Nevins 1953: vol. 1: 402)

The Transition

There is a sense in which the nineteenth century succeeded the eighteenth century as the Dark Ages did those of Greece and Rome: The ancients made rich contributions in the realms of philosophy and culture, while the medieval period yielded little of the fruits of the mind as people turned their attention to the provision of physical needs and built roads, bridges, towns, and other essential infrastructure. The eighteenth century, like the classical age, was a culmination of intellectual achievement; and it found a practical application in the architecture of government. It was the age of Voltaire, Montesquieu, and Rousseau on the Continent, of Hume, Locke, and Adam Smith in Britain; while in North America an assemblage of formerly colonial aristocrats, knowledgeable in the history of ancient governments and the leading edge of political philosophy, fashioned a new form of federal government that in time would span a continent.

The accomplishments of the nineteenth century, in contrast, were not of a philosophical or cultural sort. That century, like medieval times, saw a turning away from the pursuits of the mind to the physical provision of economic needs. Like the medieval period, the nineteenth century was a time of building the infrastructure of transportation, cities, and other economic units that formed a base for the prosperity of later times. With a few notable exceptions, the political giants of the eighteenth century—Jefferson, Hamilton, Madison, Jay, and many others—were succeeded in the nineteenth by a long line of political mediocrities; and the dynamic names of the period were the unlettered leaders of the business world—Rockefeller, Morgan, Carnegie, Vanderbilt, Harriman, and Hill. The course of events had taken a dramatic turn, and a different kind of talent emerged to exploit new opportunities and challenges in the economic sphere.

The images of the nineteenth century were those of iron and steel, of railroads, coal, and steam; of gushing crude oil surging from the hills of Pennsylvania and hauled in wooden barrels by mule-driven carts over muddy roads; of the factory housing a progeny of strange-looking machines that transformed the manufacturing process; of a polyglot wave of immigrants that manned factories, populated cities, and bought the prairie farms that financed the building of the transcontinental railroads; of a cascade of seemingly miraculous inventions from the steam engine to refrigeration and electricity, the telegraph and telephone, and the internal combustion engine; of grotesque machines of all descriptions emerging from an orgy of invention that brought vaulting leaps of productivity and the amassing of titanic fortunes, and climaxed by a legal, institutional innovation that was to organize and control this burgeoning enterprise and give a symbol to the age—the giant corporation.

The period was one of explosive growth and change in the economic system. It was at the same time a demonstration of the enormous productive and innovative force of free enterprise, and of the enormous vulnerability of that system to disruption, interruption, and breakdown. It was a system capable of remarkable self-regulation, but not consistently or reliably so. On numerous and substantial occasions the market mechanism strained, and in some it broke, posing troublesome questions for government policy.

So dramatic were the developments of the nineteenth century that there is a temptation to believe that this was the decisive turning point, with the emergence of the Industrial Revolution. Yet significant though the events of the nineteenth century were, there was another fundamental transition period that occurred much earlier that was to have continuing and expanded effects in the context of an industrial economy. It was the transition from a medieval subsistence economy to a market economy based on exchange. Subsistence economy is the production of goods needed for consumption by the producers themselves. In an exchange economy, goods are produced to be traded for other goods or for cash, which means that the producers cannot rely on their own efforts alone but are dependent on the willingness of others to trade. The critical factor is thus the ability to create exchangeable value. In such a context economic activity takes place, not just because of a need for particular goods or services, but as an end in itself, to sustain the process of exchange.

The transition from a subsistence to an exchange economy in England took place over about 150 years in the fifteenth and sixteenth centuries, through what is known to history as the "enclosure movement." The main purpose was to convert the use of the land from the tillage of crops to sheep farming, but it was also done to improve the efficiency of crop tillage (Tawney 1912, 1967). This had two dramatic effects that worked a fundamental change in the nature of the economic system. First, it vastly improved agricultural productivity, converting the essence of farming from subsistence to the production of commodities to be sold for cash. Second, it forced large numbers of workers off the land, as the restructured farming sector needed far less human labor than before. There was, however, no readily available alternative employment, resulting in the creation of a whole new class of "beggars and thieves" (Polanyi, 1944, 1957: 35–39; Tawney 1912, 1967; R. Robertson 1973: 25–26). This was a social problem of major proportions. Thus, long before the nineteenth century, in the formative stage of a market system, its vulnerability to breakdown was made painfully evident. Over time, human ingenuity devised new forms of economic activity that gave employment to the surplus population, but the process was not immediate or automatic. During this fledgling period in the transition to a market economy, the creation and preservation of employment opportunities was a prime social concern and gave rise to various forms of government intervention. One of them was by the courts, which were extremely sensitive to any arbitrary obstructions, whether private or governmental, to employment or business opportunity. The common law principles against monopolies and restraints of trade, which are the precursors of U.S. antitrust law, had their origins in this period of English economic history.

In the United States in the nineteenth century, as the farming population moved west and cultivated the vastly more productive lands of the middle-west, the resulting downtrend in the farm population was more than offset by the exploding industrial revolution, and labor was actually imported. The United States was thus spared the painful transition that occurred in England; but the fundamental change in the nature of economic activity was the same, irreversible and accelerating. The primary economic problem was no longer to produce for oneself what one needed to consume, but to produce something that one could induce others to trade for. In short, the postmedieval economy brought about a radical change in the nature of economic activity that was increasingly dependent on sustaining an ongoing system of exchange. it also meant that economic activity would become increasingly artificial and game-like.

The World of Adam Smith

> [W]e must view Adam Smith in relation to an age in which factories were tiny, the machine was still hardly more than a machine tool, the competitive system was young and struggling against eighteenth-century mercantilism and survivals of medieval restrictions which had outlived their function.
>
> J. M. Clark et al. (1926, 1966: 54)

Adam Smith (1723–1790) lived and wrote during a watershed period of economic history. The feudal economic system had gradually yielded to the eroding force of an evolving commerce in the towns(Polanyi 1944: 35–39; Tawney 1912, 1967: Pt. II, Chaps. 1, 2). These emerging markets were small, and in the still predominantly feudal context, tended toward tight control mechanisms, the guilds. This form of commercial organization survived in Smith's day as local "corporations" (Smith 1776, 1976: vol. I, Bk. I, Chap. 10, Pt. II; 140–41).

Smith was disdainful of these encumbrances, which led him to pen the single, most widely quoted aphorism in the lore of antitrust: "People of the same trade seldom meet together, even for merriment and diversion, but the conversation ends in a conspiracy against the public, or in some contrivance to raise prices" (ibid., 144). There is, however, some irony in this, for Smith followed it with a sentence dismissing the idea of outlawing such behavior: "It is impossible indeed to prevent such meetings by any law which either would be executed, or would be consistent with liberty and justice" (ibid.). Smith was, moreover, caustically critical of the antecedents of modern antitrust legislation, dismissing the statutes against engrossing and forestalling as belonging to the same class of futility as those against witchcraft (ibid., vol. II, Bk. IV, Chap. 5: 41; Dewey 1964: 416).

He saw two natural deterrents to such behavior in numerous, rather than few, producers and in geographical dispersion, both of which were common in eighteenth-century England (vol. I, Bk. I, Chap. 10, Pt. II, 140–41, fns omitted).

Smith was not much concerned about private cartels or monopolies, which he regarded as tending to self-destruct from their own inefficiencies (ibid., vol. I, Bk. I, Chap. XI, Pt. I: 165; vol. II, Bk. IV, Chap. 7, Pt. III: 112–113). He was very much concerned about monopolies conferred by the government—particularly the East India Company—not just for monopoly pricing, but for all of their inefficient performance; and his primary objection was to their exercise of powers that properly belonged to government, which he viewed these private companies as being wholly unfit to discharge (ibid., vol. II, Bk. IV, Chap. 7, Pt. III: 154–58).

The prevailing mercantilism of Smith's time led him to criticize meddlesome government restrictions and thus to appear more an advocate of laissez-faire than a closer study of his work reveals, which cites numerous exceptions to "the doctrine of natural harmony in the economic order" (Viner, 1926, 1966: 134–36; Wilson & Skinner 1976: 70).

Although Smith's world was still predominantly agricultural, the industry of his time had developed to the point where the principles of division of labor,finance, and the workings of market mechanisms could be observed, epitomized by his classic metaphor of the "invisible hand" whereby individuals, in pursuit of their own self-interest, were led to behave in ways that made markets self-regulating. There were, however, some notable omissions from the economic system that he portrayed, not because he overlooked them, but because they had yet to emerge as significant factors. Most conspicuous was the role of the corporation. The economy of Smith's day was still the world of the individual proprietor. The predecessor in his day of what is now the corporation—the joint stock company—did not impress Smith favorably and he saw very little future in it. All of the stresses and fluctuations of business he saw as requiring "an unremitting exertion of vigilance and attention, as cannot be expected from the directors of a joint stock company . . . the superior vigilance and attention of private adventurers would, in all probability, soon make them weary of the trade" (Smith 1776: vol. II, Bk. V, Chap. 1: 278). Absent a grant of monopoly or some like privilege, the only use he saw for such companies were those trades "of which all the operations are capable of being reduced to what is called a routine, or to such a uniformity of method as admits of little or no variation," citing as examples banking, insurance, canal building, and the supply of water to a great city (ibid., 279).

The last two of his examples are revealing: They do not foresee the prominent role of large, long-term fixed capital investment. Smith was sensitive to the role of capital, but he thought of it in the sense of working capital, the money a farmer spends for seed, labor, and fertilizer, or an artisan for raw materials and rent, which are returned each time a unit of production is sold. The large and long-term capital commitments that characterized nineteenth-century industry were not part of his world of the eighteenth century.

The American Scene

Colonial North America, though it had no medieval tradition, was committed almost entirely to subsistence agriculture throughout that period (Cochran & Miller 1961: 3; Hofstadter 1955: 36; *Ency. Am. Econ. Hist.* 1980: vol. II: 663). Not all the farming was of the subsistence variety; tobacco, rice, and indigo, for example, were sold for cash even in colonial times (Cochran & Miller 1961: 211). But the dominant figure of the time was the individual, "yeoman" farmer, self-sufficient, with a penchant for improvisation and a tradition of household industry (Hofstadter 1955: 36). There was, of course, some commerce in the many small towns and villages where, because of their smallness and isolation, the merchants typically enjoyed a local monopoly. This kind of monopoly was not regarded as a serious problem, the potential for abuse being checked by the closeness, customs, and mutual interdependence of these small communities, as well as the versatility of the frontier people who could serve themselves if prices became unreasonable (Stocking & Watkins 1951: 16).

The Explosion of Innovation

Innovation: progressiveness, new combinations, creative destruction, the setting up of a new production function—the idea has many labels, but the central concept is the same. The concept is much broader than its most obvious component, invention, including all changes in technique or novel undertakings that reduce costs or produce added value, a net increase in wealth. It may do this by producing the same product or service at less cost, by producing more for the same cost; or it may even increase expenditures, tapping previously idle resources to create new wealth.

Innovation also has the potential to generate exponential as well as arithmetic growth. Adam Smith's famous pin factory increased the production per worker through the division of labor from less than 20 pins a day to an average of 4,800. Today, an English worker, with the benefit of modern machinery, produces 800,000 pins a day (Pratten 1980: 93–96).

Smith was alert to the value of invention, citing as one of the advantages of a division of labor that it tended to stimulate invention. But innovation in Smith's time was still slow, and he subsumed it as an incidental benefit of the division of labor, unaware of how dramatically the relative importance of these two factors would be changed if not reversed by the end of the nineteenth century.

It was Joseph Schumpeter who first identified the importance of innovation as a dominant force in the economic system. He distinguished five different forms of innovation, or, as he termed it, "new combinations": (1) the creation of a new product, or a new quality for an existing product; (2) new methods of production and merchandizing; (3) the opening of new markets; (4) the securing of a new source of raw materials or semifinished products; and (5) organizational change, such as the corporation and the trusts of the nineteenth century. He also distinguished invention as part, but not in itself sufficient, to effectuate an innovation. The invention must be applied to take effect, which is the function of the entrepreneur (Schumpeter 1934, 1973: 66).

The vast transformation commonly termed the Industrial Revolution is dated by historians roughly from 1760 to 1830 in England and from the Civil War to 1890 in the United States. But the term—indeed the concept—is too narrow. Not only industry came into being during that century: Agriculture made great strides in productivity, reflecting scientific as well as industrial advances; and epochal progress was made in science, medicine, education, and in services generally, all developing alongside the machinery and physical plant that are associated with industrialization. The totality might better be termed the "Innovative Revolution."

The Corporation

One of the most obvious and pervasive changes in the nineteenth-century economy was the resort to large concentrations of capital investment, in contrast to the handicraft and light manufactures of earlier times. This required the collection of funds from large numbers of individuals and centralization of control over these funds in a single management. The first major need of this kind was generated by the construction of the railroads, and it was the early railroad corporations that introduced public trading of stocks and bonds and led to public disclosure of corporate finances. It was a development of profound importance for the rapidly transforming economy.

The private business corporation, which has now become a commonplace, was regarded very differently by Americans of the early nineteenth century. The need to raise large sums of capital requiring the resources of many people was rare before the nineteenth century, and in those cases where the need did arise—for public works projects such as canals and turnpikes, or for high-risk foreign trading operations—the nature of the venture embodied a plausible rationale for monopoly. Canals, turnpikes, and water systems do not admit of duplication, and the high risks of foreign trading ventures afforded a rationale for exclusivity.

This pattern was enlarged upon in colonial America, where a community spirit engendered by the need to build a new economy from scratch led to extensive government-business collaboration. This extended even into manufacturing, and it was common for the grant of a corporate franchise to be accompanied by a grant of monopoly. This became a normal way of doing business. The monopolies came to be resented, not so much for abuses as for the unevenness with which these special privileges were conferred. It was in this climate that the grant of a corporate franchise became linked in the public mind with the ideas of special privilege and monopoly.

Yet there was another and distinct motive for the early cautiousness toward the grant of the corporate privilege. It was the insight that impersonal institutions—like the medieval church—take on a life of their own that tends to exceed the natural limits of individuals. The attitude toward corporations in the early nineteenth century has been compared to contemporary fears of the computer; both have been described as soulless (Friedman, Lawrence 1973: 171–72). As a contemporary put it:

> All experience has shown that large accumulations of property in hands likely to keep it intact for a long period are dangerous to the public weal. Having perpetual succession, any kind of a corporation has peculiar facilities for such accumulations and most governments have found it necessary to exercise great caution in their grants of corporate powers. Even religious corporations . . . have proven obnoxious to this objection, so that in England it was long ago found necessary to restrict them in their powers of acquiring real estate. Freed as such parties are from the sure bound to the schemes of individuals, the grave, they are able to add field to field and power to power until they become entirely too strong for that society, which is made up of those whose plans are limited by a single life. (Ripley 1916: 472, quoting from 40 Ga. 582 [1869])

In 1802 the attorney general of Massachusetts warned that "the creation of a great variety of corporate interests . . . must have a direct tendency to weaken the power of government (Friedman, Lawrence 1973: 172, fns omitted).

This cautious attitude toward granting what was thought of as special privilege led to constitutional restrictions in some states requiring that incorporation be only by special action of the legislature. This had exactly the opposite of the intended effect, as lobbying to obtain charters proved this restraint a magnet to, rather than a shield against, corruption. Eventually, the sheer weight of numbers overwhelmed the individual approval process, which was made routine through passage of general acts (ibid.).

One lingering feature of the restrictive policy toward incorporation was to play a large symbolic role that may well have contributed to confusion in public policy. Because under the early corporation laws one corporation could not own the stock of another, the common law trust, a means of separating the power of control from beneficial ownership, was adopted to accomplish in fact what the law ostensibly denied in form. It served to centralize control over two or more separate corporate entities. But the law itself was changed to permit corporations to own the stock of other corporations, beginning with a change in New Jersey's law in 1889. Thus the trust was displaced by what have since become routine corporate holding companies. The brief epoch of the trust, however, lent an anachronistic and undescriptive label to the law that concerns competition in private business.

Together, the trusts and the holding corporation provided a vehicle with the potential to expand control indefinitely. When the dominant business form was the sole proprietorship, there were very practical limits on the geographic scope and volume of business that could be controlled by a single firm. The corporation, however, was infinitely expandable, capable of absorbing any number of businesses and exercising a unified control over all. This new way of doing business thus threatened to undermine the factors relied upon by Adam Smith to overcome the tendency toward collaboration among competitors—large numbers and dispersal.

Differing Markets of Agriculture, Industry, and Labor

Another basic change affecting the workability of the self-regulating market during the nineteenth century was the emergence of some very basic differences between the markets of agriculture, industry, and labor. The labor market failed because of the gross disparity in bargaining power between employer and employee. The differences between agriculture and industry are at once more subtle and more interesting in their implications for the functioning of the self-regulating market.

The most basic difference between agricultural and industrial markets is the ability of industry, and the inability of agriculture, to adjust production in the short run to the level of demand. A steel company can expand or contract production as demand increases or diminishes, producing in response to specific orders. The farmer has no such option. He plants in the spring for an entire season and takes his chances on the weather, pestilence, and the bounty of other farmers. Nor can he, like a manufacturer, reduce pressure on prices in a falling market by reducing production. Because each farmer has too small a portion of the market to affect it by his own action, he gains nothing by cutting back. Since each farmer reasons the same way, the cumulative effect is to maintain production, thereby further lowering prices. There is here no invisible hand guiding each individual, in the pursuit of his own profit, to do what is best for all. It became a common lament of the farmer that he sold in a competitive market and bought in a protected one, as manufacturers gained tariff protection shortly after the War of 1812 (Faulkner 1960: 210–309).

The situation grew worse throughout the nineteenth century. Agriculture was an icon of American political life, the quintessence of Jeffersonian values. This attitude had emerged during the long colonial period when most farming was for subsistence or produced cash crops for a ready market in North America or a protected one in England. As the settlement of the West progressed, and agriculture shifted rapidly to the production of cash crops (Mayhew 1972), the capacity of the market to absorb the ever-increasing bounty of the farm became increasingly pressed, at times overwhelmed; and still the government continued to encourage settlement. The farm sector became overexpanded, but overproduction did not result in cutback. The farmers remained in place and suffered or prospered according to the accidents of weather and foreign wars (Hobsbawm 1975: 138, 175–77).

Not all agricultural markets were the same: Dairy products and other perishable commodities serve local markets in which some adjustment of supply to demand is feasible, and the cost of feeding livestock imposes limits to the volume of profitable production, but grain markets are characterized both by the minor incremental cost of producing additional units and by international markets which makes impossible any adjustment of supply to demand by farmers alone (ibid., 138, 175–77).

On the industrial side, too, there were differences between markets: The railroads were something of a special case with their heavy fixed investment and extensive overbuilding, their mixture of monopoly here and cutthroat competition there, though other heavy industry mirrored at least some of the railroads' problems (Ripley 1916: xiv). The railroads, in fact, were faced with a problem analogous to that of agriculture—long-term fixed capital put them, like the farmer, in the position of being unable to adjust their supply commitment according to fluctuations in demand.

Instability and Combination

As the economy became industrialized, it became increasingly clear that there was some kind of rhythm to the expansion and contraction of industrial production that introduced a new form of economic hazard. Early panics in 1817–1822, 1828–1829, and 1837 were followed after the Civil War by recurring downturns of increasing severity: 1872, 1884, and 1893 were the worst years, but that of 1873 brought on a long depression that lasted until 1879 and was unmatched in severity until the Great Depression of the 1930s. One writer has characterized the entire period from 1873 to 1897 as 25 years of which 14 "were viewed by contemporaries as times of recession or depression" (Heilbroner 1977: 106).

The problem was seen as rooted in the very productivity of the new age of machine production, which tended to "outstrip the absorptive ability of the markets" (Diamond 1963: 11). In its early stages, the rise of machine-based industrial mass production only reinforced faith in the competitive system. Manufactured goods were a new source of competition for handicraft industry, which still survived, and the opening up of new markets by rail and canal expanded opportunities for everyone (Stocking & Watkins 1951: 19–20). But mass production gradually drove out most handicraft production; and thus the growing use of machine production, which lay at the heart of the explosion of productivity, also contained the seeds of instability. The necessary operation of the expensive plant at near capacity levels tended to saturate markets and drive prices down. Yet every glimmer of new markets attracted a frenzy of expansion, resulting in overexpansion and idle plant and equipment (Diamond 1963: 9–10).

The very conditions that attract capital investment thus tend to attract too much; production expands beyond the needs of the market, and competition intensifies as each producer tries to sell his maximum output. So even in the industrial sector, which has more capacity to adjust to short-run market fluctuations than agriculture, it was not enough to avert substantial instability, and the reflexive response was combination (Cochran & Miller 1961: 60–61).

The Specter of Monopoly

The railroad was a symbol of the age. Its physical presence was both impressive and pervasive. It was in many places a monopoly—a grudging, surly, arrogant monopoly. The attitude of railroad clerks toward shippers and the traveling public seethed with indifference and hostility (Adams 1875: 394, 399–401). The railroad was also a creator of other monopolies, as through its discriminations it selected which of its customers were to survive and which to perish. Those who dealt with the railroad where it was a monopoly got a vivid and bitter taste of that kind of system.

As instability and competitive pressures were leading to increasing "combinations" throughout industry, there emerged the "Great Anaconda," the Standard Oil Company. Huge concentrations of capital, and a general belief in ever-increasing economies of scale, contributed to an impression of growing concentration and centralization in business. Many believed this a good thing, a natural and inevitable tendency. Rockefeller and Morgan were among them. It was an age in which monopoly had become palpable, aggressive, threatening, hated, and feared (Dudden 1950; 1957).

An Economy of Games

The word "game" is used here in its colloquial sense, not that of abstract mathematical game theory (Von Neuman & Morgenstern 1953; Samuelson, in Stiglitz (ed.), 1966: vol. 3: 136 n. 7). The essential characteristics of a game are that it channels behavior according to artificially structured rules; that both its progress and its outcome are influenced by both the structure of the rules and random conditions and circumstances in which it is played; and that the behavior is unnecessary, but pursued as an end in itself. The game concept stands in contrast to the traditional conception of economic activity as serious business needed for survival. Yet ever since the enclosure movement in England improved the productivity of agriculture to the point where a significant part of the population became surplus, it has been necessary for that surplus population to generate products and services having exchangeable value. This involves both ingenuity and a contrived element of scarcity in what is offered, so that it will, in fact, have value in exchange.

The result has been an increasingly complex system in which access by most of the population to necessaries—however defined—is dependent on an intricate system of exchange including the most dispensable of luxuries. And this has been so for a long time. As early as the seventeenth century a Frenchman with the unassuming name of Pierre le Pesant de Boisquillebert observed that this progress from a few simple professions to hundreds in the pursuit of "opulence and excess . . . creates a perilous situation . . . that which has been instituted to allow the enjoyment of the surplus only, acts, when the measures have been misconceived, to deprive of necessities" (Routh 1977: 59). Our economic system is thus highly dependent on artificial, game-like activity.

Another respect in which economic behavior has become increasingly game-like is the motive for gain—identified by the same writer who saw the significance of the enclosure movement, Karl Polanyi (Polanyi 1944: 54). This factor is running riot in modern business, where the amassing of wealth as an end in itself, wholly unrelated to any need for goods or services, is consciously pursued as a competitive game.

Economic activity is also game-like in its mind-boggling diversity. The rules, the skills required, and the competitive conditions of a professional football game, a chess match, and a Sumo wrestling encounter are worlds apart, and economic activity is just as diverse. Every line of business, profession, and employment is a separate and distinct game; and the rules—not just the legal constraints, but all the economic parameters—vary widely, and in kind, from one game to another.

Not the least of the random elements that affect the game of business is the role of government. Government has throughout history injected various nonmarket influences that affect economic behavior. In many cases this is a deliberate response to some perceived malfunction. It has been a common historical experience that the shift from a subsistence to a trading economy has generated maladjustments that prompted government intervention, either by reason of economic or purely humanitarian concerns (Polanyi 1944, 1977: 38–39). In other cases, government distorts market processes through unintended effects of actions taken for other purposes, such as taxes or national defense. Economic activity, therefore, often reflects not just the natural play of economic forces but also intentional, arbitrary, and random effects of what might be termed "the governmental wild card."

The analogy to games suggests another dimension of insight into the nature of modern economic activity. Professional league sports, where economic and game activity literally come together, require continuity and a measure of balance to perform their basic entertainment function. These objectives are sometimes furthered by adjustments of the rules, as through player drafts that favor the less successful teams and disfavor the more successful. There is an obvious parallel here to the antitrust laws and business, about which more, much more, will be said later.

To a large degree the rules of the game in business are a natural test of economic performance. But in the increasingly complex economy that evolved in the nineteenth century, a growing proportion of the rules involved random elements: a bounteous foreign harvest depressing farm prices, the vagaries of the business cycle, and arbitrary or discretionary decisions such as private combination and the governmental wild card. The results of the game were thus subject in decreasing proportion to "natural" economic forces and, increasingly, to random events and arbitrary or discretionary decisions, both private and governmental.

As the nineteenth century drew to a close the game was breaking down at points, and it drew the first congressional response: First the railroads in 1887, and then more broadly, with the Sherman Antitrust Act of 1890, while yet a decade remained of the turbulent nineteenth century.

PROLOGUE: THE RAILROAD PROBLEM

> In the absence of national legislation, the railroads have naturally resorted to the only methods by which they could unaided secure any degree of stability and uniformity in their charges—consolidation and confederation. The final outcome of continued consolidations would be the creation of an organization more powerful than the government and perhaps beyond its control.
>
> *Cullom Report* 1886 (B. Schwartz 1973: vol. 1: 61)

The railroads, which played so central a role in the new age of innovation, were also the harbinger of another new factor in the changing economic order—market malfunction. The malfunctions were several, of differing kinds, and collectively raised the issue of the adequacy of market forces and the proper role of government intervention when they fail. The roads embodied almost all of the factors that tend toward instability in markets in which long-term capital investment in a highly specialized plant makes it impractical to adjust supply flexibly to the level of demand, leading to the paradoxical problems of monopoly in some places and cutthroat competition in others.

The building of the roads was carried on in an atmosphere of virtually universal enthusiasm. Government, both state and federal, smiled on them, pampered them, and lavished subsidies and prerogatives to speed their completion. Once in place, however, their many problems produced irritations among nearly all whom they served, spawning a welter of politically active and often mutually conflicting interest groups. First it was the farmers of the West, distressed over the level of rates where the roads exerted virtual monopoly power; in the East, farmers complained that the very rates the western farmers thought too high were unfairly low compared to their own (Benson 1955). These were joined by New York City merchants complaining of discrimination that disadvantaged them as against their competitors in other cities (ibid.).

Some of these complaints produced legislation at the state level, but not the national level. It was yet another level of aggravation—the breakdown of the competitive process—that led the railroads to reverse their own earlier opposition to regulation and join the call of their aggrieved patrons for the federal government to step in.

The formation of a business based upon the accumulation of large amounts of capital from scattered individual investors produced problems at the outset, for which the discipline of the marketplace had no practical solutions. The construction phase of railroad building broke all records for that form of financial abuse known as stock watering (Benson 1955). It also revealed another gap in market discipline. Corporate insiders were able to circumvent all competitive discipline by organizing their own construction companies to build the railroads, at vastly inflated prices, thus further enriching themselves and watering the stock. Although not all roads were constructed this way, by the 1860s and 1870s it had become the general practice (Locklin 1972: 139, 240). As these abuses make clear, the real profits in railroads during this period were made in building rather than running them. The distortion was so extreme that in some cases roads were built for the sole purpose of forcing a competitor to buy them out (Gilchrist 1960: 44). The result was a vastly overburdened capital structure, with severe pressures on railroad managements to charge "all that the traffic would bear," and it led to a wave of bankruptcies.

Yet railroad management soon learned that "driving a rival into bankruptcy was a consummation devoutly *not* to be desired (Benson 1955: 49). The bankrupt road was relieved of interest and dividend payments, while the plant remained in place and the purchaser at the bankruptcy sale started with a lower cost base (Schwartz 1973: vol. 1: 333). The unremoved excess capacity led to another problem—discriminations.

If the farmers of the West were to sell their products in the markets of the East and export them to Europe, the cost of transportation could not rise about a certain level without choking off the trade altogether. Thus, the competitive price of agricultural products set a ceiling on long-haul rates for western agriculture. The roads cut rates on the long hauls and charged all that they could on shorter hauls, where the total transportation charge was not so constrained by the price of the cargo (Brown 1977: 272–73; B. Schwartz 1973: vol. 1: 282; Benson 1955: 95). A similar problem arose with respect to rates between different geographic points (Benson 1955: 29–31, 42–43, 53–54; Gilchrist 1960: 34) and among different shippers (Benson 1955: 71, 135; Locklin 1972: 315).

The problems, however, were not all on the customers' side of the market. The overbuilding in the East led to cutthroat competition between the railroads, to which the primary defensive response was "pooling."

The concept behind a pool is that competing roads agree to accept a percentage of the total business rather than seeking to compete it away by rate cutting. The pools were bitterly assailed by the railroads' critics for their obvious tendency to eliminate competition and establish monopoly power (Gilchrist 1960: 33). But the ardor of this sort of criticism was blunted by continuing rate wars and an overall decline in the level of rates. The final impetus toward federal legislation lay not so much in the formation of the pools as in their failure to solve the underlying problem (Kolko 1970: 30, 38–41, 67; Benson 1955: 209, 230, 234–35).

As pools proved ineffective, resort was had to consolidation to substitute "tight" for "loose" combinations. The tendency was underway, and a source of concern to politicians, but it had not gone far enough to solve the problem from the railroads' perspective (Kolko 1970: 67).

As the overcapacity and rate wars continued to defy all private attempts at solutions, the railroads, which at first had fiercely resisted all proposals for government control, came to view the political option as the only practical solution to their problem.

The pressures for federal regulation of the railroads persisted over so long a time, and from such diverse and conflicting sources, that the nature of what finally emerged has been the subject of some controversy. It was early viewed as an uprising of progressivism, the people acting through government to assert public control over the monopolistic powers of private business. In this the Granger movement was seen as playing the key role (Kolko 1970: 20–27). One of the first "revisionist" writers, Lee Benson, emphasized the role of New York City merchants who were alarmed over the prejudicial effect of railroad rate structures on their own city, and who for a time made common cause with the farmers of western New York (Benson 1955). Gabriel Kolko stressed the role of the railroads themselves under the pressure of the continuing rate wars. Although differing in emphasis, their ultimate conclusions seem agreed. What can be said with some certainty is that all of these forces contributed, though with differing effectiveness, and cumulatively brought about the decision to intervene in 1887.

The main pressure for legislation came from the Senate, under the leadership of Senator Cullom of Illinois. There were substantial differences in the approaches of the two houses, despite their agreement on the basic issues and the need for legislation to end discrimination. The Senate was more sympathetic to the railroads' point of view than the House, which reflected the western farmers' preference for lower rates and more competition.

Senator Cullom introduced the Senate bill and a carefully detailed report, both of which bore his name (Schwartz 1973: vol. 1: 31). The philosophy upon which the bill was drafted reflected a notable lack of emphasis on monopoly pricing and considerable stress on controlling excessive power and the protection of smaller enterprises, emphasizing the problem of discrimination (ibid., 38, 91, 107).

Both houses agreed that discrimination should be barred and that rates should be fair and reasonable. But on three issues—pooling, long-haul and short-haul rate disparities, and the establishment of a commission—the two houses were sharply divided.

The essence of the division was that the western states, where the railroads still held substantial monopoly positions, saw the solution in increased competition through law enforcement; but the Senate, reflecting conditions in the East, was sympathetic to the problem of *excessive* competition, for which it favored an administrative solution (Kolko 1970: 16, 38, 42–43).

In the Senate there was a disposition, even on the part of so prominent a champion of competition as Senator Sherman of Ohio, to accept certain restrictions on competition among the roads so long as there was some form of public control over the making and enforcing of them. Senator Platt of Connecticut defended the practice of pooling at length (Schwartz 1973: vol 1: 329–36), and he attracted support from Senator Sherman, who argued for permitting the new commission to permit individual pools if it found them in the public interest:

> Does the Senator from Vermont say that the rule, and sole rule of competition should prevail? If so, then take away the power of this commission, and let the railroads fight it out—cut each other's throats. . . . The pool is to secure the steadiness of rates. The effect of this bill, by destroying such agreements, neutralizes all agreements made in the interest of the public as well as those adverse to such interest. (Schwartz 1973: vol. 1: 426)

Pooling was a device for controlling competition, not monopoly. And the fact that Senator Sherman, who was deeply concerned by the trust problem, freely conceded that the railroad problem was in some measure the result of a malfunction of the competitive process, provides a revealing perspective on the senator's attitude toward competition. It was not an absolute belief in competition as an automatic regulator; there was a readiness to make concessions in the competitive regime to achieve other public purposes. This was the prevailing view in the Senate, but not the House. Competition was still thought to be the answer there, and on this point, pooling, the Senate conceded, though effectively prevailing because it got its commission.

The long-term significance of the commission was, however, not the fact of its establishment, but the prescient insights about its inherent problems that emerged from the debates. The administrative agency envisioned by the act was viewed in two sharply contrasting lights by its supporters and opponents.

The Cullom Report's concept of the commission was that "Congress would provide a commission of men who were at once honest, intelligent, and experienced" (Schwartz 1973: vol. 1: 31, 106). Some House members equated the commission's future members to Justices of the Supreme Court (ibid., 281).

In contrast, the House floor leader, Congressman Reagan, put his finger on the fundamental problem that accounts for the largely disappointing performance of the federal regulatory agencies—their narrowly specialized roles:

> [T]he answer has heretofore been made that we trust the President to appoint our judges, and why not to appoint railroad commissioners? The answer is that judges are not selected to deal with one single great interest, but for the general administration of the law . . . while these commissioners are to deal with questions which relate to the duties of common carriers alone . . . and interests involving billions of dollars, concentrated in a few persons, some of whom have proven themselves utterly unscrupulous. (ibid., 272)

The problems of the railroads were open and well known. Market malfunctions occurred in other sectors too during the nineteenth century but were not as clearly perceived. In one, the most spectacular of them all, the full story was actually suppressed. This brings us to that very different case, the Standard Oil Company.

3

The Saga of Standard Oil

> The growth of a large business is merely a survival of the fittest... the American beauty rose can be produced in the splendor and fragrance which bring cheer to its beholder only by sacrificing the early buds which grow up around it. This is not an evil tendency in business. It is merely the working out of the law of nature and the law of God.
>
> John D. Rockefeller (Nevins 1953: vol. 2: 348)

> All the fortune I have made has not served to compensate for the anxiety of the period. Work by day and worry by night, week in and week out, month after month.
>
> John D. Rockefeller (Flynn 1932: 201)

The stereotype of the pre–1911 Standard Oil Company must rank among the larger misperceptions of American economic history. The true story has been told in a few specialized studies of Rockefeller and of the company, but these did not appear until after a vastly different and simplistic view had been firmly fixed in the public mind; and when these more balanced accounts did appear, they at first came masked in the gray garb of scholarly literature.[1] They also did not appear until after the Supreme Court–ordered breakup of Standard Oil in 1911, which removed the problem from the public consciousness; and they were written from the perspectives of history and biography, not of antitrust policy. More basically, the true story is so fundamentally at odds with conventional economic theory that most economists, particularly authors of historical textbooks, have ignored it.

The stereotype pictures Standard Oil as a greedy monopoly that destroyed its competition so that it could exact monopoly profits from consumers. Its breakup by order of the Supreme Court is seen as a vindication of the principle of self-regulating free markets, a triumph for consumer welfare.

In fact, the price of refined petroleum declined by over 90 percent from 1864 to 1894, a period that embraces the heyday of the Standard Oil "monopoly" (Bezanson 1954: 468; H. Rep. No. 3112, 50th Cong., 1st Sess., App. Standard Oil: 115 (1888); Clark, Victor 1929: vol. 2: 519; Kirkland 1956: 7) and it rose after the company was broken up (Abels 1965: 273–76; Nevins 1953: vol. 2: 382–83). Even one of Standard's most inflammatory critics, H. D. Lloyd, conceded that prices decreased during the "monopoly" period (Lloyd 1894: 430–31). Lloyd argued, as did other critics, that the price declined less than it otherwise would have, but that is not to say that the problem was excessive prices (Nevins 1953: vol. 2: 369–70).

The purpose to gain monopoly control actually served as a restraint on the company's pricing policy, since competition was never completely eliminated and the company was aware that too profitable prices would attract unwelcome competitors (ibid., 67, 148). Monopoly was sought for reasons of order, not exploitation. The price complaints of contemporaries were much less vigorous than those of subsequent commentators. Standard's prices were not considered excessive until President Roosevelt set out to prove they were, and quality was considered the best, at least in the United States.[2]

Far from being a vindication of the merits of the competitive system, the Standard Oil experience was the result of one of its most dramatic failures: Standard's reach for monopoly was incited by a chaotic failure of the competitive system in the crude oil–producing and –refining industries. It is, indeed, Rockefeller's judgment that has received the vindication of history, as both state and federal governments have since imposed mandatory controls on crude oil production in reaction to profligate waste under free market conditions after the breakup of Standard Oil.

Yet another misconception that emerged from this episode has been the impression, gaining increasing currency in recent times, that antitrust is primarily, if not exclusively, a consumer welfare measure (Bork 1978). A closer look at the dramatic history of Standard Oil, however, makes clear that what most touched the political sensitivities of the country was not price gouging of consumers, but a combination of outrage at the afflictions the company visited upon its hapless competitors and suppliers, and fear of the concentration of power within a single company. It was on the businessperson's side of the market, not the consumer's, where the politically meaningful offenses occurred.

The roots of these distortions trace directly to the stubborn refusal of Rockefeller and his colleagues to explain themselves. Their policy toward the press and legislative committees was the baldest form of "stonewalling," which Rockefeller himself later acknowledged was a mistake (Nevins 1953: vol. 1: 121).

Lacking an understanding of the true nature of the problem, journalists, politicians, the public, and even scholars seized on the only apparent, but false, explanation for the company's actions—to monopolize the industry for the purpose of wringing inflated prices from consumers.

It should be noted that while the focus here is on the events that led to the adoption of the Sherman Antitrust Act in 1890, the saga of Standard Oil continued well after 1890. The trust itself was declared illegal under a state law in 1892 (Nevins 1953: vol. 2: 230–32); and the holding company declared illegal by the Supreme Court in 1911 was not even formed until early court decisions under the Sherman Act had given erring signals that it would not violate the law (Nevins 1953: vol. 2: 241). Some of the most dramatic developments that sealed the company's image did not appear until after the passage of the Sherman Act (Lloyd 1894; Tarbell 1904, 1966). Although they thus had no influence on that legislation, they contributed to the historical perception of the Standard Oil Company and its continuing influence on law and policy (Abels 1965: 222–26; Flynn 1932: 328–29; Nevins 1953: vol. 2: 331–33, 354, 363, 366; cf. Thorelli 1955: 329). Moreover, many of the facts recounted in later works were widely publicized before 1890 through the press (Nevins 1953: vol. 2: 140–41; Lloyd 1881) and legislative hearings. So they are included here, with due qualification.

PETROLEUM IN THE LATTER NINETEENTH CENTURY

Oil was used for lighting then. But crude oil is a bouillabaisse of chemicals, ranging from light, explosive gases to the volatile liquids naphtha and gasoline, to light and heavy fuel oils, to the solidity of asphalt. Only one of these, kerosene, had the right balance to make a safe fuel for illumination. A barrel of crude oil was only about 60 percent kerosene, some fractions of which were used for lubricants and for refinery fuel; but close to half of every barrel was wasted (Nevins 1927: 403; 1953: vol. 1: 26). If the refiner mixed the kerosene with a little naphtha or gasoline, he got a larger yield—and the consumer an occasional explosion. In Europe and the West lamps were blowing up with alarming frequency (Abels 1965: 164–65; Lloyd 1894: 129, 408–9, 412–

16; Nevins 1953: vol. 2: 68). "Standard" Oil was an assurance to the favored consumer in the eastern United States that the product was pure kerosene (Abels 1965: 65).

ROCKEFELLER

John D. Rockefeller was an improbable candidate to play the role of archvillain of U.S. industry. He grew up in Cleveland under the strict religious tutelage of his mother and the keen business instincts of his father (Nevins 1953: vol. 1: 8–9). "Both father and mother . . . had taught him business thrift, foresight and enterprise." But he was also "narrow; he knew nothing of art, letters and science, and cared nothing for them" (ibid, 15). This narrowness was reinforced by his father's decision that college was unnecessary for a business career. He attended a commercial school for several months before seeking his first employment (ibid., 10).

With the narrowness, there was also stability. Rockefeller's life revolved around the three pillars of religion, business, and family (ibid., 7–8). His temperament was that of a conciliator: He did not quarrel with or dictate to his business associates; he reasoned with them. He held his ascendency in the Standard Oil Company through the respect he earned from his associates, not through financial control or dictatorial power over them (ibid., 399).

In an age marked by flamboyance and unscrupulousness in U.S. business, Rockefeller was an island of virtue. The stock of the Standard Oil Company was never watered. Rockefeller sold stock to his colleagues in the company and offered it in exchange for companies he purchased, but he did not offer it for sale on the public exchanges (Flynn 1932: 4–5, 392–94; Abels 1965: 210–11). He explained his reason thus: "In the early days the risks of the business were great," so that if listed on the exchange its price would have been subject to violent fluctuations, and he "preferred to have the attention of the owners and administrators of the business directed wholly to the legitimate development of the enterprise rather than to speculation in its shares" (Rockefeller 1909, 1973: 92). Nor did he seek government largess, either through subsidies or tariff protection or through a legal monopoly chartered by the state legislature (Abels 1965: 237).

How could a person of such deep moral and religious convictions, such honesty in his commercial dealings, so unsullied by the frauds widely practiced by other business moguls of the time, come to be hated and despised beyond the worst of them, pilloried as the quintessence of immorality in business (Flynn 1932: 4–5)? The answer is instructive, all the more so because of the striking absence of base motives in Rockefeller's personality. It was not vile motives but an intelligent response to conditions in the oil business that led Rockefeller and his colleagues to a course of action that was to prove socially and politically intolerable.

Allan Nevins, a distinguished American historian and Rockefeller's biographer, portrays him as neither saint nor villain, nor greedy. To Rockefeller business was the "Great Game," and he was superbly like today's corporation executive, the business gamesman: "His object was to distinguish himself by superlative achievement. He knew that he had great abilities, and meant to use them. It was the achievement, not the money, that counted most" (Nevins 1953: vol. 1: 19, 76). "Rockefeller . . . praising a man who took joy in his work, referred to the Great Game: 'That is it—accomplishment! . . . One builds a ship . . . but knows he will do still better with the next one he builds. Or one builds a railroad. It has 65-pound rails. His next railroad will have 100-pound rails, not iron, but steel. . . . That's the thing—accomplishment, playing the game' " (Nevins 1953: vol. 1: 19).

Rockefeller began his career as a bookkeeper and clerk in a firm of commission merchants, which brought him early into contact with the mushrooming oil business. Drake's pioneer oil well was opened in Titusville, Pennsylvania, in 1859 and triggered a rush to the area that soon came to be known as the Oil Regions.

Rockefeller had already attained such stature within the Cleveland business community that he was commissioned by a group of his colleagues to visit the Oil Regions and report his findings. He came quickly to some firm conclusions: One was that the production of crude oil was both wasteful and highly risky, but that refining, because of high margins between the price of crude oil in the Oil Regions and refined oil prices in the cities, offered "a glittering opportunity" (Nevins 1953: vol. 1: 21). Rockefeller and his partner Clark joined with an English petroleum engineer, Andrews, in "a little side issue" to their commission merchant business, organizing the refining firm of Andrews, Clark & Company in 1863 (ibid., 23).

OVERPRODUCTION

The speculative boom had begun in crude production in 1864 and continued through 1866; it spread to refining and lasted there until 1867 (ibid., 42). With profits high in 1865–1866 the number of refiners in Cleveland reached 50 in 1866; as their number increased "they became more fiercely competitive. . . . They fought for bargain supplies of crude oil, for freight cars, for skilled hands, and, above all, for sales (ibid., 49). "Many of these," as Rockefeller knew, "were tiny establishments" (ibid., 50). The predictable consequence was not long in coming: "Overproduction, overproduction . . . this was to be the curse of both the well-owner and refiners for years to come" (ibid., 51). The cause of overproduction in refining was not only the attraction of boom period profits but also the little capital required to set up a refining plant (ibid., 50). But the more basic problem was in the production of crude oil.

Depression came in 1866–1867. Growing overproduction led to a sharp break in the price of crude (House Hearings 1888: Standard Oil: 19; Abels 1965: 18, 58; Nevins 1953: vol. 1: 51). The problem was the growing number of new strikes, as the owners of lush new wells were doing well because of their high volume even at prices so low that smaller producers could not survive (Nevins 1953: vol. 1: 54–55).

The resulting oversupply spread the depression to the refining industry, and in 1867 and 1868 dozens were closed in Cleveland and Pittsburgh (ibid.). Standard was one of few to remain profitable even under these conditions, but the company's executives were not unconcerned (Rockefeller 1909, 1973: 80).

The industry as a whole had by this time developed to the point where all the key elements were in place for the business melodrama that was about to ensue. Let us pause here to survey this industry and the peculiar conditions that resulted in one of the most dramatic failures of a competitive market as an automatic regulator.

THE SHAPE OF THE INDUSTRY AND THE KEY ROLE OF TRANSPORTATION

The production and marketing of petroleum products divided itself very early into several distinct functions: the production of crude oil from wells in scattered locations; the transportation of the crude to refineries where it was transformed into a variety of usable end products, which themselves had to be transported to marketing centers; and the local retail distribution to the consumer. Each was a distinct business, with peculiar characteristics of its own.

The production of crude oil was much like agriculture: The product was fungible, the producers small and diverse, and the incentive for each was to produce the maximum output from his property. The individual well owner had a sunk capital in the cost of drilling his well; if overall production drove down the price per barrel, he could not improve that price by reducing his own output. No one had a large enough share of the market to do that. So, if prices fell, the only rational way for the individual well owner to maintain his revenue was to produce to the limits of his capacity. Adam Smith's proposition that the level of production regulates itself automatically in response to price did not fit the conditions of the crude oil–producing industry.

The refining of crude oil in these early days was something of a cottage industry. The refineries were cheaply constructed, and the early spectacular profitability of the business led to proliferation and overbuilding.

Retail marketing was another distinct function, typically carried on by independent businesses, and even more easily entered than refining.

Transportation was another dimension and played a key role in Rockefeller's business strategy. Production was concentrated in a narrow area, but the market was worldwide. The means of transport, first by railroad and water vessel, and later by pipeline, were all capital intensive, and thus sensitive to the economies of large volume and to each other as competitive alternatives. Rockefeller understood very early the critical importance of transport costs, and of the need for sheer size to gain a negotiating advantage with the railroads. He also made skillful use of competing water transport, other railroads, and, ultimately, pipelines.

The vulnerability of the railroads was of prime importance. Volume by itself in oil shipments was not the only concern of the roads. Heavy production volume could produce "costly irregularities in the demand for cars, locomotives, and yard space" (Carr 1962: 14). A steady, predictable rate of shipment was the primary objective of the railroads, and this could be assured them only by the larger refiners, to whom they were willing to concede reductions in freight rates and other advantages (ibid.; Abels 1965: 63–64, 127).

In 1867 Rockefeller gained a new partner, Henry M. Flagler, who made transportation his special province, manipulating the competitive vulnerabilities of the railroads to water carriers and other roads to obtain both lower rates and rebates (Nevins 1953: vol. 1: 52–53). Rebates were technically illegal but widely used; Standard was not alone in this practice (Abels 1965: 59–70, 99, 203–4; Tarbell 1966: 18–19; Lloyd 1894: 464; Nevins 1953: vol. 2: 131 and vol. 1: 65–69: Carr 1962: 77–79, 126–27; Friedman, Lawrence 1973: 165; *Scofield*, 43 Ohio State Reports 571 (1885); House Hearings 1888: Standard Oil: 124).

Rockefeller was firmly convinced of the justice of rebates because of the benefits the railroad received, not only the volume of shipments but also their steadiness and the further capacity of a large shipper to serve as an "evener" of traffic. These were substantial benefits to the railroad, and neither Rockefeller nor his competitors thought it wrong that the large shipper should receive some compensation for them. The competitive dangers inherent in this situation were compounded by the short-sightedness of the railroads. As they increased Rockefeller's rebates in response to his growing volume, they further strengthened his hand to compel still further reductions (Abels 1965: 64).

The introduction of the railroad tank car gave Rockefeller yet another lever. The railroads, to minimize their capital outlays, let Standard purchase the cars, which enabled Standard to continue to get preferred rates, even without outright discrimination and rebates (Carr 1962: 72–77, 98; House Hearings 1888: Standard Oil: 574–619; *Handy*, 31 Fed. 689, 693 [1887]).

With the advent of the pipeline, Standard both began construction of its own and the buying out of independent pipeline operators, thus further strengthening its grip on transportation—through vertical integration.

"OUR PLAN"

Neither the internal efficiencies of Standard Oil, which had emphasized quality in all aspects of its operations from the beginning, nor its advantage in transportation, even in combination, were sufficient to cope with the problem of overproduction. The years 1868–1873 were years of depression in the Oil Regions, and the refiners suffered too (Nevins 1953: vol. 1: 77–81). The Petroleum Producers' Association of Pennsylvania was organized in 1869, but "it did not dare face the real cause of depression—too many wells" (ibid., 78; House Hearings 1888: Standard Oil: 1–40). The fluctuations in the price of crude were chaotic. In 1861 the price of a barrel ranged from $20.00 to $0.10 (Abels 1965: 58). In the spring of 1862 a combination of well owners tried to hold the price at $4.00, but some were selling for $0.35 a barrel—less than one cent a gallon (Nevins 1953: vol. 1: 21).

The problem in refining was the same as in production: excess capacity (Nevins 1953: vol. 1: 78–79; Rockefeller 1909, 1973: 81–82). Years later Rockefeller "still recalled vividly the dropping prices, the vanishing margin of profit, the sickening fluctuations and uncertainty. 'A panic had been on for a considerable time in the oil refining business . . . resulting in loss to nearly all refiners' " (Nevins 1953: vol. 1: 96). The Standard Oil Company, the strongest in the country, might well survive, and Rockefeller had no anxiety for his personal future because of the size and diversity of his investments; but "he was convinced that he could not let the industry as a whole drift into deeper chaos" (ibid., 97).

Rockefeller's concept of the necessary solution "called for the consolidation of nearly all oil-refining units into one great organization, which would eliminate excess capacity and stop price-cutting." Rockefeller and Flagler were confirmed " 'in the idea that to enlarge our own Standard Oil of Ohio and actually take into partners with us the refining interest would accomplish the protection of the oil industry as a whole.' " The board of directors authorized the purchase of other refiners pursuant to this design, dubbed by Rockefeller as "Our Plan" (Nevins 1953: vol. 1: 99–100).

AN ASSIST FROM THE RAILROADS

The railroads, too, had a problem. Competition for the vast oil traffic had turned profits into losses. Tom Scott of the Pennsylvania offered a plan that would solve his problem as well as that of the leading refiners.

Scott sought agreement on a higher freight rate that would be paid by all refiners. Those participating in the plan, however, would receive a uniform rebate. Refiners not participating not only would receive no rebate, but a drawback would be paid on their own shipments to the participating refiners. The agreement went so far as to amount to an express business alliance between the railroads and the favored refiners, including a commitment by the railroad to raise or lower its rates as needed to overcome competition from nonparticipating refiners (Thorelli 1955: 93). Participation in the plan was to be through a specially chartered and still unused corporation, the South Improvement Company (Thorelli 1955: 93; Nevins 1953: vol. 1: 107; Tarbell 1966: 29).

The plan was originally opposed by Rockefeller and Flagler (Carr, 1962: 27–30; Montague 1973: 22; Nevins 1953: vol. 1: 99). They later agreed, and actively supported it (Nevins 1953: vol. 1: 100), largely out of deference to the railroad interests whom they understood it would be unwise to offend (Abels 1965: 71–75; Nevins 1953: vol. 1: 103–4).

When news of the scheme leaked (Abels 1965: 76), the reaction in the Oil Regions was explosive, what Ida Tarbell dubbed "The Oil War of 1872" (Tarbell 1966: 34–35). The South Improvement Plan was never put into effect. The Pennsylvania quickly succumbed to the Oil Regions, signing an agreement that promised no further rebates—a promise that was broken within a week (Abels 1965: 101).

Rockefeller had not viewed the South Improvement Plan, even after he embraced it, as a substitute for "Our Plan." The remarkable fact is that all of the uproar in the Oil Regions over the South Improvement scheme, which never went into effect, was a side show to the main event going on in Cleveland. Rockefeller had already made great strides in buying out his competitors in Cleveland in 1871 before the South Improvement scheme in 1872 (Nevins 1953: vol. 1: 132–34) but then used it to induce further conquests (ibid., 136–37). When the Oil Regions learned of Rockefeller's virtually complete takeover of Cleveland, their reaction was outrage (Tarbell 1966: 42). This episode instantly transformed the image of the Standard Oil Company from that of a respectable firm into that of a monopolistic monster, the "Great Anaconda" (Tarbell 1966: 41).

THE LIMITS OF MONOPOLY: THE TRUST

With acquisitions culminating in 1877 and 1878, Standard had eliminated all major competition and had a near monopoly in both refining and pipelines. In terms of its total market share, Standard had reached its peak, about 90 percent of the refining business in 1888, 80 percent in 1893, and 82.7 percent from 1893 to 1899 (Nevins 1953: vol. 2: 54). Even at the lowest end of this range, Standard's market share essentially met the minimum objectives of its leaders, who felt that to "maintain 'order' they must prevent outsiders from doing more than one-fifth of the business" (ibid.; Abels 1965: 202).

Given this enormous power and the desire for monopoly, why did Standard not succeed in taking the whole market through predatory undercutting of its competitors, as it was so often accused of doing? Standard's executives did consider the idea, but that was not practical (Nevins 1953: vol. 2: 65). Rockefeller asked for a reckoning of the possibility, directing one of his associates in 1883 to " 'see how much we could afford to decline the market if we could get the entire business in refining, taking into account the profit and the extra crude we would thereby pump' " (ibid., 65–66). The response made clear that there would be no profit in such a course; for even if Standard cut to cost, the independents would continue to make oil and all margin would be wiped out (ibid., 65–66; Abels 1965: 202).

This did not, however, mean turning soft on the competition. The very fact that Standard had replaced "a savage competition" with "a unified control which lifted the oil business to a highly profitable level" had once again made the business attractive to outsiders (Nevins 1953: vol. 2: 54). This fact had a restraining effect on price even where Standard did not face competition (ibid., 67).

Standard's leadership, while abandoning the attempt at total monopoly, therefore still had reason to exert pressure on the surviving competition, and it did so with a flexible strategy that combined a limited tolerance toward those not worth the expense of fighting, with selective price cutting where the threat was sufficiently serious (ibid., 66).

Although the company had achieved its objective of control in refining by 1877–1878, the "trust" had yet to appear. Unlike its many imitators, Standard did not need the trust to establish centralized control it already had through interlocking ownership (Nevins 1953: vol. 1: 392–94; Flynn 1932: 250). It was resorted to because the state of Pennsylvania had imposed a personal property tax on any corporation doing business in the state, based on the company's entire capitalization, wherever located. If other states did the same, the cumulative taxes could exceed the company's entire capitalization (Nevins 1953: vol. 1: 392). To avoid this, the 40 companies of the Standard were reorganized so that no company continued to hold property outside of a single state (Carr 1962: 65–66; Hidy & Hidy 1955: 44).

This was the first use of the trust on this scale, and it provided a model for numerous imitators (Nevins 1953: vol. 1: 393). Rockefeller took pride in having made this pioneering contribution, though he recognized that it was an accidental by-product of his quest for stability: "The time was right for it. It had to come, though all we saw at the time was the need to save ourselves from wasteful conditions" (ibid., 402).

HORROR STORIES, STONEWALLING, AND A LEGACY OF CONFUSION

Most of Rockefeller's acquisitions were accomplished by quiet negotiation based on persuading individual refiners in this depressed industry that they could not make it on their own; but the extent of his reach for market domination brought him into conflict with a few who would not accept his argument, and the resulting confrontations only reinforced the monster image of Rockefeller and the Standard Oil Company.

One of the most spectacular was the "War with the Pennsylvania." The management of the Pennsylvania Railroad was concerned at the lack of competition in oil refining and undertook to enter the business through one of its subsidiaries. When Rockefeller learned of the plan, he sought to dissuade the railroad's management. Rebuffed, he struck with hammer blows, cutting prices, cutting off shipments on the Pennsylvania, and using other assorted acts of aggression. The Pennsylvania, crippled by the Great Rail Strike of 1877, surrendered, selling all of its oil-refining assets to Standard, thereby leaving Rockefeller even more powerful than before (Nevins 1953: vol. 1: 232–42; Abels 1965: 121–25).

This episode was followed by the "Crisis of 1878." Standard's successful war against the Pennsylvania left the Oil Regions with no one but Standard to whom they could sell their oil. Rockefeller was now referred to in the newspapers as "Lord of the Regions" (Abels 1965: 125). At the same time a new glut was developing, and Standard, as the monopoly purchaser, was to bear the full calumny of the Oil Regions for the drastic fall in prices that ensued. New discoveries were being made in a variety of locations, and production skyrocketed (Nevins 1953: vol. 1: 290; Abels 1965: 136; Flynn 1932: 212). A New York Chamber of Commerce expert wrote that the producers were "persistently forcing the yield beyond all former experience and hope of a sound market" (Nevins 1953: vol. 1: 291). "[T]he producers were helpless. It was impossible for many to stop the wells for fear of damage by saltwater; unable to store, they had no choice but to pump oil onto the ground, which many did" (Abels 1965: 137). Despite Standard's heroic efforts at building new storage capacity—conceded by even its harshest critics (Tarbell 1966: 88; Nevins 1953: vol. 1: 318; Abels 1965: 136)—new wells were being connected even faster and oil was "running to waste" (Nevins 1953: vol. 1: 319). As the overproduction continued and prices plummeted to 70 cents a barrel, the producers adopted a resolution that " 'the shortest way to $2.00 oil is through $0.25 oil. Resolved, that we favor pushing the drill as rapidly and diligently as possible until the goal of $0.25 is reached' " (Abels 1965: 138; Flynn 1932: 213; Nevins 1953: vol. 1: 317).

Standard warned that its capacity was reaching its limits and pleaded, futilely, for a curtailment of the drilling (Abels 1965: 136). Finally, its capacity overwhelmed, Standard announced that it would take no more than one quarter of the oil offered for storage, and that the rest would have to be sold immediately—at a discount (ibid.). Producers saw this as a pure squeeze; and in their delirium, these arch opponents of monopoly cried, "Why force us to compete with each other?" (Flynn 1932: 213). Rockefeller was vilified, not by consumers protesting high prices, but for not artificially propping a depressed price.

There were also episodes of aggressive actions taken against independent pipeline owners, and of their eventual takeover by Standard (Lloyd 1894: 108, 112; Nevins 1953: vol. 1: 350; Tarbell 1966: 101–3, 105–6). There was a great scandal over a minor act of sabotage to a refiner in Buffalo (Tarbell 1966: 138–42; Lloyd 1894: 246–97) and over a widow who claimed that she had been short-changed in the sale of her husband's business to Standard (Abels 1965: 113–20; Lloyd 1894: 73–83). Standard also kept close tabs on its competitors, giving rise to charges of espionage (Nevins 1953: vol. 2: 77–78).

Then there was the spectacular case of a handwritten note to a railroad complaining that it had failed to charge its usual high discriminatory rate on a shipment by an independent competitor, concluding with the colorful admonition, "Please turn another screw" (Abels 1965: 197; Nevins 1953: vol. 2: 76–77; House Hearings 1888: Standard Oil: 619–20). The story became a sensation and haunted Standard executives for the rest of their lives (Carr 1962: 69).

The point of recounting these episodes is not to rekindle animus against the historic Standard Oil Company, nor to encourage the criminal law mentality of the Antitrust Division. It is, rather, to show that there was a common element in all of these provocations, which had nothing to do with excessive consumer prices, but rather with harm to business interests.

It is in this distinction that we find the answer to the question posed at the beginning of this chapter: How was it that the consummately scrupulous businessman, Rockefeller, came to be regarded as the archvillain of U.S. business while indulging in none of the financially unscrupulous practices so typical of his time? The accusation of overcharging the public was neither novel nor exciting; but to deprive people of the opportunity to earn a livelihood in the business of their choice was something else. It was the latter of which Rockefeller stood convicted in the court of public opinion.

The crisis of 1878 drew the first political reaction. State legislative investigations began in Ohio in 1878, and by the Hepburn Committee in New York in 1879 (Nevins 1953: vol. 2: 130–36). It was in these forums that Standard executives first displayed the open contempt that they consistently held toward all government investigations of Standard Oil, refusing to answer the simplest and most obvious of questions. A sampler: One executive of a company that had been acquired by Standard, when asked if he was a member of the Standard Oil Company, replied, "If I was, I think that is a personal question." "When the trust's secretary was asked for the proper name of the combination, his reply was: 'The Lord only knows; I don't. An indescribable thing." When asked if " 'Two mills a ton mile for five hundred miles would be a dollar a ton?' " he replied, " 'I am not able to demonstrate that proposition.' " He was then asked, " 'You have some arithmetical knowledge?' " to which he replied, " 'I cannot answer that question' " (Lloyd 1894: 465–67, fns omitted). A key executive described his role in the company as a "clameror for dividends," a response that gave Rockefeller special delight (Flynn 1932: 219). Nevins characterizes their performance as "flippant, unresponsive, disrespectful" (1953: vol. 2: 133–34). It was a calculated policy, and a mistake, which Rockefeller eventually conceded, but not until many years later (Nevins 1953: vol. 1: 121). The actual market problems that led Rockefeller to act as he did were thus not explained, and the resulting vacuum was filled by an inaccurate assumption of an exploitive purpose, a legacy of confusion that endures to this day.

Rockefeller, throughout his business career, had refused to talk to the press. Following his retirement, in the course of an ocean voyage to visit a daughter in Europe, he consented to be interviewed by a reporter. He complained that he was misunderstood, that his critics were his competitors. The reporter suggested that this was his own fault. Replied Rockefeller, "Perhaps it is" (Flynn 1932: 423).

NOTES

1. Nevins (1953) is the most comprehensive. Flynn (1932) is a shorter, also balanced, account, as are the more recent Abels (1965) and Carr (1962). The stonewalling of the Standard witnesses at the only contemporary legislative hearings (Hepburn Committee in New York (1879) and the House Committee of Manufactures (H. Rep. No. 3112, 50th Cong., 1st Sess. (1888)) rendered those hearings virtually useless as a source of meaningful information. The Standard Oil case of 1911 (221 U.S. 1) did not address the underlying motives for Standard's behavior. Neither the *Report of the U.S. Industrial Commission* (vol. 1: 9, 95 (1900); vol. 13: XXIII, CXVII, CXVII-CXXIII (1901)) nor the Bureau of Corporation's *Report of the Commissioner of Corporations on the Petroleum Industry* (2 vols., 1907) probed the purposes behind Standard's behavior.

2. Abels 1965: 211. The *Report of the Bureau of Corporations* (1907) viewed Standard's prices as "exorbitant" (cf. Mayhew 1972). The earlier *Report of the U.S. Industrial Commission* was skeptical of the price complaints (vol. 1: 20 (1900); vol. 13: CXVII-CXVIII (1901)), though it may have been influenced by Standard Oil lobbying (Flynn 1932: 374–75).

4

The Legislative Odyssey of the Sherman Act

A PLAGUE OF TRUSTS

The railroads and the Standard Oil Company were, in certain obvious respects, special cases. Size alone set them both apart from other business; and the cause of market malfunction in each case was rather an extreme condition—the extraordinary capital intensive nature of the railroads and the atomistic chaos of the nascent oil industry. Yet in lesser degree these and other causes of market breakdown developed in many other lines of the newly emerging businesses that sprang from the innovative surge of the nineteenth century.

Combinations

The business response to these problems was consistently one variation or another on one basic theme—combination. It took many forms: trusts were the obvious examples; but there were also pools, syndicates, cooperatives; and even the integrated organization of a single corporation, embracing people, machines, land, and financial resources, was thought of as a form of combination (R. Robertson 1973: 343; Thorelli 1955: 63–66, 70–71, 82–85; Ripley 1916: xi–xxi; Cochran & Miller 1961: 143–44; Seager & Gulick 1929, 1973: ix–x; Stocking & Watkins 1951: 32–33). But the primary significance of the term referred to the unification of formerly competing enterprises to ameliorate the competitive pressures of the marketplace.

"Where combination is possible competition is impossible" (B. Schwartz 1973: vol. 1: 335). This fatalistic pronouncement from the debates on the railroad problem soon came to represent a widespread view of the competitive dilemma facing industry generally. In market after market, where standardized commodities sold in competition with one another and productive capacity came to outstrip demand, some form of combination was resorted to for the sake of stability (Lloyd 1884). Andrew Carnegie explained the process thusly: Unusual profits lead to new firms and expanded productive capacity, and demand is soon fully satisfied. Supply soon becomes greater than demand, and prices fall—to and below cost. The theory says that here the trouble will end because goods will not be produced at less than cost. This is true of small proprietorships employing only a few journeymen and an apprentice or two, for whom it was easy to limit or stop production. In enormous establishments with $5 or $10 million of capital and with thousands of workers, it costs the manufacturer less to run at a loss than to stop production altogether. Other firms are in the same position, and so a trust is formed (Carnegie 1889, 1902, 1933: 130–31). A similar explanation was offered by the U.S. Industrial Commission (U.S. Industrial Comm. 1901: vol. 13: v).

Pools were among the earliest and most primitive devices, enjoying a brief heyday from about 1873 to 1899 (R. Robertson 1973: 344; Ripley 1916: xi–xiv; Cramer 1972: 411; Seager & Gulick 1929: 86–91). Real stability, however, resulted only when the competing firms submitted themselves to a single control. This difference was described in terms of loose versus tight combination: Loose combinations were all forms of cooperation between firms that retained their separate identities, whereas tight combinations referred to outright merger or consolidation through a trust. Combination was embraced by businesspeople as a necessity but viewed warily by those on the outside as a menace to small businesspeople, farmers, labor, and the consumer.

The "Trusts"

The term "trust" in the era of the 1880s through the early decades of the twentieth century acquired a more general meaning than the legalistic concept of controlling diverse corporations by a single group of trustees. Just as the term "Watergate" in the 1970s came to represent all forms of abuse of government power, "trust" around the turn of the century came to connote all forms of abuse of private business power (Thorelli 1955: 84–85). The railroads were not trusts, but the railroad problem and that of the trusts were seen as linked.

As a legal device the trust enjoyed only a very brief heyday. When New Jersey in 1889 amended its corporation law to permit corporations to hold the stock of other corporations, the only reason for resort to the trust device disappeared; the former trusts reclothed themselves as holding companies and blended into the landscape (Stocking & Watkins 1951: 31–32). But the label stuck, and it remained a popular political bogey.

The power of these vast aggregations of capital to influence government policy was growing rapidly and ominously. The outbreak of the Civil War has been attributed by some historians to the breakthrough of the protectionist forces of the industrial Northeast over the long-prevailing agricultural, free-trading preferences of the South (Faulkner 1960: 306–9). The war provided the rationale for huge tariff increases that were not scaled down when hostilities ended (Taussig 1931: 164–181). The influence of business over government throughout this period was so strong that the tariff system operated, in effect, as an exempt, cartelized exception to the rule of the market (Robertson 1973: 371; Josephson 1938, 1966, 451–52). Railroads dictated to state legislators, and as businesses grew in size and consolidated in the form of trusts, they manipulated legislatures, both state and federal. This growing power of private business became an issue of increasing political concern. The revolt by the Grange in the West, and the early stirrings of what was to become the Populist movement in 1890, were already alarming conservative, probusiness leaders in the Congress (Josephson 1938, 1966: 341–44; Lloyd 1881: 317; Lloyd 1884; Hofstadter 1955; Dudden 1950; 1957).

The House Hearings

Senator John Sherman's Senate Finance Committee, which produced the bill that led to the ultimate legislation, did not hold hearings on the problem. Another Senate committee conducted a study of the Beef Trust but did not issue its report until after the Sherman Act had become law (S. Rep. No. 829 (1890)). The principal legislative hearings were conducted over two years by the House Committee on Manufactures, in 1887–1889. That committee, however, proposed no legislation, issued only two reports, each less than three pages in length, to which it attached transcripts of the hearings, and abstained from making any recommendations "owing to present differences of opinion between the members of the committee" (H. Rep. No. 3112 (1888); H. Rep. No. 4165 (1889)), quoting from No. 4165).

The committee focused on just four trusts, though reporting that "the number of combinations and trusts formed and forming in this country is . . . very large, and affects a large portion of the important manufacturing and industrial interests of the country" (ibid., No. 4165). It proffered no comprehensive list on the ground that "new ones are constantly forming and . . . old ones are constantly extending their relations so as to cover new branches of business and invade new territories" (ibid.).

The four trusts targeted in the hearings were Sugar, Whisky, Oil, and Cotton Bagging. The hearings were significant in one respect, not because they catalogue a spectacular collection of corporate abuses, but rather because in *none* of the four cases examined do we find evidence of ruthless monopolists bent on the exploitation of consumers.

One of the "trusts," Cotton Bagging, did involve an admitted overcharging, but that was a one-time result of a speculative position into which the parties had been virtually forced as a defensive reaction to government tariff policies (H. Rep. 4165: Cotton Bagging: 131–34). Another, Standard Oil, continued its policy of stonewalling, thus doing nothing to forestall whatever hostile inferences might be drawn as to its motives. That hearing produced numerous allegations of monopolistic behavior with respect to forcing competitors out of business, price cutting, price discrimination, and the like, but not excessive consumer prices (H. Rep. No. 3112 (1888): App. Standard Oil; Mayhew 1972).

The other two trusts examined were more representative, and each followed a familiar pattern. Sugar refining and the distillation of alcoholic beverages both involved the processing of a readily abundant agricultural raw material in a plant not expensive to construct and so conducive to widespread entry when prices were favorable. In both cases, an overcapacity problem developed. The purpose of the Sugar Trust was to rationalize production, channeling it during periods of seasonal fluctuation to the most efficient refiners and completely shutting down the less efficient, but without putting them out of business (H. D. Havemeyer, H. Rep. No. 3112 (1888): App. Sugar: 101). The Whisky Trust likewise involved a combination of most of the distillers so that some of the plants could be shut down entirely (Jenks 1889: 301–5).

A Hung Jury?

The committee's cryptic report concluded that "the nature, form, and causes of trusts and combinations, and . . . all others in existence are formed in substantially the same way as those referred to in such testimony" (H. Rep. No. 4165 (1889): 1).

The questioning of the witnesses that appeared on behalf of all four trusts revealed a predisposition of the interrogators to prove that these trusts were demonic schemes to wring inflated prices from consumers. The trust issue was politically "hot," and the charge seemingly clear. Yet the committee, after extensive hearings over two years, confessed itself unable to compose a report, even differing majority and minority reports, because of differences among its members.

The committee chose not to articulate what those differences were. But one possible explanation emerged from the obvious slant of the questioning and the failure of the testimony to bear out its expectations: There was no convincing evidence of pricing abuse toward consumers, but there was, on the contrary, affirmative evidence that prices had declined. The only case of "unreasonable" pricing even arguable from all the testimony resulted from the admitted corner in cotton bagging and that transitory speculation was clearly not a scheme to exploit consumers but a defensive reaction to an irrational situation for which government was mainly responsible. The Whisky Trust, like Standard Oil, showed evidence of declining rather than rising prices, and the Sugar Trust showed no more than a modest price increase in a depressed market situation. Every one of the trusts examined was a defensive reaction to distressed market conditions.

A Witches' Brew

The latter nineteenth century produced a confluence of forces in the United States, the like of which occurred nowhere else. First was the sheer size of the continental scope of the U.S. market. Unlike Europe, which was carved up into numerous protected national markets, large businesses in the United States were free to expand across the entire continent, resulting in private concentrations of power the size of which alone produced reactions of alarm. Second, was the stark contrast between the conditions of industry and agriculture. This was compounded by the coincidental fact that their interests were identified with broad geographical regions—the industrial Northeast and the agricultural South and West.

Of profound significance was the plight of the American farmer. United States agriculture in the nineteenth century was torn between three distinct forces—economic, ideological, and geographical—that were to produce a unique kind of political reaction. The economic factor was a combination of the large-scale production made possible by the cultivation of the vast flatlands in the U.S. West and South and the inefficiency of market mechanisms to work as an automatic regulator of supply and demand for cash crops. Ideology worked in two distinct ways. One was the Jeffersonian romanticism of the farming ideal, conceived in the image of subsistance agriculture but unthinkingly transferred to a farming community that produced cash crops, leading to a vast overexpansion of supply. At the same time, the ideology of independence and faith in free markets tended to blind public perception of the basic unworkability of agricultural markets. In this context, the contrasting situation of industrial markets, where both protectionism against international competition and combination against domestic competition were available and utilized, produced an extremely troublesome political brew. Farmers looked on in rage as their own situation fluctuated between prosperity and depression through competitive forces that they were ideologically conditioned to accept, while industry was able to escape this discipline. Farmers, who had to purchase their necessities from industry, were acutely conscious that they were selling in one kind of competitive market and buying in a distinctly different one.

Unlike the railroad problem, that of the trusts was not focused on the problems of a particular industry. The problem of the trusts was generalized, their only common features being those that most irritated the public and politicians alike. They were all lumped together in one hazy public perception of evil that for a generation would be identified as the trust problem.

THE CLIMATE: A POPULIST MYTH AND THE MILLIONAIRES' CLUB

The basic problem noted in the preceding sections regarding railroads and the plague of trusts was rooted in the very different kinds of markets in which agriculture, labor, and industry functioned. As a practical problem this was obvious to all; but there was an important *ideological* barrier to comprehension, and this was that the idealism of free competition and free markets obscured the fact that the heart of the problem lay in market malfunction.

The failure of agricultural and western interests to appreciate fundamental problems for the market mechanism in their own sector led them to feel aggrieved that they were playing by different rules. Conservative, probusiness Republican politicians like Senator Sherman and Marcus Hanna saw the collision inherent in these differing perceptions, and they also saw abuses on the business side. As members of a party identified with business, their motivation was to save it from itself. And so there formed a strange unity of purpose between the two antagonistic political interests: the farmers in their protests, and the politician defenders of big business seeking to eliminate the provocations so as to divert more extreme measures of political reaction.

The leadership that emerged in this situation thus came, not from the agitators of the West and South, but from the probusiness side. It is a standard line of writers seeking to promote economic theory as a rationale for antitrust legislation superior to its political inspiration to characterize the latter as "Populist" (Bork 1978: 5–6; Areeda & Turner 1978: vol. 1: 27–31). But the Sherman Act was not "Populist" legislation. It passed in exactly the form that it was written in the fifty-first Senate, perhaps the most conservative, probusiness Senate in history (Letwin 1956 "Congress": 248; Letwin 1965: 53; Josephson 1938, 1966: 434), and known as the "Millionaires' Club" (Josephson 1938, 1966: 444). This was at the initiative of Senator Sherman, who had been praised at a Republican nominating convention as a man with whom big business could feel comfortable (ibid., 355), and whose manager in his presidential campaign was Marcus Hanna, the man most closely identified with forging the alliance between big business and the Republican party (ibid., 413). The Sherman Act was passed in 1890, the year that the Populist party was just getting organized.[1]

Thus, the legislative setting in which the Sherman Act passed was not a victory by those feeling most victimized by the new economic order; it was, rather, a deft response by those who saw the necessity of dealing with their complaints in a way that would not destroy what they perceived as a vital national force.

SENATOR JOHN SHERMAN

Senator John Sherman had a long and distinguished career in the Senate, and he was one of its most influential members (Kerr 1908). He was a perennial bridesmaid in his quest for the Republican presidential nomination, and his final frustration in this regard prompted him to seize the initiative in pressing for legislation on the trust problem. Sherman believed that his bid had been thwarted by the bribery of some of his delegates with money supplied by the Match Trust.[2]

He returned to the Senate with a sense of missionary zeal to pass an antitrust law. The normal home within the Senate for bills on the subject of trusts would have been the Commerce Committee or Judiciary Committee, but Sherman moved to corner the entire subject in his own Finance Committee. His rationale was that the only constitutional authority Congress could invoke successfully against the trusts was the tax power. He succeeded in this, and all bills were referred to his committee, including one based on common law principles that its author had tried to have sent to the Judiciary Committee (19 *Cong. Rec.*: 6041, 7512–13 (1888); 20 ibid., 1461–62 (1889)).

SHERMAN'S THEORY OF HIS BILL

When Sherman introduced his bill, however, he announced a different rationale. Reversing his earlier position, he now found the commerce power sufficient authority. The substance of the bill he drew from the common law of the states:

> It does not announce a new principle of law, but applies old and well recognized principles of the common law to the complicated jurisdiction of our State and Federal Government. . . .

> The purpose of this bill is to enable the courts of the United States to apply the same remedies against combinations which injuriously affect the interests of the United States that have been applied in the several States to protect local interests. (21 *Cong Rec.*: 2456 (March 21, 1890))

He grounded the need for a federal law on the jurisdictional limits of the states to enforce these principles (ibid.).

Sherman opposed criminal sanctions on the ground that the subject was too new to warrant the imposition of criminal penalties. He also thought the absence of criminal penalties would enable the courts to interpret the act more broadly as a remedial measure (ibid., 2456, 2562–64). This was an early casualty of the amendment process. Those favoring a criminal sanction argued that individuals could often not afford to sue, so the government must (ibid., 2569). And, it was added with some conviction that some of the things these trusts were doing were criminal (ibid., 2469, 2567).

Sherman stated his philosophical position emphatically as opposition to the concentration of power in private hands:

> If the concerted powers of this corporation are entrusted to a single man, it is a kingly prerogative, inconsistent with our form of government, and should be subject to the strong resistance of the State and national authorities. If anything is wrong this is wrong. If we will not endure a king as a political power we should not endure a king over the production, transportation, and sale of any of the necessities of life. It we would not submit to an emperor we should not submit to an autocrat of trade, with power to prevent competition and to fix the price of any commodity. (ibid., 2547)

Sherman made clear that he was as concerned about the ability of the small businessperson to survive as about the exploitive powers of the trusts:

> I am not opposed to combinations in and of themselves; I do not care how much men combine for proper objects; but when they combine with a purpose to prevent competition, so that if a humble man starts a business in opposition to them, solitary and alone, in Ohio or anywhere else, they will crowd him down and they will sell their product at a loss or give it away in order to prevent competition, and when that is established by evidence that cannot be questioned, then it is the duty of the courts to intervene and prevent it. (ibid.)

Senator Sherman cited chapter and verse in support of his common law theory. He cited several cases in which U.S. state courts had refused to enforce contracts because they were part of a scheme to monopolize; and with reportedly some emotion he read a lengthy extract from a Michigan Supreme Court case refusing to enforce a bond obligation because it was part of a scheme to monopolize the match business—the trust that had bribed away his delegates at the Republican convention (ibid., 2457–59; Letwin 1956 "Congress": 253).

CHAOS

The legislative debates leading to the passage of the Sherman Act were taken up mainly with constitutional questions about what the federal government could do. No formal report was issued by the Senate Finance Committee, which reported the bill, nor did it conduct public hearings. The place of the report, however, was taken by a long speech by Senator Sherman on the Senate floor (from which the above extracts were taken) in which he spelled out very clearly the rationale on which his bill was based. Equally illuminating is the course the bill followed on its way to enactment.

Amidst the continuing agonizing over constitutional questions, the bill attracted a growing number of amendments, which Senator Sherman accepted without question. He seemed oblivious to matters of detail, intent only on getting some kind of bill enacted. The continuing onslaught of amendments, including conceptual approaches quite different from Sherman's original bill, rendered the collective whole a bundle of incoherence (Kerr 1908: 203). As this process continued, repeated motions were made to refer the bill to the Judiciary Committee for redrafting, Senator Sherman's change of rationale having removed the premise for placing it in the Finance Committee. Sherman fought these motions bitterly, pleading that delay would mean no legislation at all. But votes favoring referral were greater on the second motion than on the first, and on the third carried the day after the following remarks by Senator Platt (21 *Cong. Rec.*: 2731).

Senator Platt's decisive speech explained at length and with some passion why he could not vote for the bill in its then-existing form. His remarks are some of the most explicit on the substance of the law in the entire debate. He thought it intolerable that all measures to bolster distressed prices should be illegal.

> [T]his bill proceeds on the false assumption that all competition is beneficial to the country, and that every advance of price is an injury to the country. . . . I am entirely sick of the idea that the lower the prices are the better for the country, and that any effort to advance prices, no matter how low they may be, and that any arrangement between persons engaged in business to advance prices, no matter how low they may be, is a wrong and ought to b repressed and punished. (ibid., 2729)

He proposed instead a standard of fair and reasonable prices, but he found Senator Sherman's bill inconsistent with that result (ibid.).

Immediately following these and further remarks by Senator Platt to the same effect, the Senate reversed its earlier votes and referred the bill to the Judiciary Committee under a tight deadline of three weeks on March 27, 1890 (ibid., 2731). The Judiciary Committee reported back in one week, on April 2 (ibid.; Letwin 1956 "Congress": 254).

"IN THE FORM OF TRUST OR OTHERWISE"

The Judiciary Committee was a group of conservative lawyers without any notions of social or economic engineering. Senator Sherman had explained his theory in terms of enacting nothing more than existing common law principles, and the committee took this guidance quite literally. The archival records show that the only concession to the politics of the time made by Senator Edmonds, who dominated the actual drafting, was the inclusion of the single phrase "in the form of trust or otherwise" (Letwin 1956 "Congress": 254).

The entire bill with its accumulation of amendments was stricken and the judiciary's substitute replaced it. Gone was the reference in Sherman's bill to full and free competition, and to increasing prices, among the other casualties. Sherman announced that he would vote for the bill, "not as being precisely what I want, but as the best under all the circumstances that the Senate is prepared to give in this direction" (21 *Cong. Rec.*: 3145).

Senator Kenna of West Virginia enquired concerning the meaning of monopoly in Section 2 of the bill, asking whether a man who by his own skill gains a monopoly, if that makes him a culprit. Senator Edmonds, who reported the bill for the Judiciary Committee, answered no, that monopoly had a specific meaning. Senator Hoar, the chairman of the committee, then explained that " 'monopoly' " is a technical term known to the common law, that it is "a mere technical term which has a clear legal signification. . . . It is the sole engrossing to a man's self by means which prevent other men from engaging in fair competition with him" (ibid., 3152). Kenna then asked why, if it was an offense at common law, is there a need for the bill; and Hoar explained that there is no common law of the United States, only of the respective states themselves, and that the bill would merely extend the same principle to interstate commerce (ibid.).

The bill passed the Senate without amendment, 52–1 (ibid., 3152–53). It was not amended in the House, and it passed without a single dissenting vote (ibid., 5953).

NOTES

1. Hicks (1928); Pollack (1962). Hofstadter (1955: 108), in listing the legislative successes of the Populist movement, makes no mention of antitrust, either

federal or state. See also Thorelli 1955: 361–62 and Dudden 1950 and 1957. Nor does the label fit the legislation of 1914, the Populist party having expired with the election of 1912.

2. Thorelli 1955: 168 discounts this factor as motivating Senator Sherman, but all the evidence corroborates it. Senator Sherman, in his autobiography, *Recollections,* expresses a feeling of "resentment" over what he regarded as a "corrupt New York bargain" (pp. 793, 795); and his chapter entitled "The Sherman Act" is devoted almost entirely to his Silver Purchase Act, with only a perfunctory reference to the Antitrust Law, which also expresses a tone of resentment (p. 821). Most revealing is the extraordinary effort he made to direct all bills on trusts to his own Finance Committee, causing the president of the Senate to overcome his own inclination to commit them to the Commerce Committee or to the Judiciary Committee (19 *Cong. Rec.*: 6041, 7512–13 (1888); 20 ibid., 1461–62 (1889)). See also Letwin 1956 "Congress": 253 (citing the special personal interest of Senator Sherman in reading from a Michigan case denouncing the match monopoly) and ("Origins") 253 and 1965: 87.

5

Antitrust as Economic Policy

THREE LEVELS OF RULES

It was noted in Chapter 1 that there have been three different approaches to antitrust policy: the moral view of the problem as one of wrongdoing to be dealt with through law enforcement; the efficiency/consumer welfare view; and the rules-of-the-game concept in the legislation of 1914. This last, the rules-of-the-game concept, is not so simple as it may at first appear, for there are different types of rules that perform distinctly different functions, and those differences are of fundamental importance to a clear view of what antitrust policy is all about.

The rules of all games fall into three categories, which might be thought of as three different levels: Level 1 is present in all games; it defines the essence of the game: the number of points scored by driving a football into the end zone, a soccer ball or a hockey puck into the net, and so on. A second level of rules performs a distinctly different function and appears in only a select group of league sports. Level 2 rules have the purpose of deterring types of behavior that circumvent that which the level 1 rules are designed to produce. Thus in sports such as American football, soccer, hockey, and basketball there are types of conduct deemed foul, a concept of wrongdoing. And there is yet a third level of rules, singularly distinct from the other two and fundamentally different in nature. Unlike level 1 and level 2 rules, all of which are strictly neutral as between the participants, level 3 rules discriminate between them, tilting the board, leaning against the most successful competitors, and in favor of the least successful. This seemingly perverse policy is based, not on considerations of efficiency or fairness, but on an overriding policy to maintain balance and continuity in the competitive process.

The most obvious examples of level 3 rules are the systems of player drafts in professional league sports, in which the teams that finish with the poorest records are given the top draft choices, and those that finished ahead must stand in line behind them. A pure market system would tend to the opposite bias, with the most successful, and prosperous, teams more advantageously positioned to attract the best young players. It has been the virtually universal recognition that such a process, though it would likely yield the most superior teams, would unbalance the competitive tension that provides the essential entertainment value that makes the sport economically viable. The same concept appears in such individual sports as tennis and golf, with the seeding of top-ranked tennis players and the handicap system in golf.

Now lay the antitrust laws alongside this tripartite division of the rules of games: There is no element of level 1 rules in antitrust. The counterpart of level 1 rules in business is commercial, labor, and tax law. Antitrust, in its Sherman Act incarnation, is clearly a level 2 rule, punishing with both civil and criminal penalties acts deemed inherently wrongful.

The legislation of 1914, however, is a case of predominantly level 3 rules. There are no criminal penalties. Although several types of specific conduct are prohibited by the Clayton Act, which is in part a level 2 concept, all of these prohibitions are qualified in terms of their effect on competition. The prohibition of price discrimination, tying agreements, and exclusive dealing are all provisions designed to keep firms in a position of strength from using that strength to exclude competitors. There is no criterion of efficiency or consumer benefit. The value being protected is the preservation of a competitive context in business.

The distinction between level 2 and level 3 rules is the essence of the argument presented here, not to the exclusion of level 2 rules as civil, not criminal, violations, but with the emphasis on level 3 as the true focal point of antitrust policy.

THE JUDICIARY AS ECONOMIC POLICY MAKER I: QUIBBLES OVER THE COMMON LAW (1897–1927)

The concept of the legislative authors of the Sherman Act was simple and straightforward: Two basic principles developed by the courts at common law regarding monopolization and contracts in restraint of trade were being incorporated by reference into federal legislation so that the courts could apply them on a nationwide basis. Some judges early on construed the law in precisely this way, citing common law precedents as the basis for their decisions interpreting the Sherman Act (*Jellico*, 43 Fed. 898 (1890); *Trans-Missouri*, 58 Fed. 58 (1893); *Addyston*, 85 Fed. 271 (1898). But the Supreme Court was not among them. What the Supreme Court did amounts to nothing less than wreaking mayhem on the Sherman Act, choking off the very body of precedents that was intended to guide its interpretation in favor of a set of per se rules that were literally made up out of whole cloth. What happened may be seen as a drama in three acts, with one central villain—the Supreme Court's turn-of-the-century refusal to consider legislative history as a source for the interpretation of legislation.

Act 1 was the *Trans-Missouri* decision of 1897 (166 U.S. 290). The case was brought by the government against a railroad pool. The pool was one of many formed during that era of railroad overbuilding, which resulted in rate wars, cutthroat competition, bankruptcies, and general chaos in the industry (Chap. 2). The pool, according to the facts as found by the trial court (53 Fed. 440 (1892)), and affirmed by the Court of Appeals (58 Fed. 58 (1893)), was a conscientious effort to strike a fair balance between the railroads and their customers, among other things setting tariffs at rates considered fair to both sides. The trial court evaluated the facts in the light of common law precedents that approved contractual restraints entered into for a legitimate purpose and which were reasonable in the restraints they imposed. The Court of Appeals followed the same approach, agreed with the findings of the trial court, and found no violation of the Sherman Act.

The Supreme Court, in a sharply divided 5–4 decision, reversed. Both the majority and minority were agreed on one point: The legislative history of the Sherman Act could not be considered as a source for interpretation of the act. But this barrier was seemingly rendered moot by another rule of statutory interpretation: that when a statute employs terms that have a technically established meaning at common law, the common law as it stood at the time of enactment will be used as a guide to interpretation. This seemingly simple solution, however, foundered on a quibble.

The five-man majority opinion turned to the common law and found that it had changed over time. The earliest cases had declared all contractual restraints of trade illegal across the board. The first cases, which produced this strong reaction, involved the sale of a business in which the seller contracted not to compete with the new owner. The Court, focusing on the contractual prohibition of practicing one's trade, found the provision so offensive as a matter of social policy that it would not be enforced. With later cases, however, the courts came to see the reasonableness of such an undertaking as essential to making a business salable and so came to accept such restraints when limited to terms reasonably calculated to accomplish that purpose (Letwin 1954: 376–79). The five-man majority concluded from this history that not all restraints were illegal at common law; and citing, with emphasis, the language of the Sherman Act, which declared "*every* contract in restraint of trade" to be illegal, it concluded that the Sherman Act differed from the common law standard, which therefore could not be used as a basis for interpreting the statute. In dissent, Justice White, who would later become chief justice and author the historic *Standard Oil* decision of 1911, argued that the common law standard should be applied. He answered the majority's argument with the contention that as the common law changed to accept some contractual restraints as reasonable, the usage of the term "contract in restraint of trade" changed also, being applied only to those restraints held to be unreasonable. Contracts imposing only reasonable restraints were not labeled as "contracts in restraint of trade." Applying the common law standard in this light, Justice White and three other justices viewed the railroad pool, which included price fixing, as legal.

Justice White did not support his argument by reference to legislative history, which he conceded to be inadmissable under the Court's then-prevailing rule. (This was an aberration; the Court has since accepted legislative history routinely as a source of statutory interpretation. (*Mo. Pac. R. Co.*, 278 U.S. at 278–79 (1928); *Apex*, 310 U.S. 469 (1940)). Had the history been consulted it would have definitely supported White's view and shown the majority to be wrong, for, as we saw in Chapter 4, it was not part of the legislative authors' intention to make any change in the substance of the common law. The issue so sharply divided the Court that it was reargued in another case involving a railroad pool the following year with the same result (*Joint Traffic*, 171 U.S. 505 (1898)).

Act 2 in the drama was the *Standard Oil* case of 1911 (221 U.S. 1). The vast body of scholarly commentary on this decision is remarkable for what it overlooks, for this decision was highly bizarre by the normal standards of appellate decision making. Why bizarre? Because one of the most basic rules of appellate decision making is that a court will decide only those questions that are necessary to resolve the case before it, leaving untouched all issues not critical to the result. The *Standard Oil* case was a quintessential monopolization case. The trial court found that Standard Oil had monopolized and attempted to monopolize; the Court of Appeals affirmed unanimously, and all nine justices of the Supreme Court agreed. Here was a case that by normal standards called for nothing more than a summary affirmance. Why, then, did Justice White write an elaborate opinion on the interpretation of the term "contracts in restraint of trade" to establish the historic Rule of Reason? The answer is comprehensible only in light of the *Trans-Missouri* decision. Justice White saw an opportunity to overrule that precedent and persuaded all but one of the justices to go along with him. To do so he had to misrepresent the state of the common law. In order to drag the "contract in restraint of trade" language into this monopolization case, White asserted that monopolization by private parties was not an offense at common law, citing the English Monopolies Statute that was directed against the establishment of monopolies by the government (221 U.S. 1 at 10). He was not alone in this error (Taft 1914: 7–8; cf. Wilberforce, Campbell & Ellis 1966: 19, 21, 22, pars. 105, 113; Letwin 1954)), which was one more reflection of the failure to consult legislative history. Senator Sherman, in his speech to the Senate, cited a number of common law cases that held private monopolization to be offensive, and he quoted at length from a Michigan case that refused to enforce a simple corporate bond because it was part of an overall scheme to monopolize the match industry. Moreover, Senator Hoar, when queried on the Senate floor as to the meaning of the offense of monopolizing, replied that it was a technical term with an established meaning at common law (21 Cong. Rec. 3152 (1890); Destler 1967: 134–35, 146; Dudden 1950: 493).

His reference was not to the word "monopoly," but to "engrossing," one of three closely related common law terms, the other two being "forestalling" and "regrating" (Letwin 1954: 381–82; Taft 1914: 7–8). All may be described in today's language as various forms of getting a corner on the market. In the postmedieval English economy the occasional shipments of supplies to numerous small towns enabled sharp operators to meet the incoming merchant before he got to town—forestalling—and buy up his entire supply, which was then resold at a tidy markup. This was for a time a statutory criminal offense, but the legislation was later repealed because it also banned desirable forms of retailing. The practices nevertheless remained offenses at common law (ibid.).

Overlooking both the legislative history and the common law background, Justice White argued that the Section 2 prohibition against monopolization could not stand on its own but had to be construed in light of Section 1. This sleight-of-hand accomplished, he then launched into his famous Rule of Reason opinion, purporting (somewhat tongue-in-cheek) to overrule *Trans-Missouri*.

No one called him on his faulty logic for dragging in Section 1 (except Walker, Albert 1911), but Justice Harlan refused to go along on the overruling of *Trans-Missouri*. Harlan and White were the only members of the *Trans-Missouri* court still sitting, and Harlan had voted with the majority in 1897—and had not changed his mind.

Chief Justice White was seemingly successful in his purpose. His opinion cited *Trans-Missouri*, though not his own dissent; and after a ritual argument that the result there could be reconciled with the *Standard Oil* decision, he declared the latter opinion to prevail on any points of conflict. He must have regarded his triumph as complete.

But it was not. Justice Harlan in a vehement dissent held to his literalist *Trans-Missouri* view that the Sherman Act declared illegal all contracts that restrained trade, reasonable or unreasonable, and he accused the majority of judicial legislation by reading the word "unreasonable" into the statute. Again, had anyone consulted the legislative history, Chief Justice White would have been conclusively shown to be right and Justice Harlan wrong; but no one did. White's own opinion expressly eschewed legislative history, citing *Trans-Missouri* on that point, and it also did not repeat his argument in dissent in *Trans-Missouri* of the changing usage of the term "contract in restraint of trade." In consequence, Harlan's dissent appeared highly plausible, and a general perception that he was correct may well have influenced the Court's treatment of the Sherman Act for half a century thereafter.

Another feature of White's opinion may have contributed to this result. Unlike then Circuit Judge William Howard Taft's famous *Addyston* opinion (85 Fed. 271), the two lower court decisions in *Trans-Missouri* (53 Fed. 440; 58 Fed. 58), and a few others, White's opinion did not include extensive citations of common law precedents. Rather than conveying the impression these other opinions do, of arguing that the present result follows from a chain of specific precedents, White's opinion took, rather, the form of his own freehand restatement of the law. A general reference to common law precedents was consigned to a footnote, and the body of the opinion was simply White's own statement. The uniform treatment of the *Standard Oil* decision, both in other cases and the literature, has been to regard it as an original creation, a starting point, as though the Rule of Reason was created there, rather than establishing a link between the Sherman Act and earlier common law precedents. What in effect happened was that the Rule of Reason became disembodied from the common law. Instead of acting as a vehicle for connecting the language of the Sherman Act to common law precedents, only the Rule of Reason itself survived, and even that only as stated in Chief Justice White's opinion, not through earlier common law precedents.

Act 3 of the drama was the *Trenton Potteries* decision of 1927 (273 U.S. 392). The Court was confronted with a set of facts somewhat like *Trans-Missouri*, and the defense was made, based on *Standard Oil*, that the prices agreed upon were reasonable. The opinion, which cited *Trans-Missouri* favorably (273 U.S. at 398), was a step backward in that direction. It injected a new idea, one that did not appear in the common law, of per se offenses, which were not to be judged by the standard of reasonableness. The link to the common law had been effectively severed, the one clearest intention of the Sherman Act's authors totally rejected.

The Court has on later occasions affirmatively declared common law precedents to be relevant guides to Sherman Act interpretation, but the

Court has for so long not followed this course that there has been a large hiatus in the case law development that it is probably too late to close. The *Trans-Missouri* majority's mistaken quibble over the meaning of the term "contract in restraint of trade" has thus had a permanent and distorting impact on the law.

And the quibbles continue. Robert Bork's academic writings, though at one point declaring unequivocally that the only conscious intent of the Sherman Act authors was to enact the common law (Bork 1966: 22) nevertheless argue that the statute did not do so (ibid., 36–37). His reason is that there was conflict in the cases at common law, thus making impossible any coherent rule that could be applied by the courts, and that the selection of cases cited by Senator Sherman was an unrepresentative, artificial construct. Neither point is well taken. Conflicts in the cases come with the territory in the common law; judges are accustomed to pick and choose, as Bork himself notes that Judge Taft did in his *Addyston* opinion (Bork 1978: 27). Also, it is a misreading of Senator Sherman's speech to say that he was making an artificial construct of the law. The senator was not purporting to describe the whole of the law, only to cite a few illustrative cases to show that the common law courts had addressed the problems at issue (Chap. 4).

The quibbles, though ill-founded, have prevailed, as we shall see later in this chapter ("Judiciary II").

TINKERING WITH THE ECONOMY: THE LEGISLATION OF 1914 AND AFTERTHOUGHTS

Congress was coming to accept the economic policy implications of antitrust legislation by 1914. The kind of obvious predatory practices that led to criminal penalties in the Sherman Act proved to be the exception rather than the rule, which brought the underlying economic problems closer to the surface, though this was still not widely perceived. Especially frustrating to the lawmakers was the fact that the growth of "trusts" was neither stopped nor visibly slowed by the enactment of the Sherman Act, and their proliferation continued even under the vigorous prosecution policy of President Theodore Roosevelt.

Congress was also beginning to focus on some of the more obvious defects of the Sherman Act as a device for controlling business: Its broad, vague language was a parody of the kind of clarity and specificity customary in regulating commercial matters. A need was also felt to adjust practical problems through an administrative mechanism, and the announcement by the Supreme Court of the Rule of Reason served as a spur for Congress to assert itself in the making of policy.

The economic dilemma was also now becoming quite obvious to some segments of opinion. President Roosevelt came to the belief that the trusts in some form or another represented economic inevitability; and because such concentrations of private power were excessive, he favored resort to regulation (Hofstadter 1955: 245–47).

Two different approaches developed in the Senate and House (Kintner 1978, 1980, 1982). The Senate felt the only need was to make the content of the law more specific by enumerating specific prohibited acts. This was attempted through the Clayton Act bans on anticompetitive mergers, tying and exclusive dealing agreements, price discrimination, and interlocking boards of directors. The House, on the other hand, saw a need for a flexible approach and the need for administrative expertise. President Wilson, though agreeable to this, insisted that the Sherman Act should be left as it was; the result was a compromise in which the House got its administrative agency while the Clayton Act embodied the Senate's approach—and the Sherman Act was left untouched.

Both the Clayton and FTC Acts embodied what has been referred to here as level 3 concepts: rules designed to offset in part the advantages enjoyed by more powerful firms, and to affirmatively aid the survival of small business. The Clayton Act ban on price discrimination was intended to prevent large retailers from gaining an edge over small business through volume discounts. The ban on tying agreements was also an offset to the market power of large and powerful firms.

An element of conscious policy making was also injected. Each of these practices was singled out as potentially, but not necessarily, harmful to competition, and so each was hedged by a qualification that the effect of the practice "may be substantially to lessen competition or tend to create a monopoly." Here, Congress (1) intervened directly in business decisions on grounds of economic policy rather than because they were wrongful or criminal, (2) introduced the word "competition" as a criterion of the law that required the courts to exercise discretionary judgment, and (3) made explicit the protective purpose of antitrust legislation, even at some possible loss of efficiency.

Afterthoughts: The point was made in Chapter 1 that all of the conceptual elements of present legislative antitrust policy were in place by 1914. Significant legislation was to follow, but it was in the nature of plugging loopholes, not adding new concepts. The Robinson-Patman Act of 1936 concerning price discrimination and the Cellar-Kefauver Act of 1950 on mergers were reaffirmations and tightening of ideas already present in the legislation of 1914. Other legislation has addressed procedural matters, but the fact remains that the substantive core of U.S. legislative policy has not advanced beyond the probing insights of 1914.

THE STILLBIRTH OF THE FTC

> Now let me make this prediction. I have often been warned not to make prophecies, but let me make the prediction that if the Trade

> Commission is at all successful... in less than 10 years you will never hear of an action to dissolve a monopoly under the Sherman ... law.
>
> Senator Borah (Kintner 1978: vol. 3: 2582)

To the many businesspeople and their attorneys who have experienced the burdens of litigation and other intrusions by the FTC into the conduct of their businesses, the suggestion that this agency was stillborn will seem strange indeed. To be sure, a bureaucracy was created, and though much criticized for ineffectiveness (Stone, 1977; Kirkpatrick, 1969, 1989), it has been a factor that business has had to reckon with. What was stillborn was the agency that its legislative authors thought they were creating—an expert body knowledgeable in the realities of the business world, whose sheer expertise would overshadow and eventually eclipse the Sherman Act (Blaisdell 1932: 255–56, 288–90). In comparison to its primary foreign counterparts, the directorate of the European Commission responsible for competition matters, and the West German Federal Cartel Office (FCO), the FTC has nothing like the power, authority, and prestige of these foreign institutions; even at home it is overshadowed by the Antitrust Division of the Department of Justice.

The reasons for this disappointed expectation cannot be proved definitively; but there are, with the benefit of historical hindsight, a number of factors that appear to have played a major role in this debacle.

First is the failure to fold the Sherman Act into this newly formed administrative agency. This was not an oversight; it was the universal determination of both President Wilson and Congress, on both sides of the aisle, not to make any change in the Sherman Act by this new legislation. Ordinarily, when Congress reaches the conclusion that an area of economic policy making requires the expertise of an administrative agency, the agency is given full authority over the entire legislative scheme. The very general, even vague, language of the Sherman Act made it a natural object for submission to the new administrative agency; but the prevailing political mood at the time still viewed antitrust largely in terms of criminal behavior.

A second factor that stunted the growth of the FTC was a combination of overly restrictive Supreme Court decisions, which have since been overruled by the Court, and a series of weak political appointments in its early years (Blaisdell 1932: 259–90).

A third factor is the institutional structure of the FTC. This has two dimensions. One is the fact that the Commission is a collegial body that does not speak with one voice, as does the head of the Antitrust Division in the Department of Justice. This dimension of the problem is compounded by the fact that the Commission is outside the executive branch, which tends to minimize its influence on policy. The second dimension of the institutional problem is that despite its nominal status as an independent agency, it is politically an agency of the Congress and so vulnerable to whatever political winds may be blowing at the time (Nader et al. 1972: 323–25, 333). The Antitrust Division in fact enjoys greater political independence than the FTC.

Finally, a fourth factor may be that the mission of the FTC was fundamentally misconceived. As expressed in the lead quote to this section, the primary concern of the Congress in 1914 was monopoly, and the purpose behind creating the FTC was to nip monopoly in the bud. United States policy at that time was preoccupied with monopoly. The fact that substantial market problems may arise short of the extreme case of monopoly may suggest that the FTC's mandate to prevent monopoly was in some measure a case of generals fighting the last war.

THE JUDICIARY AS ECONOMIC POLICY MAKER II: MECHANISTIC POLICY

An Overview

To describe the judiciary as an economic policy maker sounds like a contradiction in terms. It is a role stoutly denied by many judges and especially by enforcement officials. The criminal sanctions in the Sherman Act provide some credence to a Justice Department official's view of his office as just that of the cop on the corner, enforcing the law as it is, and to the court's view that it is performing the same function. Finding facts is a purely judicial function, as is the determination of whether those facts amount to a violation of law.

But the criteria of the legislation itself unavoidably raise questions of economic policy. Does a contract or combination unreasonably restrain trade? Does a merger, a price discrimination, or an exclusive dealing agreement impair competition or tend to result in monopoly? Whichever way such questions are answered is to make economic policy, whatever the state of mind of the decision maker. If policy is put out of mind altogether, it is nonetheless made by default.

Moreover, the very concepts taken over by the Sherman Act from the common law were pure exercises in judicial policy making. There is a species of cases in which the courts, lacking any statutory mandate, will on their own motion refuse to sanction a contract or other document on the ground that what it seeks to do is inherently repugnant to public policy. It is on this ground that the courts refused to enforce contracts or wills conditioned on abstention from marriage, contracts entered into by children, and the like. The rule against contracts in restraint of trade arose from this same tradition. The courts were alarmed at the prospect of a man signing away his right to earn a livelihood (Wilberforce, Campbell & Ellis, 1966: 35–36); and the evils of monopoly were likewise invoked even to the point of declaring illegal a royal grant of a monopoly by Queen Elizabeth (ibid., pars. 104–39, pp. 18–34; Letwin 1954). The common law offenses of engrossing, forestalling, and regrating—that is, cornering the market—which were the model for the Sherman Act ban on monopolization, originated in judicial decisions based on social policy values (Letwin 1954: 368–73; Taft 1914: 17–18). Antitrust concepts are thus firmly rooted in the most explicit exercises of judicial declarations of public policy.

There have been some judicial decisions in this tradition under the Sherman Act, such as the Supreme Court's first strong antitrust ruling barring a railroad merger in the *Northern Securities* decision of 1904 (193 U.S. 197); and Judge Learned Hand's opinion in *Alcoa* (148 F.2d 416, 429 (1945)): "Throughout the history of these statutes it has been constantly assumed that one of their purposes was to perpetuate and preserve, for its own sake and in spite of possible cost, an organization of industry in small units which can effectively compete with each other." Other strong decisions were the Supreme Court's decision in 1912 announcing the principle that the owner of an essential facility must grant fair access to other users (*Terminal RR of St. Louis*, 224 U.S. 383), in the Court's decisions declaring illegal tying and exclusive dealing contracts (*Northern Pacific*, 356 U.S. 1 (1958); *Standard Stations*, 337 U.S. 293 (1939)) and group boycotts (*Klor's*, 359 U.S. 207 (1959)), and in decisions refusing to accept exclusionary practices in local geographic markets where the defense was that they were only fractions of a much wider geographic market (*Indiana Farmers'*, 293 U.S. 268 (1934)).

But these bold policy declarations are atypical. The most truly judicial conservatives—Holmes, Frankfurter, both Harlans—did not make any significant contributions to antitrust and might even be described as having been uncomfortable with it. The Supreme Court declared its support for Hand's ruling in *Alcoa* but did not adopt his broad policy pronouncements (*American Tobacco*, 328 U.S. 781, 813–14 (1946)); Neale 1970: 112).

The main policy impact of Supreme Court rulings for approximately 50 years, from 1927 to 1977, was in the pronouncement and application of per se rules. During this period the Supreme Court took particular delight in this concept, which greatly facilitated the process of judicial decision making (*Northern Pacific*, 356 U.S. 1 (1958)). This era came to an end in 1977 with the *GTE Sylvania* case (433 U.S. 36), which for the first time overruled a prior decision declaring a particular business practice illegal per se.

Since then the Court has lost its enthusiasm for the per se approach, which has left something of a vacuum; and that vacuum has tended to be filled by Chicago School doctrines of efficiency and consumer welfare (*Reiter*, 442 U.S. 330, 343 (1979).

The Judiciary as Judiciary

In recounting the performance of the judiciary in the context of antitrust it is important to keep in mind the basic function of the judiciary, which is to decide individual cases. Add to this the basic nature of antitrust policy—to override business decisions made by businessmen—and the awkwardness of the judiciary in such situations is not difficult to explain.

The problem is not the same in all cases. There is a clear distinction between tight combination (single-firm concentration) and loose combination (cartel behavior) cases. The loose combination, restraint-of-trade cases generally do not present particularly difficult problems for the judiciary. The judiciary itself invented the rules, and their application to particular facts is the ordinary grist of the judicial mill. The tight combination (monopolization) cases, on the other hand, often find the judicial fish out of water. The consequences of finding a violation to have occurred are likely to find the court in the position of deciding how a business should be organized differently than the way businesspeople themselves had done it, as Judge Greene has been called upon to do in the AT&T case.

But the distinction is not quite as clear-cut as just described. Some restraint of trade cases involve second guessing a business decision as to how, for example, a retail distribution system should be organized, and most monopolization cases involve mainly claims for monetary damages or injunctive relief of a behavioral sort, without splitting up the offending concern.

The misfit between the judiciary's functions of deciding individual cases and the social override purpose of antitrust policy thus does not arise in all cases. There is, however, a more fundamental and pervasive problem. The nature of the judicial system is inherently decentralized. Individual courts are deciding individual cases on a broad variety of subject matters, of which antitrust cases are a small proportion; and the central problem in all cases from the judge's perspective is which party should prevail. The judge is not engaged in formulating broad programs of social and political policy (with some exceptions, mainly at the Supreme Court level). This element of incoherence is compounded by the widely varied viewpoints of different judges, especially when issues of social or political policy are involved.

This is not said to fault the judiciary or to argue that it has no proper role in an overall antitrust scheme. The point is, rather, that too much of a policy-making role has been left to an institution that has only rarely shown itself capable of rising to the occasion and that, arguably, when it did so, may not have been acting its most judicial. Further, to make the point that where the legislative purpose is to establish an economic policy, the diverse, uncentralized structure of the judiciary makes this virtually impossible. One Court of Appeals may decide a case 180 degrees differently than another; but if it wishes to do so, there are any number of ways that it can mask its opinion to conceal the conflict. In theory, Supreme Court review tends to reconcile such conflicts, but in reality that Court reviews but a fraction of the cases in which they occur. The reliance on the judiciary as the first line in formulating and applying what is essentially a policy-making function virtually assures that policy will not be applied consistently, and that has been true of U.S. antitrust policy.

Before leaving the subject of the judiciary as judiciary another and distinctly different point should be made, one that has been remarked often. The judicial system, for the purpose of facilitating the performance of its basic function, deciding cases, has developed elaborate discovery and trial procedures that are both costly and extremely time consuming. This poses two distinct problems in antitrust cases. One is the extensive discovery practice that arises in cases going to a company's business practices, which causes much delay and expense. These discovery rules were formulated having in mind the normal judicial docket, which usually involves less complex matters than an antitrust case. The mixture of these rules with the voluminous factual materials involved in antitrust cases has resulted in a proliferation of "monster" cases.

The second problem is a question that has been raised as to the suitability of normal trial procedures to the ascertainment of complex economic issues raised in antitrust litigation (Dession 1949: 1271).

The Judiciary as Legislator

It was noted at the end of "Judiciary I" that Justice Harlan's dissent from the *Standard Oil* decision was off the mark in accusing the majority of judicial legislation, for the Rule of Reason was much more in tune with the legislative intent than his own literalist interpretation. But no one at the time defended Justice White's opinion on the ground stated here, and the question of whether there should be a legislative correction was considered though rejected in the course of the legislative debates of 1914 (Kintner 1978: vol. 2: 1349 and vol. 3: 2509, 2784–85, 2804).

Although the Rule of Reason escaped legislative revision, the Court itself changed course in 1927 and effectively frustrated Justice White's effort to connect the Sherman Act to the common law. In addition to the failure to invoke the legislative history, another factor may have resulted from the fact that Justice White's rationale for raising the issue of reasonableness was a subterfuge. Had there actually been an issue as to what constitutes an illegal contractual restraint in the *Standard Oil* case, White's opinion likely would have been studded with citations to earlier common law precedents, which would have established the connection to the common law. Instead, White's opinion was written in the abstract, as a kind of freehand restatement of the law. As such, the opinion is regarded as the origin of the Rule of Reason, the personal creation of Justice White, rather than as the forging link between the Sherman Act and the common law.

Whatever the reasons, the Court in the *Trenton Potteries* decision of 1927 (273 U.S. 392) effectively severed the link between the Sherman Act and the common law by inventing a new concept of per se rules, which carved out whole areas that would not be appraised under the Rule of Reason but by absolute rules invented by the Supreme Court (Oppenheim 1952).

It is true that the Supreme Court has since affirmed that common law precedents are relevant to the Sherman Act; but these have been isolated incidents, not a general return to common law principles. Rather than examining each case under the common law standards, the Court was making up rules, acting more like a legislature than a court.

Price Fixing: A Bootstrap Felony?

It is not the point here to defend price fixing as a general principle. The point is, rather, that price fixing is more a symptom than a disease, and that what it is a symptom of is something that most economists and all antitrust ideologues refuse to admit: of markets that are not efficiently self-regulating.

That agreements between competitors setting the prices they charge is behavior harmful to the public interest has legal precedents dating as far back as Roman times (Wilberforce, Campbell & Ellis 1966: 20–21; Rahl 1971 ("Overview"): 766). It is explicitly proscribed by the leading European antitrust regimes cited here as models of a more realistic policy. But those prohibitions are not absolute. Exceptions are possible and have been made. The common law prior to *Trenton Potteries* generally disapproved of price-fixing agreements, but not unconditionally (Peppin 1940).

The Antitrust Procedures and Penalties Act of 1974 for the first time declared price fixing to be a felony (88 Stat. 1706 (1974); 15 U.S.C. Secs. 16(b)–(i) (1976)), so that it is, in fact, law. How this came to pass is an object lesson in bad government and how policy should not be made. It is in large measure a result of the Supreme Court's acting more like a legislature than a court over a span of 50 years.

United States courts, on one occasion or another, have followed three different rationales to the conclusion that agreements between competitors on price are illegal. The first was the *Trans-Missouri* decision of 1897, reading the Sherman Act literally as outlawing "every" contract that restrains trade, ostensibly overruled by the *Standard Oil* decision of 1911. A second rationale was offered by Judge Taft's *Addyston* decision of 1898 (85 Fed. 271), based on numerous common law precedents. But the Court of Appeals in *Trans-Missouri* cited different precedents (58 Fed. 58), and more recent scholarship has shown that the common law rule was not the inflexible rule adopted by Taft or the Supreme Court (Peppin 1940).

The third, and definitive, rationale was provided by *Trenton Potteries* (273 U.S. 392 (1927)). The Court pointed to nothing in the legislative history that expressed congressional concern over price fixing—there was none. In fact, the only reference to it in the Sherman Act debates, as pointed out in Chapter 4, was Senator Platt's empassioned criticism of Senator Sherman's bill because it would *not* have permitted price agreements to assure merchants a fair price during depressed times. Senator Platt's speech was immediately followed by the vote that sent Sherman's bill back for rewriting by the Judiciary Committee, and that committee unanimously reported the bill that became the Sherman Act.

The Court did not express judicial outrage at price fixing as inherently criminal. Its rationale was simply one of judicial convenience: Courts and prosecutors cannot be expected to be making judgments from day to day about whether prices agreed upon between competitors are reasonable. Common law courts had done so (Peppin 1940), but no mention was made of this. (The Court did at the end of its opinion reject some common law cases that the losing party had cited as inapplicable, which may have been true as to the facts in *Trenton Potteries*, but the opinion contains no acknowledgment that the common law cases did not follow a per se rule). The Court did make some comments at the end of its opinion that it saw no useful public purpose in agreements of this kind, but this was an afterthought, not the primary impetus to its decision, which was plainly a consideration of judicial convenience.

The Sherman Act, contrary to Senator Sherman's own inclinations, carried criminal penalties. Those penalties were inserted in reaction to some rather spectacularly outrageous behavior by various of the nineteenth-century trusts. There is no significant evidence linking criminal penalties to concerns over consumer welfare. The emotional concerns in Congress were with what powerful businesspeople were doing to powerless businesspeople.

There is in place a criminal statute. The Supreme Court has declared a bright line rule. Officials in the Justice Department, both career employees and political appointees, through a process of natural selection, tend to associate big business with moral wrongdoing. What the Supreme Court addressed as a consideration primarily of judicial convenience was translated by the enforcement bureaucracy into a matter of high policy. Criminal enforcement is the Justice Department's prime mission. The notion that price fixing is criminal behavior has become an institutional obsession in the Justice Department. Even in the 1980s, with antitrust enforcement at low tide, the shrillness of the cries from the Antitrust Division for putting businesspeople in jail for price fixing is at an all-time high (Starling, 57 *Antitrust L.J.* 157 (1988); 46 ibid., Issue No. 2: 431–80, 508–42, 545 (1977).

By law bankers, farmers, insurers, exporters, and others are granted immunity to fix prices (ABA Antitrust Section 1984: 599–713). For a period of many decades there was an amendment to the Sherman Act permitting retail price fixing under which a businessperson could be found guilty of violating the law for not complying with a price-fixing agreement—to which he was not even a party (*Report* 1955: 151–52)!

How did price fixing become a felony under U.S. law? When the essentially regulatory character of antitrust litigation settlements had become sufficiently obvious to generate corrective legislation, the Antitrust Division decided to try to salvage something for itself and persuaded Congress to change the word "misdemeanor" to "felony," and that is how price fixing became a felony (*U.S. Code Cong. & Ad. News* 1974 (1): 1383, 2572).

The point of recounting this history is not primarily the issue of price fixing itself, but the distortion of policy. The coincidence of the judicial bright line rule with the Justice Department's criminal enforcement responsibility has led to an exaggerated preoccupation with a subject matter that is of secondary importance to the main political purpose of the antitrust laws, which is the preservation of a competitive context. The impact of this exaggeration, moreover, has been compounded by a second coincidence, the simplistic doctrines of economic theory that overstate the role of price. This has led directly to the present policy vogue that views the only legitimate purpose of antitrust as mandating price competition as an aid to consumer welfare. This almost exactly reverses the political value judgment expressed in both the Sherman Act and the legislation of 1914, which sought to preserve freedom of opportunity in business, even if this meant somewhat higher prices that might result from a more efficient monopoly (*supra*, Chap. 4, Chap. 5).

The Judiciary as Regulator

In the U.S. legal system, an outgrowth of the English, there is a historical distinction between two kinds of powers that may be exercised by a court. One, associated with the ancient courts of law, is simply to grant or deny judgments requiring the payment of a sum of money. The other, for which a special category of courts of "equity" was created, is the power to require a party to do or refrain from doing an act; this is a decree known as an injunction. The two court systems have long since been merged, but the distinction between these two types of power, and the standards for exercising them, continues to this day.

In exercising its equitable powers a court has virtually unlimited discretion to "fashion" or "tailor" its decree to the peculiar facts and circumstances of the case before it. The Sherman Act, from the very beginning, conferred upon courts the authority to exercise their powers of equity in its enforcement. Since what is at issue in an antitrust case is a firm's behavior in the marketplace, the forward-looking nature of equitable relief places a court in the position of doing very much the sort of thing that regulatory agencies do vis à vis firms within the scope of their regulatory jurisdiction. This fact has long been recognized (Timberg 1950; Neale 1970, which at numerous points refers to the effect of a court's finding of an antitrust violation as subjecting the defendant to the regulatory jurisdiction of the court; Massell 1964: 98–162; Boyer 1983; Kalodner 1978; Isenbergh & Rubin 1940), and it has recently been accorded the status of legislative recognition. The Antitrust Procedures and Penalties Act of 1974 (15 U.S.C. Secs. 16(b)–(i)) imposed procedural requirements on the issuance of decrees in antitrust cases essentially like those imposed on a regulatory agency: calling for publication of the proposed decree, its rationale, and its projected "competitive impact," with a waiting period to provide an opportunity for public comment.

A court in this situation is thus drawn into making judgments involving economic issues that are not the normal grist of the judicial mill (*U.S. Code Cong. & Ad. News* 1974(1): 6544–46). And the problems of fashioning a forward-looking decree are so different from those involved in adjudication of past facts that they have been said to involve entirely different mental processes (Timberg 1950: 634).

The quintessential example, of course, is the breakup of AT&T (Peters 1985; Lavey & Carlton 1983; MacAvoy & Robinson 1983; Green 1984). This enormous economic policy action was taken through the approval of a consent decree by a single district court judge. That decree, and its amendments, governs such basic business decisions as what businesses the surviving firms may enter, their pricing policies, and their geographical scope of operations. The decree in fact to a large degree displaces the regulatory function of the Federal Communications Commission (FCC) (MacAvoy & Robinson 1983). The question of the appropriateness of looking to a single district court judge to be making these kinds of far-reaching economic policy decisions has been often raised in this setting. The point is not to criticize Judge Greene, whether one disagrees with him or not. He is only doing the job the law requires of him. And he may, as an individual, be exceptionally well qualified to handle these problems. But the contrast between the traditional role of the judiciary and the economic policy issues presented by this case serves to underscore the conflict between the role of the judiciary and the fundamental nature of antitrust policy.

Policy as an Incident of the Judicial Process

If antitrust policy is recognized as economic policy, it would seem logical that it be formulated and administered in terms of economic policy. That is a task of which the judiciary, as an institution, is incapable. The fact that this responsibility has nevertheless been conferred upon the judiciary has resulted, predictably, in the policy itself being shaped by considerations relevant not to economic policy but to the institutional idiosyncrasies of the judiciary.

The most obvious instance is that detailed above, of how the issue of price fixing became bloated out of all proportion because of the judicially perceived lack of capacity to adjudge the reasonableness of agreements between businesspeople regarding price.

But this, and all of the other per se rules, is not the only respect in which the internal workings of the judicial system affect the substance of policy. It was noted earlier that the judicial system is largely decentralized, and that differences between the views of individual judges often bring about different results depending on the particular court that decides a case. This results in a phenomenon known to the legal profession as forum shopping, which is not unique to antitrust cases, but which is in no wise exempt from it.

Judges as Oracles of the Law

In England and the United States judicial opinions play a larger role in originating law than in such continental systems as the French and German. This is because the French and German systems originated in a tradition of highly systematized, codified statutory Roman law, whereas no such tradition existed in England. Early English courts were forced often to decide issues of legal principle on which there was no legislation to guide them. Thus it was in the written opinions of courts that much Anglo-American law originates, with the result that courts in our system have come to be looked upon as the "Oracles of the Law" (Dawson 1968: xi).

However, as the late Prof. John P. Dawson of the Michigan and Harvard Law Schools, a master of the case method was at pains to point out, judges are not legislators. Their function is to decide cases, not to write laws (ibid., 413). The tendency of American lawyers to look upon courts as Oracles of the Law carries a special hazard in the field of antitrust. The failure by the Supreme Court to link the Sherman Act to the common law has rendered the Rule of Reason a hollow shell, devoid of the insights of the common law, and the per se rules an exercise in abstract speculation.

THE PROSECUTOR AS ECONOMIC POLICY MAKER

Pure Policy

The attorney general was perplexed, perhaps a trifle irritated. In July of 1969 the Antitrust Division, on behalf of the Department of Justice, had just made public a scathing attack on the Mandatory Oil Import Program, questioning its importance to the national security and recommending major changes in its administration to favor "independent" oil companies at the expense of the majors (*New York Times* 8/14/69: 1). There was not much new in this. These same arguments had been urged repeatedly by the Division for years—and ignored—within the internal councils of government.

What was different this time was that the argument was presented publicly, in circumstances that made the offended elements in the oil industry very nervous. A growing list of administrative exceptions and questionable uses of the quota allocation system, for purposes having no clear relation to oil import control, and culminating in the notorious proposal for a free port at Machiasport, Maine (*New York Times* 12/28/69), resulted in widespread industry demands for a thorough review of the whole system. What the industry wanted was to clean up the administrative mess that the program had become. To their horror, the job was given to George Shultz, then Secretary of Labor, who was willing to consider such unthinkable questions as whether the program should be continued at all. He insisted that all presentations to his cabinet-level task force be made upon the public record. When the Antitrust Division fired its missile into this incendiary situation as a public document, the level of pain within the industry was quickly made known to the attorney general.

The attorney general was not an antitrust lawyer. John Mitchell had come to the Department of Justice at a time of mounting national concern over crime in the streets; and he thought of the Department in terms of the federal government's equivalent of a sheriff's office, whose job was to put crooks in jail. What, then, were these madmen in the Antitrust Division doing meddling in sensitive issues of national security and economic policy?

There followed a hurried briefing for the attorney general on what had by then become the customary role of the Antitrust Division as an advocate of procompetitive policies within the government, in addition to its basic function as prosecutor of antitrust violations. The Division had built into its charter by regulation the role of policy advocate for competition within the executive branch.

This meant an increasingly active and public role for the Division in the regulatory commissions whose mandates involve some trade-off between competition and other public policy objectives (Baker 1970, 1976 ("Banking"); 1976; ("Mecca"), 1976). The OMB clearance process, which establishes the administration position on all domestic issues, consults the Department of Justice on all competitive policy issues. The Division commonly represents the administration's views in Congressional hearings on matters affecting competitive policy, ranging far beyond the antitrust laws themselves.

The Prosecutor as Prosecutor

There is a deeply imbedded psychology in the Antitrust Division to view its mission in terms of morality, its ultimate goal to go after "bad guys" and put them in jail. This attitude differs from the policy aspects of the policy just described, in which most members of the staff are not interested. Indeed, most of the career staff have the same view of antitrust enforcement as John Mitchell's perception of the sheriff's office.

This perception has deep historical roots. Robert Bork quotes "a nationally prominent attorney, who later became an Associate Justice of the Supreme Court" : " 'Antitrust . . . is in the good old American tradition of the sheriff of a frontier town: he . . . merely walked the main street and every so often pistol-whipped a few people' " (Bork 1978: 6). Fittingly, a collection of the correspondence of Thurman Arnold, one of the most vigorous of antitrust prosecutors, and also something of a Renaissance man, was published under the title *Voltaire and the Cowboy* (Gressley 1977).

The Juxtaposition

The dual role of prosecutor and economic policy maker has led to the situation, which reached its peak during the years of the Warren Court when the government was winning all its cases, of establishing the heads of the enforcement agencies as the effective decision makers in antitrust cases (Kauper 1968). This led to a kind of tea leaf reading process, in which members of the private bar looked primarily, not to court decisions, but to the stated policy of the enforcement officials as a source of guidance in advising their clients. This led one lawyer to comment that while "the speeches of the Department of Justice are extremely helpful

. . . the effect of legislation by speech is an interesting concept" (Copp, John S. 1971: 991).

Another facet of the present administrative structure that has proved frustrating to the private bar is that there is no reliable way of ascertaining the government's position in advance. There is, to be sure, a procedure for advance consultation, but any approval is not binding on the government (ibid.).

And yet a third problem that arises from the prosecutor's dual role is an occasional conflict of interest. A dramatic instance of this kind occurred, also during the regime of John Mitchell, and also involving the oil industry.

The Organization of Petroleum Exporting Countries (OPEC) was then at the height of its power, and the major U.S. integrated oil companies wanted to negotiate with the cartel on a joint basis. The head of the Antitrust Division, Richard McLaren, did not like the idea because of the tendency such collaboration would have to induce cooperative behavior between these major companies, and he refused their request for an informal clearance. This decision was overturned by the president, and the Justice Department ultimately had to defend that decision in court, which it did—successfully. The problem was resolved, but the system itself was inherently flawed. McLaren's position was legitimate as a policy function; but his dual role as prosecutor as well as policy advocate put him—and the government—in an embarrassing position.

The Great Cyclops and Another Legacy of Confusion

We come here to a point of fundamental importance, noted earlier in Chapter 1. Because of the institutional separation of the FTC and the Antitrust Division of the Department of Justice, the latter approaches the policy aspect of its function from a tunnel-vision perspective of the Sherman Act alone, unenlightened by the insights of the legislation of 1914, as well as the legislative judgments reflected in the regulated sectors of the economy. This point is elaborated later in this chapter.

The Rockefeller legacy of confusion was described in Chapter 3. Another legacy of confusion has resulted from mixing notions of criminality with economic policy in an institution dominated by a criminal enforcement mentality.

ANTITRUST AS HOKUM: CONSULTATION WITH A FRIENDLY CYNIC

> A humbug based on economic weakness and incompetence.
>
> Oliver Wendell Holmes (Letwin 1965: 53)

> There may be a few lawyers left in... [Justice and FTC] who sincerely believe that such laws... could restore capitalism to something like its pristine individualist form.... No one expects them to be effectual, whether the government wins or loses.
>
> Irving Kirstol (1978: 9–10)

In what otherwise purports to be a work of nonfiction, resort must be made to one fictional setting. There are several reasons for this. One is that the viewpoint presented in this section is a composite: views of this kind have been voiced by numerous people over many years but not marshaled in a comprehensive way that gives coherence to the argument in a way that permits it to be tested. Another reason is that a full statement of this viewpoint must include some questionable points and facts, as well as confidential sources, that should not be identified with any real person. Thirdly, to present the argument fairly it should be given the benefit of some spirited advocacy, with which the author would not wish himself to be identified.

It is important that this viewpoint be delivered cheerfully. It is not the intention here to reproduce the frenzied hostilities of the Muckrackers or the Naderites. The spirit is rather that of Thurman Arnold, whose puckish cynicism in his *Folklore of Capitalism* (1937) proved a serious embarrassment when he was later nominated to be assistant attorney general in charge of the Antitrust Division of the Department of Justice (Gressley 1977: 39–40). Some of his bark will be recognizable here, but the argument presented is much broader than Arnold himself invoked. Arnold, though a vigorous partisan of antitrust policy, was also sensitive to the logical flaws and incompleteness of that policy. We will encounter some of his ideas here; but he is only one of many contributors to this composite argument of the closet critics of antitrust policy.

There must needs be a foil; and for this we turn to the circulating body of bright young lawyers who hold appointive positions just below the chief of the Antitrust Division. Here we need not so much a fictional composite as anonymity, for the role is taken from real life and could be played interchangeably by any one of the scores of lawyers who have filled these staff positions over the decades.

The setting is an evening of the American Bar Association's ritual spring gathering in Washington, D.C., at the Shoreham Hotel, during one of the many private parties staged by various private law firms at a variety of sites in the hotel. But we must choose a time about a decade before the present, when the staff of the Antitrust Division was true believing in its sense of mission, not possessed of the demolition mentality that has prevailed during the 1980s. Let us return to a point in time shortly after Richard McLaren's departure from the Antitrust Division, the mid-1970s, a high point for traditional antitrust doctrine.

This ABA gathering brings together a full range of government enforcement officials, their staffs, and the private bar. Many of the government staffers are primarily interested in furthering their post-government careers in private practice and so are especially interested in meeting members of the private bar. Even so, they are still full of the ebullience of the enforcement mentality necessary to their present government positions, some being naively ignorant of what their future private employers will expect of them.

And so we may picture one such staffer sharing a drink with a wizened senior partner from a prominent private firm, resulting in a classic conflict of generations. To give a youthful image to the young staffer, let us call him Dennis; the senior lawyer will be Oliver. The conversation develops along classic lines, Dennis spouting the official line about the importance of competition to the national economy and the vital role played by the antitrust laws in preserving competition. Finally, Oliver has had all he can take.

Oliver: Oh, come now. Some time after you have had a little more experience in the real world you will come to understand that the antitrust laws are just for show; they don't really change anything in business.

Dennis: How can you say that? Sure, nothing much happened for the first dozen years or so after the Sherman Act was passed, but from the time President Theodore Roosevelt broke up the merger of the Great Northern and Northern Pacific with the *Northern Securities* case in 1904 the merger was actually stopped and the Sherman Act became a real force.

Oliver: Ah, you think you've got me there; but that case only serves to prove my point. Antitrust changes nothing in the real world. In that case the merger was stopped, but only temporarily. The railroads' lawyers made a rather eloquent argument to the Supreme Court that though the Court's decree would be respected, monopoly in the circumstances of that case was inevitable (Moody 1904, 1968: 446–50). When the ICC ultimately approved that merger, it turned this argument into a prophecy.

Dennis: That is all the more reason why the Division is working to put the ICC out of business.

Oliver: This case is not an isolated incident. The ultimate victory of the railroads has its parallel in the many large corporations that have survived intact despite the antitrust laws. The government lost its cases against the Sugar and Whisky Trusts. The United States Steel Corporation, General Motors, RCA, General Electric, and many others were all "trusts," as that term was understood around the turn of the century.

Dennis: But you haven't mentioned some of the government's major successes: the breakup of the Standard Oil Company; the suits against the American Tobacco Company; the first *Alcoa* case that resulted in the creation of a competitive oligopoly where once there was monopoly; the successful suits against the Meatpackers' Trust and against the predatory practices of the old National Cash Register and Corn Products companies. And the AT&T break-up was no small accomplishment.

Oliver: OK. Let's start with Standard Oil. Couldn't find a better example of my point that antitrust is more show than substance. The show here was spectacular. A huge company was broken up. It was a famous victory. But look at the results. Prices to consumers went up. The value of Rockefeller's stock tripled. The split-off companies were assigned different geographic areas and so did not compete with each other. There was no ostensible benefit to the public, which wound up paying higher prices, but there was a real benefit to the company. In addition to the increased profitability, the split-off companies provided new opportunities for managers that had been stifled below layers of bureaucracy in the larger company. The real beneficiary was Standard. In hindsight, they probably realized they should have done it themselves voluntarily. Why do you suppose AT&T caved in without a serious fight? Andrew Carnegie had no fear of monstrously large companies. As he put it, "The bigger they are, the harder they fall."

Dennis: There are many antitrust supporters who are less than pleased with the way the Standard Oil decree was structured. But to the extent that you contend that the split-off companies were more efficient, some good was done by the antitrust intervention.

Oliver: Sure, I'll give you that. Mind you, I'm not arguing that antitrust is a bad thing, just that it is more smoke than substance. Now let's come to another of your famous victories—Alcoa. On the surface this example looks pretty good for you. A monopoly industry got some competition. But the antitrust laws were so ineffective in bringing this about that the actual result came from another arm of the government. The major practical change was the establishment of two new competitors by the sale of plants that the government controlled because of wartime conditions. The antitrust law alone did not accomplish this result. And even with this outside help, the government's victory has not displaced Alcoa as a firm of dominating force in the same market it was convicted of monopolizing. The same is true of meat packing and corn refining. National Cash Register has been taken over by competitors, but that was not because of antitrust actions. On the other hand, consider what happened without antitrust intervention at all in the sugar-refining industry. The government lost its antitrust suit, but the industry gradually evolved into an oligopoly similar to what happened in aluminum, with no help from the antitrust laws.

Dennis: One problem I have with your approach is that you are looking only at what happened in specific antitrust cases. The deterrent effect of a successful prosecution in preventing things that otherwise would have taken place is impossible to demonstrate or quantify, but there is widespread agreement that this effect has been large.

Oliver: There is probably something to that, but more likely in the context of specific restrictive practices, and our discussion to this point has been focused on the monopolization side of the law. Before changing the subject, let's test your proposition in the context of industry concentration, ostensibly what antitrust policy is mainly about. Consider these simple facts. The Sherman Act was passed in 1890. Not until 1914 was the idea of merger control added to the legislation. But that was another example of all show and no substance. The 1914 act restricted mergers accomplished through the purchase of stock, but not of assets. The loophole was as wide as the prohibition. This loophole was not closed until 1950. That means that the development of the American economy up to 1950 took place under an almost total absence of antitrust restraint.

Dennis: No one is happy about that history, but we still believe that the successful Section 2 prosecutions had a substantial deterrent effect. But now let's look at the other side of the law, the prohibition of concerted actions. The law has been strictly enforced, beginning with the *Addyston* case.

Oliver: Splendid! You have matched your performance with Standard Oil. Another famous victory. A group of companies was found to have violated the law by restricting competition among themselves. And with what result? The guilty parties all merged while the case was still on appeal (Bittlingmayer 1982: 202). Some practical victory for competition. You speak of deterrent effects. There is a plausible case that can be made that the very strictness of the prohibitions on concerted behavior was a powerful incentive for companies to combine during the long era when there was no effective merger control (ibid.). The greatest period of trust formation was in the decade after the passage of the Sherman Act, and there have been successive merger waves since then.

Dennis: Excuse me, I just saw someone I've been wanting to talk to.

CONCEPTUAL CONFUSIONS AND DESIGN FLAWS: THE DEVOLUTION OF ANTITRUST POLICY

There is a fundamental—and massive—conceptual confusion in the U.S. antitrust tradition as a result of the Standard Oil Company's extraordinary legacy. That legacy was characterized in Chapter 3 as a legacy of confusion, and the magnitude of that confusion is difficult to exaggerate. What appeared to be a greedy purpose to exploit consumers through monopoly prices was in fact a rational reaction to a market that did not work. Because Rockefeller refused to explain his problem and his purpose, the public, the politicians, and the economists all drew the seemingly obvious, but mistaken, conclusion that this was a simple matter of exploitation.

In this context, the problem was conceived of as monopoly, the solution to which was to break up the monopoly; and in the absence of monopoly, free market forces, which are inherently self-regulating, would suffice.

This perception, rooted in total ignorance of the true causes of the Standard Oil phenomenon, failed to see that the problem inhered in market failure rather than the wrongful displacement of a self-regulating mechanism. This misperception persists, undiluted, and indeed exaggerated, to the present day.

Senator Sherman's theory of his bill, which was adopted by the Judiciary Committee in its rewritten version, was a simple incorporation by reference of two common law concepts: contracts in restraint of trade and monopolization. The two concepts were closely linked; however, there was a subtle difference between these two concepts that no one noticed at the time, a difference that was to have major long-term consequences.

To understand the significance of this difference it is necessary to go beyond the court opinions to the momentous socioeconomic developments that gave rise to the attitude of English courts toward monopolistic behavior and contracts in restraint of trade. We have seen in Chapter 2 ("The Transition") the effect of the enclosure movement in England during the fifteenth and sixteenth centuries, which improved agricultural productivity but also caused a massive unemployment problem. Large numbers of people were forced off the land at a time when the transition from a medieval subsistence economy to a market economy had not advanced far enough to provide alternative sources of employment.

The English courts of that era were extremely sensitive to any form of legal restraint that obstructed employment opportunities. The early monopoly case, *Darcy v. Allen, or The Case of Monopolies* (Letwin 1954: 363), decided in 1603, just at the culmination of the enclosure movement, invoked some ideas that sound like those of a modern-day economist, but which in fact disclosed a more fundamental concern. The case involved a royal grant of a monopoly in the manufacture and sale of playing cards. The court commented that the effect of the monopoly would be to increase the price and lower the quality of playing cards. But the court when on to make another point: that even more important was the effect of the monopoly in depriving someone of the opportunity to earn an honest living.

> All trades, as well mechanical as others, which prevent idleness (*the bane of the commonwealth*) and exercise men and youth in labour for the maintenance of themselves and their families and for the increase of their substance . . . are profitable for the commonwealth and therefore the grant to the plaintiff to have the sole making of them is against the common law and the benefit and liberty of the subject. (Letwin 1954: 363, fns omitted; emphasis added)

This strong aversion to anything that interfered with an opportunity for honest employment accounts for the courts' strong repugnance to both monopolization and contracts in restraint of trade. In time, however, a divergence emerged in the courts' reactions to these two types of trade restriction. As to contracts in restraint of trade, the earliest such contracts involved a covenant by a merchant not to engage in the line of trade in which he was experienced. The courts at first reacted, like the court in *Darcy v. Allen*, very strongly against this obstacle to employment. Later they came to perceive that such a covenant worked to the advantage of the person bound by it because it made it possible for him to sell his business at a price that reflected the value of goodwill. To induce the purchaser to pay such a price, the buyer needed assurance that the seller would not reopen across the street and usurp the goodwill he had sold. The courts thus came to take a much more relaxed and discretionary attitude toward contracts in restraint of trade than toward monopolistic conduct. Thus the tendency, noted by both the majority and minority in *Trans-Missouri*, for the English decisions on contracts in restraint of trade to become more tolerant of what they regarded as reasonable restraints than the earlier decisions.

This change in emphasis led to some confusion, and the court in the landmark case of *Mitchell v. Reynolds* (Court of King's Bench 1711. 1 P. Williams 181, 24 Eng. Rep. 347) sought to clarify the state of the law. The opinion went through a laundry list of different types of restrictive contracts, explaining which were legal and which were not. In the course of this list, the opinion noted that if the purpose of a restrictive contract was to create a monopoly, "that would be a crime" (Oppenheim 1948: 7). In other situations described in the opinion, a test of reasonableness was used. The courts thus had distinctly different attitudes toward contractual restraints in general, of which they were largely tolerant, and monopolistic behavior, which they regarded as criminal.

The English law for a time made a statutory crime of practices labeled by a number of antiquated terms that we would today simply term cornering the market, and it was to these prohibitions that Senator Hoar referred when he was asked to explain the term "monopolize" (Chap. 4).

There was thus some tradition of criminality associated with the idea of monopolizing, and this conception was powerfully reinforced by the behavior of the more aggressive nineteenth-century trusts, such as the Standard Oil Company.

The concepts of monopolization and contracts in restraint, although emerging from the same judicial instinct to protect freedom of enterprise, thus evolved in different directions, the aversion to monopoly remaining firm, while the reaction to contractual restraints softened considerably.

When the Sherman Act, reacting to the emotion of the moment, linked both of these ideas in a single statute carrying criminal penalties, it inadvertently mixed apples and oranges. The results were unforeseeable, but of lasting significance. The looseness of the Rule of Reason approach struck the Supreme Court as unworkable in a criminal statute and so led to the creation of new and unprecedentedly rigid rules in the restraint-of-trade area. This has had the ironic effect of transferring the strong emotional reaction to monopolistic behavior to practices that were never regarded as criminal at common law, and in many cases not illegal at all. This confusion, this basic design flaw in the original Sherman Act, has had several distinct and far-reaching distorting effects on policy. First has been a vast overemphasis on price fixing as a major concern of public policy. Second, the fact that this far more rigid rule than what the common law courts had applied was adopted by the Supreme Court does not affect the recurrence of business conditions that give rise to it in the first place, which creates much business for the Department of Justice, thus leading to the development of a powerful and influential bureaucracy.

The preoccupation with price fixing, and the consequent emergence of the Antitrust Division's influence in domestic policy making, has opened the door to the influence of academic economic theory, a subject that will be addressed separately in Chapters 6 and 7. The significance of this development can be stated very simply. The entire cast of antitrust policy thinking has been oriented to the idea that the objective of policy is the promotion of consumer welfare through maximum price competition, ideally under the conditions postulated by academic economists. This is a sharp departure from, and in important respects inconsistent with, the political origins of antitrust policy in a concern to preserve freedom of enterprise, even if that entails greater costs, and primarily for the benefit of businesspeople. The enforcement emphasis on seeking criminal sanctions for price fixing, which under many circumstances was not even illegal at common law, by invoking penalties designed for deliberate monopolization is nothing less than a perversion of policy.

The linkage in the Sherman Act of both the concepts of contractual restraints of trade and monopolization in a criminal statute thus constitutes both a conceptual confusion and a design flaw. The 30-year evolution of Supreme Court rulings described in Chapter 2 in "Judiciary I" is thus a prolonged but eventually clear exposure of the consequences of this design flaw.

While in this instance a conceptual confusion can be said to have led to a design flaw, conversely there is an important respect in which a design flaw has led to major conceptual confusions. This consists in the institutional separation of the FTC and the Antitrust Division of the Department of Justice. As noted in Chapter 1, this has resulted in a kind of tunnel vision in the Justice Department that focuses on the narrow concept of the Sherman Act, largely uninformed by the more advanced insights of 1914.

The ultimate design flaw may be viewed as the conferring of too large a burden on the judiciary to perform an economic policy-making role for which it is not institutionally suited. Yet it should be noted that this is more the result of accident than either design or assignable error. From the perspective of 1914, when the Congress was engaged in creating a new administrative agency expected to eclipse judicial activity under the Sherman Act, it was only three years after the controversial Rule of Reason opinion in the Standard Oil case of 1911. The main concern then was that the Court might be too permissive. Wholly unforeseeable was the change of course by the Court 13 years later in *Trenton Potteries*, which by the nature of its severe rigidity would open up a vast area for judicial activism.

This rigid policy prevailed for almost exactly 50 years, when in 1977 the Supreme Court first revoked one of its own per se rules. Policy since then has been somewhat adrift, since the Court has neither the common law tradition nor its own long-standing per se policy to guide it. Into this vacuum has entered an increasing emphasis on consumer protection and a drift in the direction of laissez-faire, neglectful of the more fundamental purpose of the law to preserve a competitive context as an end in itself.

This accumulation of confusions and design flaws has led to what may be termed the devolution of U.S. antitrust policy. Evolution connotes the idea of growth, of successive development over the course of time; devolution, in contrast, conveys the opposite concept: degradation, degeneration. The first 24 years following the enactment of the Sherman Act in 1890 through the legislation of 1914 were clearly evolutionary in character. The Supreme Court's decisions of 1904 barring a railroad merger, which was the first major prosecution success for the government; the breakup of the Standard Oil Company in 1911; the *American Tobacco* decision of the same year (221 U.S. 106); and the *St. Louis Terminal* decision of 1912 (224 U.S. 383) establishing the essential facilities doctrine were all advances in policy. The legislation of 1914 represented a substantial conceptual advance beyond the limited idea embodied in the ggSherman Act. But at that point growth essentially ceased; for all of the advance represented by the legislation of 1914, it was incomplete and has never matured into the policy conception it initiated. The incomplete transition in 1914 from a concept of simple wrongdoing to economic policy centered in an administrative agency was followed by an exaggerated emphasis on the wrongdoing concept during the 50-year era of per se thinking. The subsequent retreat from that policy, together with the incomplete transformation to an administrative process, has reduced policy to a rudderless, mechanistic regime that is in the process of destroying itself. And thus we face the devolution rather than the evolution of antitrust policy.

6

The Theology of Antitrust: Fanciful Teachings of Economic Theory

INTRODUCTION

> You may, and I believe will, object to the correctness of many of my terms, as they will appear to you fanciful, and not always properly applied.
>
> Ricardo to Malthus (Sraffa 1952: vol. 7: 145)

> I was delighted to find in a dictionary the word mumpsimus, which means stubborn persistence in an error after it has been exposed.
>
> Joan Robinson (1978: xix)

To the extent that antitrust represents economic policy, economists are a seemingly obvious source of technical expertise. But antitrust, as a political and legal phenomenon, did not originate from the ideas associated with past or present-day economic doctrine. Indeed, the vast differences in perspective of the political, judicial, and academic economic approaches to the subject leave an impression like that of an orchestra, the members of which are not all reading from the same score. The attitude of the academic economist to this confusion is straightforward: the political and legal sources are unscientific; only the economic theory represents an objective, rational source of guidance for policy. Any appraisal of what antitrust policy is all about must address the merits of this proposition.

The conclusion proposed here and in Chapter 7 is unequivocal: It is that the present state of economic theory is an intellectual scandal, medieval theology, alchemy, falsely posturing as science in the twentieth century, an irrelevant and incompetent beacon by which to guide policy. Radical as this conclusion may appear, it did not originate with the author of the present work, as will be seen from the extensive body of criticism from within the profession cited here.

The theory addressed here and in Chapter 7 is not the whole of economic theory, but a distinct subset known as neoclassical microeconomic theory. The distinction resulted from John Maynard Keynes's demonstration of its irrelevance to real-world economic problems. The Keynesian analysis was put in a separate box called macroeconomics. The academic doctrine continued as before and has presumed to counsel antitrust policy. This is the aspect of theoretical economics that is addressed here. How this should be balanced against the empirical contributions of economists is taken up in the concluding "Postscript" of Chapter 7.

INFILTRATION

Economic theory cannot be said to have played any significant role in either bringing about or shaping the substance of the Sherman Antitrust Act of 1890. The origins of the Sherman Act make clear that it was inspired by political objectives and embodies no economic concepts beyond whatever could be read into the judicial precedents (and English legislation) on restraints of trade and monopolies—and that was precious little.

Some early signs of economic doctrine can be detected in the thinking behind the Clayton Act's modest attempt at merger control in 1914, and Woodrow Wilson's legislative proposals may have been influenced by J. B. and J. M. Clark (1914, 1971: 17). The views of economists played a large role in the legislative background of the Cellar-Kefauver merger control amendment of 1950 (Bok 1960; *Brown Shoe*, 370 U.S. 294, 311–23 (1962); Rowe, Frederick 1984: 1522–23; Hovenkamp 1985: 253 n.188). In addition, the Justice Department merger guidelines of 1968 incorporated into enforcement policy, and thereby effectively into law, the prevailing economic doctrine of that time. Their revision in 1982 and 1984 was premised equally explicitly on concepts of economic theory (Rowe, Frederick 1984: 1525, 1532).

Although as recently as 1972, a majority opinion of the Supreme Court expressed alarm at the thought of being drawn into "the wilds of economic theory" (*Topco*, 405 U.S. at 609–10 n.10 (1972)), elements of conventional economic doctrine are sprinkled throughout the jurisprudence of antitrust and have become increasingly frequent in recent years

(Rowe, Frederick 1984; Hovenkamp 1985; Crew 1986). Some far-reaching proposals for a general breakup of large firms advocated by economists have received a respectable hearing, though not acceptance, in Congressional committees in the 1970s (*infra*, Chap. 7, "Illusory Benchmark").

The Antitrust Division, beginning with the tenure of Donald F. Turner in the 1960s, appointed one distinguished young academic economist annually as a special assistant for policy advice in addition to the Division's permanent staff of economists. In 1973 this custom was institutionalized by merging the permanent staff and the distinguished outsider into a new Economic Policy Office, the director of which was a distinguished academic economist in the tradition of the earlier special assistants. The FTC, envisaged as a body of people experienced in business, has instead turned for "expertise" to economists. The latest important treatise on antitrust law and policy, coauthored by Prof. Phillip Areeda and Donald Turner of the Harvard Law School, premises its policy analysis explicitly on economic theory (1978). Economists generally boast that microeconomic theory is being increasingly recognized as the "scientific" basis for antitrust policy (Bork 1978: 117; Fox & Halverson 1984: 8, 16, 18; O. Williamson 1979: 919).

The political rejection of the far-reaching deconcentration proposals noted above in the early 1970s marked something of a watershed in the policy bias of economic theory. These proposals had been rooted in traditional theory that emphasized deconcentration of industry. With this major defeat for the orthodox policy, the field was left open to be seized by a rather extremist segment of the profession known as the Chicago School.

In 1981 the Antitrust Division came under the direction of William Baxter, who expressly invoked Chicago School theory as the basis for his own antitrust policy. Lawyers in the Division, like the FTC, were encouraged to attend classes in economics by instructors imported from Chicago (Baxter 1982: 24). One year later Baxter believed his administration had accomplished a lasting reorientation of policy (Baxter 1983: 41–42); and in 1983, the chairman of the FTC, James C. Miller, III, proclaimed the ascendancy of the Chicago School version of economic theory to the rank of orthodoxy and control of antitrust policy (Miller 1984).

THE DOCTRINE AND DOUBTS

There are some differences of detail among economists on the antitrust implications of economic theory, but there is a broad consensus that has long been the familiar position of economic theory and has gained some degree of acceptance in government policy. That is the "doctrine" referred to here. It is a composite of two root ideas. One is the concept of the self-adjusting, self-regulating market identified with Adam

Smith's classic metaphor of the Invisible Hand. The other is a body of mathematically oriented theory that constitutes the essential gospel of contemporary orthodox economic doctrine known as price theory (52 *Antitrust L. J.* 515–837 (1983); Areeda & Turner 1978; Bork 1978).

Economists do not, as a rule, distinguish these two concepts. With rare exceptions they believe firmly in both and tend to intermix them in their expositions of doctrine.[1] And so the doctrine described here is an admixture of the two. This complicates our problem somewhat because, of the two ideas, the latter only is "theory." The former, the implicit belief in an automatic self-adjusting market, is not a theoretical concept so much as an article of faith. If it may be characterized as a theory, it is a theory distinct from price theory. In this chapter and the next the primary focus is on theory in the sense of price theory; the article of faith is addressed separately in Chapter 8; but we cannot separate them completely. So the "doctrine," as used here, includes both, though the primary focus will be on price theory.

The doctrine begins with the premise that competition, properly understood, means competition in price—period. Product innovation, service, advertising, and all that passes under the label of marketing are classified separately as "rivalry"; The ultimate value is competition in price.

Second, the ideal standard of price competition is that it be completely free and undistorted, reflecting no variables other than the quantitative interaction of supply, demand, and price. For this to happen it is necessary that sellers and buyers alike be numerous enough so that none, by his decision to sell or not or to buy or not, can have any perceptible influence on price.

Under such conditions it is assumed that the price of all goods and services will be driven down to the cost of production—and more particularly, to the marginal cost of the last unit of production. In such circumstances resources are said to be allocated with optimal efficiency.

This ideal condition is contrasted to its opposite, monopoly, characterized by the capacity of a single buyer or seller to control price. Assuming that the monopolist will set whatever price will maximize his own profits, output will be limited to a level below that which would obtain under competitive conditions, and the price will be higher.

From these premises it is said to follow that even though ideal conditions cannot be realized in the circumstances of industrial markets, policy should be measured against those ideals and seek to emulate them as nearly as possible. Thus, not only complete monopoly should be suppressed, but any power of a single seller or buyer to affect price should be deterred. And while economies of scale to a degree necessitate concentration that makes the number of sellers or buyers less than ideal, the objective of policy should be to make them as numerous as possible, consistent with realizing genuine scale economies.

It is also said to follow that government as well as private restrictions that in any way interfere with unfettered price competition are undesirable, which is the basic premise behind the economists' support of deregulation proposals.

At points, the doctrine and political tendencies of antitrust policy coincide. Merger policy falls directly in line with the doctrine's purpose to maximize the number of participants in any market. The judicial rule against price fixing is also in line with the faith of economic doctrine in the price mechanism as the automatic regulator of markets. Taken literally, however, the doctrine at points collides directly with politically based antitrust policy, as we shall see in some detail. Here, it is sufficient to note that economic theory brings a bias to antitrust policy to the effect that its only rational purpose is to promote efficiency in the limited sense of minimizing costs.

Within the citadels of academe, the doctrine is not only well entrenched but also viewed as having reached something of a historic high water mark as the "scientific" basis for antitrust policy (Posner 1979; Bork 1978; Miller 1984). Nonetheless, there are a number of growing cracks in the edifice. By the standard of political acceptability, despite the recent ascendancy of Chicago School leadership in the Antitrust Division and the FTC, the staffs of these agencies remain silently hostile, and there is no evidence that Congress has been moved in that direction.

Political acceptability aside, there are abundant signs of doubt within the profession itself, and these doubts can be distinguished at two levels: (1), in the specific context of antitrust, in the major doctrinal shifts that have occurred over time; and (2), in doubts going to the underlying validity of the theory itself.

First, in the antitrust context, we find such spectacular shifts in position as George Stigler's renouncing of his own *Fortune* magazine article "The Case against Big Business" (1952; Goldschmid, Mann & Weston 1974: 414) as well as the flip by William Baxter, who as a member of the Neal Commission endorsed a far-reaching policy of compulsory divestment in business, which he later recanted ("I shifted. Is that immoral?").[2] Indeed, there followed what has been described as a wholesale history of recantation on the subject of concentration (Goldschmid, Mann & Weston 1974: 414). The issue of economic theory's role was squarely joined in a series of articles between Bork and several others in 1965 (Bork, Bowman et al. 1965), and two major attacks on the theory as a basis of antitrust policy appeared in 1984 and 1985 (Rowe, Frederick 1984; Hovenkamp 1985).

The leading textbook in the field of antitrust economics, by F. M.

Scherer (1980), describes all manner of doubts in the first chapter, and the balance of the book can be fairly described as taking up seriatim the whole catalogue of theoretical ideas about industry structure and performance and finding all of them wanting in some respect.

More broadly, and more deeply, there is an old but rapidly growing chorus of doubt and dissent about the theory itself. And these criticisms come not from a lunatic fringe but from economists of recognized stature, including no lesser figures than two presidents of the American Economic Association (AEA) in their presidential addresses to that group: Wassily Leontief, "Theoretical Assumptions and Nonobserved Facts" (1971), and Kenneth Boulding, "The Economics of Knowledge and the Knowledge of Economics" (1966.[3] The following sampling from the literature, in reverse chronological order, is indicative: Wiles and Routh (eds.), *Economics in Disarray* (1984); Eichner (ed.), *Why Economics Is Not Yet a Science* (1983); Balogh, *The Irrelevance of Conventional Economics* (1982); Robinson ("that woman"), *What Are the Questions?* (1981); Heilbroner, *Economic Relevance: A Second Look* (1976); Lekachman, *Economists at Bay* (1976); Kaldor, "What Is Wrong with Economic Theory?" (1975); O'Brien, *Whither Economics?* (1974); Ward, *What's Wrong with Economics?* (1972); Robinson, *Economic Heresies* (1971); Andrews, *On Competition in Economic Theory* (1965); Knauth: *Managerial Enterprise* (1948), *Business Practices, Trade Position, and Competition* (1956), "Monopoly Reconsidered" (1945); and Lipsey and Steiner (1975), *Economics,* which covers the inside of the front and back covers of an economics text with extracts from the farewell address of William Beveridge as director of the London School of Economics in 1937, the tone of which may be gleaned from the following extracts:

> The distinguishing mark of economic science . . . is that it is a science in which verifications of generalizations by reference to facts is neglected as irrelevant.
>
> I do not see how [members of the public who survey the controversy] can avoid the conclusion that economics is not a science but a survival of medieval logic, and that economists are persons who earn their livings by taking in one another's definitions for mangling.

Perhaps even more telling is the sensitive barometer of undergraduate student reaction, which is increasingly critical of the theory being taught in the schools for want of relevance (Heilbroner 1976: v; Ward 1972: 30).

There is indeed a widespread view that economic doctrine is presently in a period of crisis (Eichner 1983; Pribram 1983: 579ff.; Ekelund & Hebert 1983: 3). "The complacency of the 1960s, however, has given way to the nail biting of the 1970s. There is nowadays a pervasive and repeatedly expressed sense of crisis in economics" (Blaug 1978: xii). Phyllis Deane declares that "both the textbook doctrines and their practical application are being increasingly subjected to fundamental criticism" and further speaks of "faculties where orthodox theory is being actively questioned by individuals of acknowledged stature in the profession" (1978: xix).

The critique that follows thus makes no claim to originality; it is but a collection and summation of critical thought that goes back at least as far as the Rev. Thomas Robert Malthus in the 1820s.

A POINT OF DEFINITION

> The problems presented by advertising and product differentiation are simply not problems of scarcity. They are therefore not manageable within the philosophical framework of economics.
> (Sherrard 1951: 140; quoted in Robinson, Romney 1978: 872 n.2)

It is a seemingly obvious conclusion that if, and to the extent that, antitrust policy is concerned with economic policy, it is to that discipline and its practitioners that policy makers should turn for expertise, and they have often done so. There is, however, in this seemingly obvious assumption an element of semantic confusion that has basic implications for the substance of policy.

This is so because economists do not occupy all of the terrain they ostensibly claim. The word "economy" or "economics" comes to us from the Greek *oikonomikos*, the management of a household. The term, as used by economists of the "micro" variety, is equated with efficiency, the obtaining of any result with the least expenditure of resources.

But the modern meaning of the word is broader, extending to all matters concerning the creation, distribution, and consumption of wealth. The crucial difference is the inclusion of the creation of wealth. Adam Smith entitled his classic work "An Inquiry into the *Nature* and *Causes* of the Wealth of Nations" (emphasis added).

Economic theory is broadly divided between macroeconomics or income theory, and microeconomics, or price theory. The "macro" side is the wealth-creating aspect of theory. Questions of industrial organization and antitrust policy, however, are viewed as strictly "micro" issues, the allocation of resources through the price mechanism, with no account being taken of the wealth-creating side of economic activity.

The difference between these two kinds of questions is basic and pervasive. It can be seen clearly in the management of any moderate-to-large-size business. There is an indispensable need to economize, to allocate financial, material, and human resources within the firm as efficiently as possible. But there is also a distinctly innovative side to business management. Innovation, as Schumpeter was careful to explain, is a much broader concept than technological change. An advertising or marketing plan that serves only to increase sales of an unchanged product or service is also innovation and plays a vital role in a market economy.

Although both efficient resource allocation and innovation are essential to overall business success—and some managers, like Rockefeller, are capable of both—in their extreme forms they differ so fundamentally from one another that a talent for one is often the equivalent of incompetence for the other. The brilliant innovator William Durant, who assembled the General Motors Corporation, had no talent for management, which led to the succession of the master manager, Alfred P. Sloan, Jr. (Drucker 1946, 1964). Or contrast the perspectives in a modern pharmaceutical, genetic engineering, or data-processing firm between the innovative research scientist with an unlimited appetite for funds and the company's financial managers, who must establish some balance between the needs of innovation and financial survival. The relative importance of the two functions varies widely from industry to industry: In such businesses as film making, aerospace, computers, and genetic engineering, innovation is of the essence; whereas banking, insurance, railroads, and public utilities place a higher emphasis on the efficient conduct of day-to-day operations. Yet even in these extreme cases the lesser element has some role to play. Financial control is indispensable to the innovative industries, and even such somnolent businesses as banking, railroads, insurance, and utilities have their innovative needs.

Similarly, for the economy as a whole, the economic system embraces both the saving and cost-minimizing functions and wealth-creating function of innovation. And just as the individual firm cannot perform both functions with techniques peculiar to only one of them, so economic policy risks serious distortion if it is based on analytical techniques that relate to only one of the two essential aspects of the system.

Economic theory, as that term is used here, is the prevailing, orthodox theory that concerns itself only with what is believed to be allocative efficiency through price competition and that admittedly takes no account of the innovative, wealth-creating aspect of business activity. It addresses the narrower question of how resources can be most efficiently employed—or more accurately, the minimization of costs—at a given level of technology. Changes in technology, or innovation of any kind, change the assumptions on which the economists' formulas are premised and so cannot be included within their analytic framework. Their analysis is thus said to be static, incapable of accommodating the innovative forces that make for growth and increasing productivity—in essence, the creation of wealth.

The reason for this omission lies in a preoccupation with method. The subjects that price theory addresses are those that can only be dealt with in terms of abstract logic. The wealth-creating side of the economy calls for empirical study.

This omission of the empirical side of the subject matter has not passed without notice and criticism from within the profession. And the criticism is not confined to any doctrinal segment. Robert Lekachman, on the left, comments thus:

> Now to write a dissertation about an industry or a regulatory agency is exceedingly time-consuming for graduate students who start with little empirical information . . . the trick is to apply an arcane mathematical method to a small problem or available body of data, manipulate the information elegantly in a computer, and defend the results to an approving dissertation committee whose members are also eager to speed their students on paths of professional glory. . . . Ignorance of the real world is more than bliss; it is very nearly a prerequisite to a successful career in conventional economics. (1976: 184–85)

Wiles and Routh (1984: 21 n.3) make the same point. John McGee, conservative, reflects as follows:

> I now come to a delicate issue, the mishandling of which could put me out of the guild. . . . Most economists, I believe, have very little first-hand knowledge about such things [specific industrial processes, techniques and technology, the more complicated business decisions] relative to even one present-day industry, although they may have read several industry studies that were prepared as PhD theses. A few know a little about a handful of industries, and still fewer know a fair amount about perhaps one or a very few. (1974: 102)

And F. M. Scherer, centrist, declares:

> Perhaps a more serious obstacle is the characteristic indolence of economists. It is hard work to plow through file after file of company documents and to interview dozens of executives, cross-checking each observation to guard against bias and misinterpretation. It is much easier to work with census data punched into IBM cards that can be interrogated in the comfort of one's home, that answer all questions without evasion, and that never complain when bent or spindeled. (1980: 7)

To an outsider the most puzzling fact about academic economists is their indifference to the world of business, which is their ostensible subject matter. To any sophisticated businessperson, the preoccupations of economists appear unreal, even naive. The explanation for this seeming paradox lies in the dedication of economic theory to a scheme of abstract analysis that does not take the functioning of actual business as its starting point. When faced with criticisms of this sort, orthodox economists typically react as one whose most profound religious convictions have been questioned; indeed, this scholarly profession has in fact been compared to a religious cult (Eichner 1983 (book): xiii; McCloskey 1985: 7–8, 11; Rowe, Frederick 1984: 1512 n.4) and to alchemy (Hendry 1980). Robert Bork has likened his own persuasion to the Chicago School way of thinking to a religious conversion (Kitch 1983: 183).

And so our point of definition is that the term "economics" means different things to different people. This may be expressed in terms of a political analogy. In government a distinction is made between politics spelled with a big *P* (Republicans vs. Democrats) and politics spelled with a small *p* (one does not recommend cuts in social security, offend special interest groups, etc.). We may speak here of economics with a small *e* as embracing the whole generic world of economic activity, including its wealth generating aspects; and of economics with a big *E* as the narrow doctrinal world of neoclassical theory.

Why, given its obvious limitations, do "micro" economists so constrain the scope of their analysis? The answer partakes some of history, some of logic, and more than a little of psychology. In sum, it stems from the insistence by economists that their subject matter is a science.

THE SCIENTIFIC AFFECTATION

> Political economy you think is an inquiry into the nature and causes of wealth—I think it should rather be called an inquiry into the laws which determine the division of the produce of industry amongst the classes who concur in its formation. . . . Every day I am more satisfied that the former inquiry is vain and delusive, and the latter only the true object of science.
>
> Ricardo to Malthus (Sraffa 1952: vol. 8: 278–79; Bonar 1887: 175)

The Value Judgment

"They want a closed system." So an economist answers the question posed at the end of the preceding section. The drive to systematize, to find theoretical precepts, has been perhaps the most distinguishing characteristic of economic doctrine since Adam Smith. Economists never cease to proclaim to themselves and to the world that their discipline is a science. The fact that the literal meaning of the word "science" embraces a much wider range of uncertain subject matters than is connoted by the image of the "hard" physical sciences is occasionally but rarely noted in the economic literature (Stigler 1946: 3n.; Schumpeter 1954: 6–7; McCloskey 1985: 32–33, 54–57). The model most commonly invoked as the standard for economic "science" is that of physics.

This predilection for a scientific method has impressed an indelible mold on the methods of analysis used, and thereby on the values and the conclusions of economists. It is difficult to exaggerate the degree to which academic economists, in their devotion to abstract, theoretical analysis, have isolated themselves from the world of business. It is an isolation much deeper than the fact of academic aloofness implies. For economic theorists it is something of a point of honor to abjure the study of business from the inside. Geologists, archeologists, anthropologists, and so on, venture forth from their academic homes to study their subjects wherever they are to be found. But economic theorists find no such compelling curiosity to understand what makes business tick. So attached have they become to their theoretical methods that empirical study is not only neglected but disdained (Stigler 1946; 1966; 1968). Even when the actual motivations of businesspeople are viewed as worthy of serious study, the prevailing methodology has not been empirical but theoretical and mathematical (Simon 1976).

Smith, Malthus, and Ricardo

There was none of this in Adam Smith. Smith was not a narrow technician. He was a lifelong scholar who wrote on an encyclopedic range of subjects besides, and mainly before, the dozen years he devoted to *The Wealth of Nations* (West 1969: 20–21, 166; Foley 1976: Chap. 2; Skinner & Wilson 1975: 2). However, despite his own commitment to the scholarly life he was scathingly critical of the universities of his day, accusing them, among other things, of harboring "exploded systems" (West 1969: 41). When Smith began work on *The Wealth of Nations,* he conceived of it, not as a narrow work on economics, but as an "essay in conjectural history," by which he meant "the systematic study of the effects of legal, institutional, and general environmental conditions upon human progress" (West 1969: 19). Smith did not believe that man's economic problems could be isolated from their political, social, or cultural context; he had nothing but disdain for abstract analysis (Reisman 1976: 9–19). *The Wealth of Nations* has been described as "a philosophical work in that it deals with broad problems of human welfare, and it deals with them in a reasoned and unprejudiced manner" (Morrow 1926; 1966: 156–57).

Smith was described somewhat disdainfully by Schumpeter as not a theorist (Schumpeter 1954: 38–39), and Smith would have agreed. His method was empirical, not theoretical. This was no accident. Smith was not the first to struggle with the analysis of economic systems, and among the sources with whom he had early and intimate contact was the leading French writer Quesnay, of the French Physiocrat school. To the Physiocrats there was but one source of genuine productivity, and that was agriculture. The soil generated new wealth, and it was out of this wealth that artisans found their means of support. Hence, only agriculture, not manufacture, was a source of wealth (Meek 1968: 51).

Smith was not taken in by those sophistical reasonings of which he was explicitly critical in *The Wealth of Nations* (1776, 1976: vol. II, Bk. IV, Chap. 9). His background in moral philosophy had led him to a firm rejection of formalized systems of logic, notably those of the Casuists (Myers 1976: 564). In his teaching duties he gave short shrift to that portion of his philosophy course that dealt with formalized systems of logic (West 1969: 54–55). And he was particularly sensitive to the futility of applying techniques of rigorous precision to subjects like moral philosophy and political economy that were not susceptible to them. In his earlier treatise, *The Theory of Moral Sentiments* (1759), which tells something more about his philosophy of political economy than what appears in *The Wealth of Nations* (Myers 1976: 561–64; West 1969: Chap. 8), he spoke disdainfully of what he described as "frivolous accuracy" (Myers 1976: 564). Already in his time the attempt was being made to treat the subject of political economy in arithmetical terms, under the label "political arithmetic," which Smith summarily dismissed as being incapable of the exactness it professed (Hollander, Jacob 1926, 1966: 3–10).

Smith was sensitive to the error of trying to explain everything in terms of a single cause (Bonar 1922, 1967: 173). He was aware that history had seen "many philosophers who knew only their own small art well, but were brashly eager to make it the foundation for far-fetched analogies, 'the great hinge on which everything turned' " (Foley 1976: 23). He appreciated the fact that successive analytical efforts tend to simplify earlier, more complex solutions (Thomson 1965: 225), but in his approach to the subject of political economy, he was so thoroughly empirical as to be subject to the reproach that he was at times difficult to reconcile with himself (Bonar 1931, 1970: 44). His style was eclectic, leaving room for defenders of abstract theory to point out some respects in which his analysis resembled that of the later system builders (Hollander, Samuel 1979: 13–14; Ekelund & Hebert 1983: Chap. 5), but the comparison does not hold. Smith used many methods but was a slave to none and, more to the point, neither to method itself.

To Smith it was unthinkable to forego inquiry into the very questions that most interested him—the causes by which wealth is increased—merely because the answers could not be provided by techniques of scientific precision. Fully aware that they could not be answered in this way, he addressed them through empirical study and reflection and not through a formal system of deductive logic. That Smith's empirical method was in itself an important contribution is an insight mainly lost in the English-speaking mainstream of orthodox theory (Recktenwald 1976: 54, 56, 111–12).

Smith's influence in this respect was short lived, however. The issue was sharply joined after an interval of about 40 years by his two immediate successors of note: David Ricardo and Thomas Robert Malthus.

Malthus, like Smith, took the broader view of political economy, saw its central problem to consist in the causes by which wealth is increased, and openly disdained the pretensions of those who sought to make of political economy an exact science governed by principles of mathematical rigor. To Ricardo this broad and inexact concept could not be reconciled with the idea of science; he insisted on limiting its subject matter to those variables that could be manipulated in terms of pure logic. He was philosophically aligned with the French Physiocrats (Paglin 1961, 1973: 162); and because his influence in the profession triumphed decisively over Malthus, he constitutes a direct link between the Physiocrats to the neoclassical school, which is the foundation and the essence of modern economic theory. As Professor Stigler wrote in 1963, the economist of today inclines to purism, a characteristic he traced directly back to the Physiocrats (Stigler 1963: 24). It was indeed from France that the initial impetus to a more precise, calculated form of economic analysis emerged. At first out of favor in England because of a general repugnance to everything French in the wake of the Revolution, Ricardo's ascendancy paved the way for a later acceptance of French writers and their dedication to "scientific" method (Hollander, Jacob 1926, 1966: 16–19).

The debate between Ricardo and Malthus was thus of seminal importance in setting the mold in which subsequent economic theory was to develop, and nowhere has the issue been more clearly framed than in their dialogue. Their differences are all the more illuminating because they were purely conceptual. Malthus and Ricardo were good friends who corresponded, visited, and spoke with each other over many years; their disagreements were couched in civil, polite, even cordial, tones however sharp the clash of ideas (Sraffa 1952: vol. 9: 382 and vol. 8: 101, 334 n.2). And they did not disagree across the board. Each was careful to note points of agreement as well as disagreement, thus isolating and sharpening the conceptual gulf that divided them.

Ironically, these two Englishmen reversed the normal stereotypes of economic theory: Malthus was an academic, the first to hold an academic chair in political economy (Hollander, Jacob 1910, 1968: 47), with a distinct predilection for the practical implications of theory. Ricardo, a successful stockbroker whose speculations made him independently wealthy at an early age (ibid., 35) and who literally bought his way into Parliament (Mitchell 1937: 344; Spiegal 1983: 311), was inclined to pure abstract theory. Malthus and Ricardo also defended positions at variance with their personal economic interests: Ricardo, the landholder, denouncing landlords as parasites, while Malthus, with no landed interest, defended them (Malthus 1836, 1964: 216–17).

Ricardo wrote first (*Principles of Political Economy and Taxation*, 1st ed., 1817); Malthus responded in 1820 with *Principles of Political Economy*, in which he devoted an entire chapter to Ricardo, though his differences with the Ricardian approach permeate the entire work. Malthus's *Principles* was written mainly in reaction to Ricardo's treatise (Malthus 1836, 1964: v; Paglin 1961, 1973: 15), though careful to note his "very high opinion of Mr. Ricardo's talents as a political economist" and an "entire conviction of his perfect sincerity and love of truth" (Malthus 1836, 1964: 18). Ricardo, in subsequent editions of his own *Principles*, reciprocated with a chapter on Malthus. In addition, he compiled an extended commentary on Malthus titled *Notes on Malthus' Principles of Political Economy* (1820), which he showed Malthus but did not publish (Sraffa 1952: vol. 8: 373). The *Notes* did not appear until almost 100 years after his death (Ricardo 1928: ix–xi).

The conceptual issues on which Malthus and Ricardo differed break along precisely the same lines that frame the issues of economic theory today. By capsulizing the disagreement between them we gain an insight from history that explains more in a few pages than any amount of logic.

Malthus shared the aspiration of science for political economy. He referred to it consistently as such, and to further that end he compiled a dictionary aimed at standardizing the terminology (Malthus 1827, 1971). But Malthus was a man embued with the value of proportion, and his view of political economy as science was in the flexible sense in which we speak today of political science, or as in Malthus's time with respect to the "science" of morals. Like Smith, he distinguished the rigorous precision possible in certain of the physical sciences from what was possible in so complex a subject as political economy (Malthus *Principles*: 1).

Malthus saw the audience of political economy as practical statesmen (ibid., 14), and he insisted that the "first business of philosophy is to account for things as they are; and till our theories will do this, they ought not to be the ground of any practical conclusion" (ibid., 8). He saw as a principal source of error in political economy a tendency to simplify and generalize (ibid., 4–6), citing as an example the virtue of savings, which is to some degree essential to capital formation but which if carried too far would bring the entire system to a halt (ibid., 6–7). He thus found proportion to be of the essence of political economy and accepted without reservation the imprecision this implied for the "science" (ibid., 432).

Like Adam Smith, Malthus saw the primary object of political economy to consist in identifying the origins and increase of wealth. Writing in this context, he came to some very different conclusions than those of his earlier and more famous *Essay on Population* (1st ed., 1798; last ed., 1826; Everyman 1933). Morton Paglin observes in the introduction to the 1964 reprinting of the *Principles*:

The analysis and policy proposals of the *Principles of Political Economy* are in sharp contrast with those of the *Essay*: Instead of population relentlessly pressing on the means of subsistence, Malthus in the *Principles* sees vast powers of production lying fallow, with existing resources adequate for ten times the population. In place of exhortations to the working class to save and establish banks to encourage thrift, he vigorously argues against those who declare thrift and parsimony to be a virtue and national benefit, and suggests devices to encourage consumption. In the *Essay* advocates of poor employment schemes are treated with condescension; in the *Principles*, Malthus advocates public works programs. (ibid., iv–v, fns. omitted; Paglin 1961, 1973: Chap. V, 115, 137; St.Clair *Key*: 175)

For all of his insight, Malthus in his time could scarcely attract an audience. For David Ricardo had published first and already attained such stature that Malthus confessed, "I frankly own I have sometimes felt almost staggered by his authority, while I have remained unconvinced by his reasonings" (Malthus *Principles*: 18). David Ricardo, setting a pattern that is recognizable in our own day, had established a vogue of rigorous, "scientific" method that had a more powerful appeal than Malthus's empiricism.

Ricardo's point of departure was different, as well as much narrower. He asked different questions, more narrowly focused, and thus conducive to a more calculated approach. Ricardo disdained the broad inquiry into the causes and progress of wealth as not susceptible to scientific treatment. He complained of Malthus that one of his "great mistakes" is that "Political Economy he says is not a strict science like the mathematics" (Sraffa 1952: vol. 8: 331) and of too great a reliance on experience (ibid., vol. 6: 295).

Ricardo was a reluctant author. The idea of putting his ideas into writing was not his, but James Mill's (ibid., vol. 1: xv–xvi). And it took more than just a suggestion; Mill cajoled him into writing, dismissing Ricardo's protests of his limited formal education (ibid., xix; vol. 6: 321, 340; vol. 7: 60, 183–84, 199; vol. 8: 10; Hollander, Jacob 1910, 1968: 49). When he did come to write he brought the viewpoint that had made him a successful financial speculator. To the speculator it is of the essence to identify certain isolated causes that have predictable effects. It is not necessary, it is indeed undesirable and confusing, to take account of other, complicating factors. Legislators, judges, and politicians generally cannot indulge this luxury, for the essence of their work is to strike a balance between contending influences. The speculator, in contrast, thrives on narrowness (Hollander, Jacob 1910, 1968: 119–20).

Whatever problems Ricardo had with Malthus's writings on political economy, he had none with the *Essay on Population*, which he not only accepted but also incorporated in his own analysis. From the *Essay* he took the principle, or axiom, that an increase in the wages of labor results in an increase in population, thereby increasing the supply of labor and tending to depress the level of wages to the bare subsistence level (Ricardo *Principles*: 177; Hollander, Samuel 1979: 308–10, cf. 555–59; Sraffa 1952: vol. 2: 115). He also believed that the technological progress already fomenting in his time would run down like a clock (Ricardo *Principles*: xi; Landreth 1976: 100–101; Mitchell 1937: 350) and that technological improvements in agriculture would be more than offset by the combined effects of expanding population and the law of diminishing returns, as expanding population forced ever less productive land into use (Landreth 1976: 100–101).

Ricardo was consistently wrong in his predictions: Rising wages were accompanied by a decline rather than an increase in the birth rate, technological progress both in manufacturing and in agriculture continued to outstrip the growth of population, and the landlord class did not continue to grow richer at the expense of manufacturers and laborers (Blaug 1978: 698–99; 1958: 187–88; Mitchell 1937: 352; Landreth 1976: 126–27; Spiegal 1983: 336).

But his failure as a prophet did not detract from his influence, for Ricardo, by his methodology, had provided a seemingly impermeable defense to factual contradictions: He was not purporting to describe the whole of reality, only the tendencies of certain causal elements within it. If other factors in reality overcame the influence of those tendencies, that did not detract from the logic based on the interrelation of those tendencies taken in isolation. These relationships were purely logical and therefore scientific principles that could be accepted without fear of contradiction by the actual course of events (Mitchell 1937: 354–55).

To this end he sought to deal with economics like Euclidian geometry, predicated on definitions, axioms, and assumptions to fit in for the missing facts. The work has occasionally been described as "Ricardo's Book of Headaches" (St. Clair *Key*: xxiii). This categorical method, despite its logical flaws, was a large factor in Ricardo's triumph over Malthus. In contrast to Malthus's changing, contradictory views, "Ricardo offered a consistent and comprehensive system of analysis, capable of yielding solutions on questions of trade policy, monetary and fiscal policy, or any other economic problems" (Paglin 1961, 1973: 158).

What were the effects on the theory of the triumph of Ricardo over Malthus? They were several, and they were fundamental: (1) the elevation of method over substance, (2) the misuse of rigorous method, (3) the disregard of the origins and nature of wealth, and (4) the estimation of output over value.

The Elevation of Method over Substance. The most fundamental difference between Malthus and Ricardo was over the nature of the inquiry itself. Malthus asked the same question as Adam Smith: How is wealth generated and increased? His observations as to how this was done led him to identify factors that could not be measured with scientific precision, which he was willing to forego for the sake of addressing what he viewed as the relevant questions. Ricardo was not; he placed the "scientific" method at the center of his analysis, simply refusing to address any questions that could not be answered by methods of "scientific" rigor.

The Misuse of Rigorous Method. Malthus and Ricardo were divided not only over the issue of whether the scope of questions to be addressed should be limited by their susceptibility to a rigorous method of analysis; they also disagreed over what uses of rigorous method were proper. Malthus called Ricardo on this at an early point in their correspondence, citing the desire to simplify, "which . . . has induced you to ascribe to one cause phenomena that properly belong to two, and not to give sufficient weight to the facts which . . . make against your doctrine" (Sraffa 1952: vol. 6: 82).

Formal systems of logic are dependent for their validity on both symbols that always represent exactly the same thing and on axioms or laws that invariably work exactly the same way. The variables that Ricardo was manipulating, and the principles according to which he purported to describe their interactions, met neither of these requirements (Blaug 1978: 703). The proposition, for example, that population increases in proportion to the availability of food supply is an empirical observation that is more or less true under varying conditions, but by no means an invariable law. Yet Ricardo declared that "population is found to increase invariably with the means of providing for it" (Hollander, Samuel 1979: 564), and on this basis he argued adamantly against food relief for the poor, contending that it would lead only to a never-ending spiral (ibid., 564–65, 723).

Ricardo was not totally insensitive to the problem. He wrote in self-defense to Malthus that their differences "may in some respects . . . be ascribed to your considering my book as more practical than I intended it to be." His defense was that his purpose "was to elucidate principles, and to do this I imagined strong cases" to show their operation (Sraffa 1952: vol. 8: 184; Hollander, Samuel 1979: 645). Ricardo was aware, too, of the hazard of using a formal, deductive method in dealing with facts subject to numerous complicating factors, but he thought he could bridge the gap because " 'even his most abstract analysis retained a high degree of explanatory correspondence to reality' " (Hollander, Samuel 1979: 603). This attempt, in effect, to substitute for the absolute precision of logical or mathematical symbols a resort to simplifying assumptions was denounced by Schumpeter as the "Ricardian vice" (Schumpeter 1954: 472–73).

This rationale, in turn, has led to one of the most exquisite paradoxes of modern economic theory—a reliance on tendencies and assumptions and an indifference to empirical confirmation or discrediting in a discipline that purports to be scientific. Since the economic theorist, like Ricardo, is purporting only to explain the logical interrelationships between certain isolated variables under given conditions, it is a matter of indifference to him whether real-world events turn out differently (Mitchell, 1937: 354–55). The real world is beset with complications that are excluded from his models, so that their presence and effects do not invalidate it. This remarkable attitude traces in an unbroken line to Ricardo.

The Disregard of the Origins and Nature of Wealth. Ricardo's refusal even to consider the very subject addressed by Adam Smith placed a severely constricting set of blinders on all subsequent economic theory.

Where Smith had answered the question of how wealth is increased by the principle of the division of labor, Malthus, not disputing the value of this, saw a deeper causative principle in effective demand—meaning a desire to consume combined with the ability and willingness to do so (Malthus *Principles*, Bk. 1: 7, 63, 69; Bk. II, Chap. 1, Secs. 6–9: 372, 411). His argument was empirical, taking as examples the economies of Central and South America and Ireland. In these cases a cheap and abundant food source—bananas in Latin America and potatoes in Ireland—made it possible for the native population to meet their minimum needs for survival with a fraction of the effort required by the less favorably endowed English soil. But in each case, the natives chose to consume their surplus time afforded by nature's bounty in leisure and consequently lived in relative poverty compared to the more industrious English (Malthus *Principles*: 335–51). The difference in their condition was thus not rooted in the relative bounty of nature but in the willingness of the English to exert themselves to obtain conveniences and luxuries beyond the base necessities of life.

Thus, like the seventeenth-century Boisguillebert (Chap. 2, "Games"), Malthus saw the production of luxuries as essential to the production of necessities.[4] The mechanism by which Malthus saw wealth as being created and increased was exchange, by which each party gives up something that he values less for something he values more, so that for each there is an increase in value and thereby an increase in total value or wealth (Malthus *Principles*: 300, 397).

Malthus saw in this the true rationale for free foreign trade: the extension of markets, increasing the opportunity for mutually advantageous exchange, and thereby of value/wealth (ibid., 382–83, 398). Malthus thus saw one of the great benefits in foreign trade to consist in "its tendency to inspire new wants, to form new tastes, and to furnish fresh motive for industry" (ibid., 403).

The progress of wealth was thus, as Malthus saw it, not a function of population (ibid., 313), abundance of resources (ibid., 335–51), or more quantity of production, but of the ability to suit whatever is produced to the desires of willing consumers to stimulate them to exchange for it. From such a perspective the major economic problem was not the allocation of scarce resources but the mobilization of otherwise idle resources to meet an effective demand (ibid., 313). His view of the government's role was neither the activist planner of mercantilist theory nor the supposed laissez-faire of Adam Smith (ibid., 14–15). He analogized the role of government in the economy to that of a physician, cautioning that "the ablest physicians are the most sparing in the use of medicine, and the most inclined to trust to the healing power of nature" (ibid., 16).

Malthus, seeing an increase in wealth through the process of exchange, resulting in an increase in total value as perceived by both parties to the exchange (ibid., 300, 382–83, 396–97), saw an increase in wealth to follow from an increase in demand. Malthus, at this early time, had the concept of national wealth measured in terms of annual revenue, just as we today think in terms of GNP, which he referred to as "the gross annual revenue of the country" (Malthus *Principles*: 304–6). From this he argued that capital could be increased without saving through a diminution of expenditure, but through savings from demand-generated wealth (ibid., 365–66). Ricardo adamantly denied this possibility (Hollander, Samuel 1979: 111); he saw value as consisting only of physical output as produced by human labor (Hollander, Jacob 1904: 459 n.3). Malthus and Ricardo were nowhere more sharply divided than on this subject. What Malthus saw as the basic problem was the stimulation of demand to increase wealth; Ricardo saw this as no problem at all.

The economy, as Ricardo saw it, was a system for eking necessaries out of a limited stock of resources. Demand was never a problem; it was insatiable; the problem lay wholly on—to use the current idiom—the supply side. It was a zero sum game; what was gained by one party was another's loss. The concept of trade somehow resulting in a net increase in wealth was simply incomprehensible to Ricardo.

The Estimation of Output over Value. Malthus's view of the origins of wealth as springing from demand led him to stress value over quantity as the object of economic activity. He put the argument in terms of international trade carried on through barter. Again invoking the principle that wealth is increased by each party giving up something it values less for something it values more, he argued that after each of the trading partners had exchanged exports and imports, "we might be very much puzzled as to whether we had increased the *quantity* of our commodities," but by having acquired commodities better suited "to our wants and tastes than those which had been sent away," there is an increase in "the exchangeable value of our possessions, our means of enjoyment, and our wealth" (Malthus *Principles*: 397).

Value, as Malthus saw it, is thus a function, not of quantity, but of the suitable adaptation of what is produced to the tastes of consumers (ibid., 318), an elevation of a subjective over an objective criterion.

The search for an objective standard led Ricardo to favor physical output, which is readily measurable and absolute, over value, which is subject to fluctuations with varying subjective attitudes and market conditions. He repeatedly stressed this difference of view in his *Notes on Malthus*: The object of economic policy is to "increase the quantity of commodities without increasing their value" (Ricardo *Notes*: 202; Sraffa 1952: vol. 2: 373). Again: "The happiness of a country depends on the quantity of things which it has to enjoy and not on the 'value' of these commodities" (Ricardo *Notes*: 197; Sraffa 1952: vol. 2: 365). And again: "Would it not be better to have coals of less value and in greater plenty?" (Ricardo *Notes*: 7; Sraffa 1952: vol. 2: 22). This same thought is repeated in other contexts (Hollander, Samuel 1979: 546–47, 549; Ricardo *Principles*: 185; St. Clair *Key*: 190).

What conceptual differences underlay these polar extremes of position? They merit close examination because they are among the most fundamental and enduring controversies in the history of economic theory.

Their difference lay in the fact that Malthus perceived exchangeable value to have an existence all its own, rooted in the subjective valuation of buyers, wholly distinguishable from the physical commodities to which that valuation is attached. As the buyer translates his personal valuation into the willingness to expend money, value in exchange is created, and increased, and it is in this manner that wealth is increased.

This insight was a considerable advance beyond Adam Smith's explanation for the increase of wealth through the division of labor. It is not just the division of labor but also a division organized according to a system of exchange that provides the launching point for a modern economic system with an ongoing process of growth. A division of labor occurs in many forms without a system of exchange, such as occurs in primitive tribes, the home economics of the family, the feudal land tenure system, and even among social insects.

The lack of insight into the key role of exchange is betrayed by another tenet that was common to all the classical economists except Malthus—the insistence that money is an irrelevancy. Smith, Ricardo, and Say all maintained that it was commodities that traded for commodities, money being nothing more than an inert material that served to facilitate the exchange (Pribram 1983: 147, 150). Malthus alone maintained that money's role in wealth creation should not be spurned (Malthus *Principles*: 304–5; 324; St. Clair *Key*: 186, 201). It is money that gives concrete form to exchangeable value and translates demand into the creation of wealth.

To acknowledge a distinct role for exchangeable value recalls the ancient distinction between value in use and value in exchange. Smith noted the distinction, and in one of his more memorable passages, contrasted water and air with diamonds (Smith, 1776, 1976: vol. I, Bk. I,

Chap. 4: 32–33). Ricardo and Say were both aware of the distinction but, like Smith, did not see its full implications.

It is of the most fundamental importance that the subsequent development of economic theory followed Ricardo and ignored Malthus in this respect. Although the specifics of their reasoning differ, Ricardo and modern economists alike exhibit a strong bias toward a unitary concept of value, identified with physical output.

Modern economic theory purports to have explained away the difference between value in use and value in exchange, known as "the Paradox of Value," through what is termed marginal utility theory. This theory, predicated on the "Law of Diminishing Returns," holds that successive increments in the quantity of any commodity will yield gradually decreasing units of satisfaction, or utility (Kauder 1965; Howey 1960; Stigler 1950: 307, 373; Viner 1925: 369, 387). Thus, it is said that the reason water and air lack exchangeable value is that having all that we require of both, a marginal or incremental unit has no marginal utility, hence no value, and the concepts of use and exchangeable value are unified (Samuelson 1980: 412; Robbins 1970: 15; Fellner 1960: 145–46, 160; Knight 1956; 19–21).

Does this really explain away the difference between value in use and value in exchange? The case posed, an incremental unit of water or air beyond what there is any use for is one in which there is value neither in use nor in exchange. All that utility theory explains is why there is no value in exchange; but as to those units that are required and used, they have substantial use value but none in exchange. Or, to take another example, consider the research notes of a scholar, infinitely valuable to him in use, but of no value in exchange. Just as there is no positive, there is no negative correlation: Artificial kidney and heart machines are both of immense value in both senses.

Malthus did not articulate his difference with Ricardo in terms of the distinction between value in use and value in exchange, his focus being solely on the fact that value in exchange had an independent significance of its own. Others of their contemporaries and immediate successors were more explicit on this point. Say at one point made it in his correspondence with Ricardo (Sraffa 1952: vol. 9: 189), but it was perhaps best articulated by the French mathematical economist Augustin Cournot, whose conception of value was the exact opposite of Ricardo's. He posed the case of a shepherd in possession of vast pasture ground that he cannot exchange for something he might prefer. Hence, concludes Cournot, the term "wealth" must be identified with "the words exchangeable values" (Cournot 1838, 1960: 5–6).

Ricardo's statement that it is better to have more coals of less value than fewer coals of higher value would undoubtedly be true for Cournot's shepherd, for whom only subsistence values count. But in an exchange economy, where goods are produced only in response to a price adequate to stimulate their production, the value judgment expressed by Ricardo has no application. He was mixing apples and oranges, judging an exchange economy by subsistence values. A comparison of output and value cannot be made in a single proposition as Ricardo did but must be stated separately according to the context of subsistence value and exchangeable value. Malthus made the point strikingly in the following passage:

> If the roads and canals of England were suddenly broken up and destroyed, so as to prevent all passage and interchange of goods, there would at first be no diminution of commodities, but there would be immediately a most alarming diminution both of value and wealth. A great quantity of goods would at once lose their value by becoming utterly useless. (Malthus *Principles*: 301: St. Clair *Key*: 188)

From a subsistence perspective it is best to have more quantity; from the perspective of the exchange economy, more value is to be preferred. But the tendency to reduce the two propositions to one, and to conclude that output is to be preferred to value, is one of the characteristic concepts that has endured in neoclassical theory. One of the clearest examples is in the theory of international trade. Malthus's view that exchange, rooted in demand, creates new wealth provides the true rationale for free international trade, not Ricardo's argument of increased efficiency through a reduction of costs:

> If we could not import from foreign countries our tea, sugar, coffee and tobacco, our port, sherry, claret and champagne, our almonds, raisins, oranges and lemons, our various spices and our various drugs, with many other articles peculiar to foreign climates, it is quite certain that we should not have them at all. To estimate the advantage derived from their importation by their cheapness, compared with . . . [what] they would have cost, if we had attempted to raise them at home, would be perfectly preposterous. (Malthus *Principles*: 397)

Nevertheless, the insistence on output as a criterion superior to value remains a centerpiece of modern economic theory (Stigler "Goals" 1975: 284). Ricardo's classic "proof" of the advantages of international trade, which is still accepted as gospel in the textbooks (Samuelson 1980: Chap. 34: 626), is rooted in it. Ricardo purported to prove the gains from international specialization through trade by a numerical example showing that two nations making wine and cloth respectively would produce greater total units of both if each specialized in making only the one in which it had the relative advantage (Ricardo 1821, 1963: Chap. 7; Hollander, Jacob 1910, 1968: 90–92, 125–26; Hollander, Samuel 1979: 462–63). But the example takes no account of value. If the two commodities were agricultural goods, and before specialization each was being produced in just the right quantities to meet demand at a price sufficient to assure continued production, specialization resulting in greater total output would produce a glut of both commodities. As Malthus made the point:

> An extension of foreign commerce, according to the view which Mr. Ricardo takes of it, would, in my opinion, place us frequently in the situation in which this country was in the early part of 1816, when a sudden abundance and cheapness of corn and other commodities, from a great supply meeting a deficient demand, so diminished the value of the income of the country . . . the consequence of which was that, in the midst of plenty, thousands were thrown out of employment. (*Principles*: 393)

Yet economists have become thoroughly conditioned to think in terms of output as an objective standard superior to market value; and this one postulate, more than any other, has been at the heart of nearly all economic analysis as it relates to antitrust policy. The theoretical reasoning invoked against monopoly, for example, is termed the "dead weight loss" attributable to monopoly (Bork 1978: 107–10; Scherer 1980: 17–18, 22, 460, 464; cf. Weiss 1979: 1104). This is based on the obvious proposition that at an artificially raised monopoly price fewer goods will be sold than at a lower price, and this difference in the number of units produced is said to be the dead weight loss. But if we add a further factual postulate, that the commodity is wheat, and that the higher artificial price coincides with the farmer's break-even price, we see again the error in taking quantity of output as—yes—a value judgment.

Cumulatively, these specific conceptual differences reflected a fundamental philosophical difference. The literature tends to pair Smith and Ricardo as the founding classical writers of the science; but the classification is misleading. Smith and Malthus thought and wrote in a broader, more philosophical, more practical mode than did the narrow-minded technicians who chose Ricardo as their model. As Keynes characterized the debate by correspondence between Malthus and Ricardo: "Time after time in these letters Malthus is talking plain sense, the force of which Ricardo with his head in the clouds wholly fails to comprehend. Time after time a crushing refutation by Malthus is met by a mind so completely closed that Ricardo does not even see what Malthus is saying" (Keynes 1951: 117–18).

Ricardo was not so much a successor to Smith as a competing tour guide who led his followers away from the broad high road shown by Smith and Malthus into a narrow valley in which the profession has ever since not only confined itself but pressed ever deeper. He offered a different methodology than the empirically oriented Smith and Malthus, which by its very nature changed and shaped the subject matter of the inquiry itself.

From Ricardo to Marshall

The time frame beginning with the first publication of Ricardo's *Principles* in 1817 to the first edition of Alfred Marshall's *Principles of Economics* in 1890 was the period of gestation for what has come to be known as neoclassical microeconomic theory. It was a period in which not just the methodology but also the fundamental conceptual approach of economists to this subject—and more than that, the subject itself—was formed. Oddly enough, present-day economists are as a rule not knowledgeable in the details of this formative period. One apparent explanation lies in their textbooks. With rare exceptions (Robinson & Eatwell 1974: 5–47), almost all treat the subject as if it appeared full blown in its present form, filled with diagrams and mathematical equations. Indeed, the history of economic thought scarcely existed as a teaching subject well into the 1960s (Blaug 1978: xii).

There has since been a notable reaction to this void, a literal outpouring of histories of the development of economic theory (Blaug 1978: Pribram 1983; Spiegal 1983; Ekelund & Hebert 1983; Deane 1978; Landreth 1976; Lekachman 1976; Oser & Blanchfield 1975; Routh 1977; Rogin 1971; Robbins 1970; Bonar 1967; Barber 1967; Letwin 1963), in contrast to the rather limited selection up to about 1960 (Heilbroner 1961; Fellner 1960; Knight 1956; Schumpeter 1954). One of the stated motives for this growing literature has been increasing soul searching within the profession (Blaug 1978: xii-xiv; Eichner 1983; Pribram 1983: 579; Ekelund & Hebert 1983: 3).

Many of these histories, however, reflect the fact that they are written by economists who have an interest in upholding the major traditions of their profession. There is no other apparent reason for the repeated instances in which commonly accepted tenets of the theory are logically exploded without drawing the obvious conclusion that they should therefore be discarded.[5]

At the time when Malthus and Ricardo were engaged in their provocative dialogue, their subject was of great topical importance. The question of protection for agriculture, the Corn Laws, was of immediate political importance; and questions of monetary policy and the national debt were also agitating politicians, who even attended lectures and read articles on political economy (Paglin 1961, 1973: 160; Spiegal 1983: 312–13). Ricardo became a member of Parliament at the urging of James Mill to give practical effect to his views (Sraffa 1951: vol. 6: 252 and vol. 8: 10).

In the decades following Ricardo's death these questions faded from the political scene, and the continued pursuit of the intellectual subject matter reverted to academe (Paglin 1961, 1973: Chap. 6). There, with no practical consequences to turn on the results of their conclusions, academic writers were free to immerse themselves in abstractions of no interest to anyone but themselves. As Stigler has put it, "Beginning with the Physiocrats, economics began to be cultivated increasingly by scholars" "and after 1870 this orientation became, not merely dominant, but well-nigh exclusive" (Stigler 1960: 36, 38; 1963: 23–24).

A second major fact that characterizes this period is the complete acceptance of Ricardo's—and the complete rejection of Malthus's—concept of what the subject matter was all about. As Keynes put it graphically: "Ricardo conquered England as completely as the Holy Inquisition conquered Spain. Not only was his theory accepted by the city, by statesmen and by the academic world. But controversy ceased; the other point of view completely disappeared; it ceased to be discussed" (Keynes 1935: 32).

Ricardo "himself seldom explicitly discussed questions of methodology" (Landreth 1976: 123), but his immediate successors did and, indeed, gave it primacy. The two leading writers of this post-Ricardian period were Nassau Senior and John Stuart Mill (ibid.). Senior was the first to articulate the notion that political economy could be an armchair science, whose practitioners could derive their basic postulates by a process of "introspection" without the necessity of gathering empirical data from the real world (Pribram 1983: 171; Blaug 1978: 697–98; Landreth 1976: 123–25). This period, the 1830s and 1840s, thus became a watershed in the evolution of economic theory. The fundamental premise that it derived from the Ricardian influence was to emphasize abstract models and logical deductions rather than empirical investigations, which led it to the propensity to elevate theory over fact, dismissing the latter when it did not support the former (Landreth 1976: 125; Mitchell 1937: 103–4; Robbins 1935; Blaug 1978: 697–98). The leading expositor of the "science" at this stage of its development was John Stuart Mill. Despite the authority his treatise enjoyed until its displacement by Alfred Marshall in 1890, Mill's own contributions were quite limited, and he made little impression on the subsequent course of development of the theory.

Enter the mathematicians. Once the methodology of Ricardo was accepted—the isolation of a few key variables that can be manipulated with precision to show certain tendencies—the potential for applications of mathematical analysis was obvious. The first systematic attempt to do so was by the Frenchman Cournot, first published in 1838 (Cournot 1960: viii; Spiegal 1983: 508–10; Ekelund & Hebert 1983: 252–59; Schumpeter 1954: 463, 958–59). A succession of other mathematical writings followed throughout the middle of the nineteenth century (Landreth 1976: 196).

Central to this thinking was the perceived behavior of markets under fluctuating conditions of supply, demand, and price. Agricultural commodities, especially, demonstrated the tendency of prices to rise or fall in accordance with variations in supply, suggesting a mechanism inherent in the market itself, beyond the willful power of any of its human participants. This suggested an obvious analogy to the laws of physics, and specifically, of mechanics. The opposing forces of supply and demand could be compared to opposing physical forces, with an inherent tendency to reach a state of equilibrium. When such a state exists, an incremental or marginal increase on one side only will exert a decisive force, and thus the concept of marginalism became a key element in theoretical speculations (Spiegal 1983: Chap. 22; Ekelund & Hebert 1983: Chap. 13; Blaug 1978: 310–12; Deane 1978: 205; Landreth 1976: Chap. 6; Oser & Blanchfield 1975: Chaps. 12–16; Robbins 1970: 25; Fellner 1960: Chap. 13; Knight 1956: 19–25; Schumpeter 1954: Pt. IV, Chap. 5).

This perception was linked to the proposition of Adam Smith—said to be his one significant contribution to theory—that when a commodity is in short supply, its price will rise and thereby induce additional production until the supply becomes excessive, resulting in a declining price and a cutback in production, thus resulting in self-adjustment of the market through changes in price.

These concepts together sparked a quest to demonstrate mathematically that in a completely unfettered market, inherent forces would lead ultimately to a self-regulating state of equilibrium (Pribram 1983: 172; and all of the sources cited two paragraphs above). The effort was carried to its high point for the period by the attempts of Leon Walras to describe mathematically how an entire economy would reach a state of general equilibrium (Ekelund & Hebert 1983: 389–91). A recent Nobel Prize was awarded to a mathematical economist who proferred such a proof.[6]

The belief in the existence of a self-regulating market mechanism that will tend to equilibrium and some kind of overall optimality is the central concept of microeconomic theory as it developed and was further enhanced and codified by Alfred Marshall (*Principles* 1890 (revised edition 1910, 1961 repr.); Spiegal 1983: 566). It was Marshall, too, who changed the name of the subject matter from political economy to economics (Landreth 1976: 285). The publication of his treatise is said to mark the beginning of "neoclassical" economics, as distinguished from the "classical" writers Smith, Ricardo, Malthus, and Mill.

Marshall was by instinct and education a mathematician, but he also shared the humanistic goals and empirical instincts of Smith and Malthus. In his endeavor to be encyclopedic he strove constantly to keep one foot in each camp on all controversies, a tendency that much irritated those who wished for a more decisive commitment to the new, more formalistic, mathematical analysis (ibid., 288).

Marshall's role was in some respects both ambiguous and ironic. Marshall took Ricardo as his model, though unlike Ricardo he was a mathematician; and he fully elaborated the mathematical analysis that he and his predecessors had been developing throughout most of the nineteenth century. But he buried his mathematics in an appendix and was always careful to emphasize what he regarded as the limitations of mathematical techniques for economic analysis. His personal standard for the use of mathematics was severe:

> I had a growing feeling in the later years of my work at the subject that a good mathematical theorem dealing with economic hypotheses was very unlikely to be good economics: and I went more and more on the rules—(1) Use mathematics as a shorthand language, rather than as an engine of inquiry. (2) Keep to them until you have done. (3) Translate into English. (4) Then illustrate by examples that are important in real life. (5) Burn the mathematics. (6) If you can't succeed in (4), burn (3). This last I did often."[7]

Marshall was a strong believer in the importance of empirical study, and his work included much material of that nature. His followers and successors, however, preferred his formal analysis, and they used his treatise to point economic theory in the direction of formal, abstract analysis. This trend, however, did not mature until the 1960s, 1970s, and 1980s. In the interim a more pragmatic view prevailed.

A QUASI-PRAGMATIC INTERLUDE

The 1930s brought an interruption, something of an intellectual revolution against this increasingly formalistic reasoning. The Great Depression of that decade brought much orthodox theory into disrepute, and with it the concept of perfect competition, the inconsistency of which with modern industrial markets was becoming increasingly obvious. The key development was the dual appearance in 1933 of two books making essentially the same argument: Edward Chamberlin's *Monopolistic Competition* and Joan Robinson's *Imperfect Competition*. Both were written in the language of price theory, however, couched mainly in diagrams and mathematics. Robinson, who later confessed her work to be flawed, admittedly took the curves on her graphs, not from any empirical source, but from thin air—the source to which most of the basic axioms of orthodox theory have been attributed (Dewey 1969: 16; Routh 1977: 22–25; Andrews 1965: 21–23; Robinson 1981: 58).

Their influence was reinforced during the 1940s by J. M. Clark, who eschewing as well the formalistic graphs of price theory argued for a new standard of what he termed "workable competition." His analysis was empirical, painstakingly descriptive of the differing mechanisms that work in a great variety of markets (Clark, J. M. 1961). His influence was limited by the absence of any clear conclusions, and perhaps because he did not offer a new theory. Thus the textbooks grew fatter, relating both the old theories and those that refuted them (Routh 1977: 256–57, 261–62).

The concept of perfect competition envisioned atomistically small buyers and sellers, so that no individual has power over price. It has always been obvious that this is in most businesses a condition impossible of fulfillment, and it has thus served to set some bounds to the pretentions of economic theorists. The formal concepts were included in all the textbooks, but the use made of them was generally limited, as well as outweighed by empirical and other nonformal analyses. Economists drew to some extent on the models as a basis for advocating smaller rather than larger business units, but that is about as far as they went. It was a period of peaceful coexistence between economics and antitrust law, in which most lawyers regarded the theory as irrelevant (*Report* 1955: 338) and economists did not press their concepts aggressively. A few did, mainly at the staff levels in the Justice Department and FTC, but those voices never reached the level of practical policy (Knauth 1948: 174).

The beginning of the end of this period came with the publication in 1959 by Donald Turner and Carl Kaysen of a one-volume study that proceeded to argue from the premise of the "rigorous model" that certain concentrated businesses should be systematically broken up. Turner became assistant attorney general for antitrust in 1964, and during his tenure the Johnson administration produced the Neal Report (1968), advocating legislation along the lines of the Kaysen-Turner book. Senator Hart introduced a bill containing a similar proposal, to give the idea a hearing, which proved fatal (S.1167, 93d Cong., 1st Sess. 1973; Scherer 1980: 542; Goldschmid, Mann & Weston 1974: 344–45, 444–48).

THE FORMALIST REVOLUTION: ASCENDANCY OF THE CHICAGO SCHOOL

The inspiration for what is now known as the "Chicago School" was Aaron Director, an economics professor at the University of Chicago, who did very little writing but succeeded in imbuing his students with a kind of messianic fervor (Bork 1978: ix). His teaching was rooted in a rigidly consistent application of price theory, from which he challenged almost all the conclusions of the then-prevailing pragmatic analysis. This kind of purified analysis attracted a collection of first-rate minds who shared this same basic outlook that came to be known as the Chicago School. The influence of this internally consistent, mathematically oriented type of analysis exerted a growing hold on the profession. Graphs and mathematics were scientific, rigorous; and to a group of professionals by nature mathematically inclined, such concepts had an irresistibly powerful appeal (Ward 1972: 40–41). The transformation, termed the Formalist Revolution, came rather suddenly, as changes of this sort go: "Starting as a new social system of formalists . . . at Chicago and M.I.T. . . . it spread to other schools . . . and by the early 60's, all economics departments with any interest in research were feverishly stocking up on the new breed economists" (ibid., 43).

This tendency has not been accepted uncritically by all in the profession. Wassily Leontief created something of a stir when he took the occasion of his inaugural address as president of the American Economic Association to express concern over the tendency of the profession to absorb itself increasingly in abstract mathematical speculations unrelated to real-world facts (Leontief 1971). He observed that "[u]ncritical enthusiasm for mathematical formulations tends often to conceal the ephemeral substantive content of the argument behind the formidable front of algebraic signs" (ibid., 1–2). And further: "There is something scandalous in the spectacle of so many people refining the analysis of economic states which they give no reason to suppose will ever, or have ever, come about" (ibid., 2).

The devotion to scientific method has led the theory to a methodology that admittedly excludes variables of importance to the real world. Does this methodology provide insights so valuable that we need not be concerned about what it omits? To answer this question we must have some understanding of the concepts of price theory, a task the following section seeks to address as painlessly as possible.

PRICE THEORY

Price theory is the essential language and catechism of economic theory. Its special vocabulary and analytical method are the common core of basics upon which all microeconomic theory is postulated (Stigler 1946; 1966; Friedman, Milton 1976; Watson 1963; 1969).

The central concept is the use of models, of abstract depictions of basic variables and tendencies removed from the varying circumstances of actual markets. It rests upon an assumption that there are certain universal laws—the favorite analogy is to physics—that govern markets.

The basic empirical premise of the theory is the observed tendency of prices to rise when pressure comes from the demand side and to fall when it is greater on the supply side of the market (Stigler 1966: 22–24). A corollary is the tendency of supply to increase in quantity in response to rising prices and to fall in response to falling prices, with a resulting tendency to equilibrium in both cases. Because the purpose of the theory is to isolate the pure interaction of the three variables, supply, demand,

and price, it is postulated that commodities are infinitely divisible; that is, they can be bought and sold in units of single molecules like metered water, gas, and electricity, rather than "lumpy" items such as an automobile, a house, or a factory. Thus any change in one of the variables produces a minute deviation from the point preceding it, yielding smooth lines and curves that can be pictured graphically. Hence comes the term "atomistic," which is often used to describe the type of competitive market structure associated with the basic models of "perfect" or "pure" competition (ibid.; Koopmans 1970: 214–21).

This concept forms the basic foundation of the theory, which, insofar as it has been applied to questions of antitrust policy, has three facets. For simplicity of expression these may be pictured in the form of a triangle, of which the supply-demand-price interrelationship is the base and the two legs represent two other conceptual facets of the theory: one relating to market structure and the other to the interaction of costs, prices, and output.

One leg of the triangle concerns the structure of the market. The object is to isolate the pure interaction of supply-demand-price without distortion by either monopoly power or market idiosyncrasies such as brand name loyalties, locational advantages, or buyer ignorance. The basic model is described as perfect competition, and since this is an abstract concept rather than a depiction of any actual market, its description is arbitrary and varies in detail from writer to writer. Authoritative works describe its essential elements in terms of as few as 3 elements (Stigler 1946: 21; the 1966 edition raises it to four: 88) up to as many as 11 (Knight 1921, 1964: 76–81). Stocking and Watkins note that "the neoclassicists' competitive model is a mental construct with no objective counterpart" (1951: 8). The essential point is that the market be homogeneous and atomistic.

The following five elements are typical: (1) The product must be homogeneous, fungible, every unit identical to every other. There must be no brand name identification or other basis for buyers to prefer one unit to any other except for a difference in price. (2) No individual buyer or seller should command a large enough volume to be capable of influencing the market price by adding or withholding his entire producing or purchasing capacity from participation in the market. This atomistic premise actually occurs in some markets, most notably in agriculture, where wheat farmers, for example, face exactly this sort of market condition. (3) There must be complete freedom of entry and exit. Since all firms under the assumption of perfect competition will be producing at their optimal level where the price equals marginal cost, increases and decreases in output occur primarily through firms entering or leaving the market. (4) There are no locational advantages. (5) All buyers and sellers have perfect knowledge.

A distinction is dawn between "pure" and "perfect" competition, pure competition consisting of the first four elements but omitting the assumption of perfect knowledge (Stocking & Watkins 1951: 13 n.8).

The third leg of the triangle, the cost-price-output paradigm, proceeds from the assumption that every firm has what is described as a U-shaped cost curve; that is, as the quantity produced increases beyond zero, cost per unit falls to a certain point, beyond which, according to the law of diminishing returns, costs begin to increase. In this rising section of the cost curve there comes a point at which the cost per unit of each additional unit equals and then exceeds the marginal revenue, or price of the last unit produced. Proceeding from the further assumption that each businessperson's objective is to maximize profits in terms of this cost-price-output paradigm, further increases in quantity produced will stop at the point where marginal cost is exactly equal to price. The price at which marginal price equals marginal cost is thus said to be the optimally efficient price and output because at a lower level of output profits could be increased by increasing output, and beyond that level profits would be reduced.

These three sides of the triangle provide the analytical basis for price theory as a criterion for antitrust policy. Its most obvious propensities are to favor more, rather than fewer, competitors in a market, to oppose the existence of concentrated market power that permits any one firm to influence, let alone control, market prices, and to oppose all artificial restraints on market forces that inhibit an unfettered interplay of supply, demand, and price. The theory purports to prove that competition under these assumed conditions is superior to monopoly because a monopolist, (a) being able to influence price and (b) seeking to maximize his profits, will restrict production somewhat to get a higher price, resulting in less total output than under the competitive model, and at a higher price to the consumer.

The essence of price theory lies in its claimed scientific proof of the automatic, self-regulating tendency of markets through the price mechanism. Price is the universal solvent of economic theory. Left unfettered, the forces of the marketplace will work toward an equilibrium price and output level and thus to an optimal allocation of resources.

NOTES

1. Armentano 1972 is a bizarre combination: severe criticism of price theory analysis followed by unqualified acceptance of Robert Bork's views—which Bork, at least, purports to base on price theory.

2. The quotation in the text is the author's eyewitness recollection of what Baxter said. The official version, as published in 54 *Antitrust L. J.*, p. 33 (1985) reads: "And so I have changed my opinion. I have never seen that as a total demonstration of moral inferiority, to change one's opinions."

3. The two lectures cited are by no means the only critical addresses by presidents of the AEA, and indeed of other such organizations. See, e.g., Routh, Guy, *The Origin of Economic Ideas*: 20–24 (1977). The two singled out here bear the most directly on "micro" theory, which is the sole concern of the argument presented here.

The author gratefully acknowledges the assistance of Stedman B. Noble, an economist, in research for sections of Chapters 6 and 7.

4. *Principles* 1836, 1964: 334. Adam Smith, too, made this observation in *Moral Sentiments* (1759, 1976): "The pursuit of wealth 'is a necessary deception which rouses and keeps in continual motion the industry of mankind' " (West 1969: 93).

5. Mark Blaug's *Economic Theory in Retrospect* (1978) is one of the more spectacular examples. See, especially, pp. 701–7, 720, 724. Landreth (1976) makes repeated references to this tendency, which was also criticized by Joan Robinson (preface to *The Economics of Imperfect Competition*, 1969 ed.).

6. Gerard Debreu, *New York Times* 10/23/83: F15; *Washington Post* 10/18/83: A18b and 10/19/83: B3a. His "proof," however, was heavily dependent on the making of admittedly unrealistic assumptions. Cf. Morisihima, "The Good and Bad Uses of Mathematics," in Wiles & Routh 1984: 51, 68–71.

7. Pigou 1925, 1966 repr.: 427; Landreth 1976: 288. Marshall's greater caution toward the use of mathematics may have stemmed from his insights as a mathematician into the limitations of such techniques (Keynes, 1951: 157–60; Spiegal 1983: 563; Coase 1975: 25; Brems 1975, 583).

7

Flaws in the Theory

The theory has long been under attack from many angles within the profession. Some of the criticisms are so obvious that they are raised and countered in the price theory textbooks themselves. Other, and more penetrating objections, to which no good answers have been found, are simply ignored. To intermingle these various objections could confuse the significance of the more substantial criticisms with others to which the defenders of the theory have more or less plausible answers. The dividing line is necessarily somewhat arbitrary, but there is a reasonably objective standard: Those flaws that are conceded and answered in the leading textbooks on price theory are treated here as "conceded"; those that the textbooks normally do not address are classified as "unconceded."

CONCEDED FLAWS

Unreality

The oldest and most widespread criticism of the theory, unreality, is addressed mainly to just one leg of the price theory triangle, the conception of the ideal form of market structure in terms of perfect or pure competition. It is obvious that no industrial market can be organized in the atomistic form posited by the concept of perfect or pure competition.

The standard answer to this criticism is that it does not matter that the ideal type can never be realized; its value is as a standard of comparison, to which other, actual market structures can be compared. (See, e.g., Blaug 1978: 629–30, 700–701.) The favorite analogy is to the concept of a perfect vacuum in physics: a state that never occurs but the properties of which prove useful in analyzing conditions that imperfectly approach it.

The Variable Elasticity of Price and the Role of Cost

The essence of the theory lies in the assumed cause-and-effect relationship between supply (output), demand, and price. The theory, as we have seen, thinks of these relationships as perfectly symmetrical, that is, each minimal change in one of the variables will produce a corresponding change in the other two, and in the direction posited by the theory. Actual experience, however, demonstrates that the interaction of supply, demand, and price is rarely symmetrical. The term "elasticity" is used in economics to describe the degree to which changes in one of the three variables act on the others. The variations are extreme; for example, high quality meats are highly elastic, whereas such staples as salt and ink are hardly elastic at all, with all degrees of variation in between. This fact is so pervasive that the price theory texts all bring it out. What they fail to mention is the obvious fact that to the degree that price is not fully elastic, the basic mechanism of price theory is not applicable. It is an exception to the theory, and undeniable.

A second major exception to the theoretical interaction of supply and demand as the determinant of price is the key role played by the cost of production. This is one respect in which David Ricardo stood on solid ground. He acknowledged that supply and demand had an effect on prices, but he argued that this was true only of transitional periods when the market has to adjust to changing conditions. The rest of the time Ricardo held that price is determined by the "natural" price. The term "natural" is offensive to twentieth-century ears, but if we translate it to mean approximately what Ricardo meant, we can call it "cost" (Stigler 1958), and there is ample empirical evidence that cost is a major—though surely not the sole and not a precise—influence in the price of most commodities. There is no way the difference in the price of a tomato selling for a few cents and a new automobile for $17,000 can be explained in terms of supply and demand.

There are thus two undeniable exceptions to the premise of the interdependence of supply, demand, and price: (1) the varying degree to which such interdependence has been observed and (2) the role of cost as a determinant of price irrespective of supply and demand.

The General Theory of the Second Best

In a seminal article published in 1956, R. G. Lipsey and Kelvin Lancaster presented a mathematical argument demonstrating that under market conditions that do not meet the perfections of Pareto optimality (perfect competition in all markets), specific changes in the direction of greater competition would not necessarily increase and could even decrease welfare (Scherer 1980: 24–29, 463–64, 599–600). Their thesis has never been disproved, and it remains a constant point of weakness in the theory. Its implication for policy is that this entire conceptual structure based on reasoning from ideal model types tells us nothing reliable, since adjustments made to more nearly accommodate the conditions of the models may be counterproductive. F. M. Scherer candidly labels it a "counsel of despair" (ibid., 28).

Economists have sought to console themselves with the observation that the conditions under which such counterproductive results would obtain are rare and idiosyncratic, so that the special case is of little practical importance (ibid.; Rakowski 1980; Elzinga (1977: 1209–11; Bork 1978: 113–14). This may well be true, and for this reason critics of the orthodox theory cannot gain a whole lot of mileage from this technical flaw in the theory. Its appraisal is difficult and complex, and so the issue remains murky from both sides. It thus marks a safe form of concession and takes its place in the textbooks along with other strawman criticisms of the theory.

The Theory of the Firm

> ... and after all, none of us trusts the price system when we deal with ideas that we care about.
>
> Kenneth Dam (Tollison 1980: 76)

The term "theory of the firm" can be confusing to the uninitiated because it suggests the existence of some specific theory about a firm, or about firms in general. No such single theory exists; the term rather refers to an entire body or field of theoretical inquiry that comes under this particular label. Fritz Machlup in 1967 identified some 21 concepts of the firm (1967: 26–28).

What the theory of the firm is generally about is that portion of economic activity that is organized outside the marketplace within the administrative confines of the firm. The firm is said to exist because the transactional cost of allocating resources through competitive market prices is greater than doing so administratively within the firm (Coase 1937, 1952; Scherer 1980: 89–90).

Joan Robinson traces the origins of the theory of the firm to Alfred

Marshall, who was troubled that the conditions of perfect competition—a concept he did not favor (Stigler 1965 "Essays": 252 at n.42; 1962; Marshall 1910, 1961: 540)—would be unstable, having a tendency to break down and lead to monopoly. He reassured himself on this score by analogizing individual businesses to trees in the forest that grow and eventually die off to be replaced by others (Marshall 1910, 1961: 457, Chap. IV, secs. ix-xiii; Robinson, Joan 1981: 11; 1971: 97; Spiegal 1983: 570). Marshall, of course, was writing before the large, institutional corporation had become an enduring landmark on the economic scene (Williams 1978: 92).

When the full implications of the theory of the firm are appreciated, they present a far more serious challenge to the theoretical structure than the enigmatic "theory of the second best." The theory of the firm is a veritable antithesis of price theory as an ideal mechanism for resource allocation. What the theory of the firm says is that to the extent that allocation of scarce resources is the economic problem, administrative mechanisms rather than the free market is the more efficient solution. And this is not just theory; there is an abundant empirical documentation of the superiority of conscious management over unguided market forces in allocating resources (Chandler 1977, reviewed 14 *J. of Econ. Issues* 797 (1980); Drucker 1946, 1964).

What apparently saves the theory from the logical consequences of this obvious conclusion is probably a mixture of the sheer confusion of ideas that parade under the broad tent labeled the theory of the firm and, more important, the sheer enormity of what it portends for a long and solidly entrenched line of dogma—its total irrelevance to the real world.

One is tempted at this point to proclaim checkmate. What is already conceded by that corner of the theory that relates to the firm is enough, logically, to compromise the entire structure of neoclassical theory. But the wise chess player surveys the whole board before leaping to conclusions, and there remains much that we have not yet examined.

The Exclusion of Innovation

Theoreticians have always conceded that economics based on a system of abstract, deductive logic cannot accommodate the factor of innovation. Ricardo was not troubled by this because he thought the stream of innovation would eventually peter out, leaving a stationary state (Landreth 1976: 100–101). John Stewart Mill found the idea of progression actually subversive of welfare (ibid., 134, 139–40; Mill 1848, 1963: Bk. IV: 748–49) and so cheerfully disregarded it. Joseph Schumpeter argued the weakness of the theory on this ground most emphatically, so much so that his concept has remained outside the orthodox theory. The modern tendency among the orthodox is to concede the point but dismiss it as unimportant because progressiveness cannot be measured with any precision (Kaysen & Turner 1959: xvii; Bork 1978: 132). If you cannot count it, ignore it. And this, we are asked to believe, is science!

Before turning to the unconceded flaws in the theory we note two intermediate concepts—monopolistic or imperfect competition and workable competition—that depart from the fundamental assumptions of the theory but have addressed different questions rather than challenging it directly; and a third alternative concept—"creative destruction"—that is not so much a description of defects in the theory as a very different conceptual approach.

DEPARTURES FROM THE THEORY

Thus three major concepts have intruded themselves into the dialogue and literature of economic theory that depart in varying degrees from basic price theory. They are unrelated to each other and do not represent any coherent attack on the theory itself, though each identifies some weakness in the traditional theoretical scheme.

Monopolistic or Imperfect Competition

The Great Depression of the 1930s led to dissatisfaction with the unrealistic assumptions of the model of perfect competition (Stigler 1965 "Essays": 256; Landreth 1976: 392–93). This atmosphere led to a warm reception of two books that appeared within six months of each other in 1933, making much the same argument: that the model of perfect competition was not relevant to modern industrial markets (Chamberlin: *Monopolistic Competition;* Joan Robinson: *Imperfect Competition*).

Their attacks were thus focused primarily on one of the three legs of the price theory triangle, that relating to market structure. Chamberlin frankly disputed that pure or perfect competition was an ideal standard (Chamberlin 1946: 25, 173–75). But their analysis also challenged in some degree the base of the triangle—the tendency of price, supply, and demand to change in reaction to one another. As Joan Robinson put it in the introduction to the 1969 edition of her book: "Even in a seller's market where output is up to the limit set by capacity, firms usually prefer to lengthen delivery dates or ration consumers, rather than to choke off demand by raising prices today for fear that it might be permanently lost. Movements of demand affect profits strongly, but prices hardly at all" (1969: viii).

Chamberlin also qualified the automaticity of the supply-demand-price relationship, focusing on nonprice competition: "Price adjustments are, in fact, but one phase, and often a relatively unimportant phase, of the whole competitive process. More and more is price competition evaded by turning the buyer's attention towards a trademark, as by competing on the basis of quality or service" (1946: 73).

These contributions did not displace the earlier concept of perfect competition. As one historian of economic theory observes puckishly, the textbooks simply grew fatter, the refuted theories continuing to be published along with those that refute them (Routh 1977: 17, 256–57, 261).

Workable Competition

John Maurice Clark was one of the more distinguished economists who challenged the basic precepts of price theory. We shall come to his contentions in this respect shortly ("Empirical Studies"). Although he gained no following for these heretical views, he did introduce a new concept that became a permanent part of the economic doctrine.

Clark argued that the conditions of perfect competition being impractical of attainment, economics should strive for some more realistic standard by which to set the goals of policy. This he proposed be termed "workable competition" (Clark, J. M. 1940), and the term stuck.

Workable competition is like perfect competition in one respect—there is no one universally accepted version of it. F. M. Scherer's version of the contemporary concept is something of a laundry list of all things idealized by economists, consisting of 16 elements, including the maximum number of traders consistent with economies of scale, independent decision making by firms without collusion, that "production and distribution operations should be efficient and not wasteful of resources," and so on (Scherer 1980: 42).

This is not theory; it is, rather, a position, a compromise between reality and the unrealistic conditions postulated by the theory. It is a commonsense type of concept, vague enough to be the basis for a broad consensus, which it had in fact become by the 1950s (Oppenheim 1952). Together with the concepts of monopolistic and imperfect competition, it gave economists some kind of conceptual framework for dealing with the world as it actually existed. But as recognized by some of the scholars who participated in the 1955 Attorney General's National Committee to Study the Antitrust Laws: " 'the doctrine' of workable competition is only a rough and ready judgment by some economists, each for himself, that a particular industry is performing reasonably well" (*Report* 1955: 339). George Stigler's put-down has become classic: "To determine whether any industry is workably competitive, therefore, simply have a good graduate student write his dissertation on the industry and render a verdict. It is crucial to this test, of course, that no second graduate student be allowed to study the industry" (Stigler 1956: 505).

The indeterminate variations that can follow from this standard are elaborated in an article by Stephen Sosnick (1958). The major practical effect of this concept, though derogating from the idea of perfect competition, may have been to protect it by providing some commonsense company that distracts attention from the unreality of the theory.

Creative Destruction

At about the same time that J. M. Clark was questioning some of the essential tenets of price theory, another prominent, but unorthodox, economist mounted an even more basic assault on the theoretical concept of competition. Joseph A. Schumpeter's *Capitalism, Socialism and Democracy*, first published in 1942 (1950), attacked the assumptions of perfect competition from two distinct angles: On the one hand he questioned its capacity for automatic self-adjustment, and on the other, he posited a completely different concept of competition than that employed in the theory. We postpone the first of these points to the discussion of unconceded flaws in the theory and focus here on the major alternative that he offered to the orthodox concept of competition.

Schumpeter, perhaps being overly optimistic, asserted that "Economists are at long last emerging from the stage in which price competition was all they saw. As soon as quality competition and sales effort are admitted into the sacred precincts of theory, the price variable is ousted from its dominant position" (ibid., 84). Schumpeter argued that "in capitalist reality" it is not the price competition pictured in the textbooks that counts

> but the competition from the new commodity, the new technology, the new source of supply, the new type of organization (the largest unit of control, for instance)—competition which commands a decisive cost or quality advantage and which strikes not at the margins of the profits and the outputs of the existing firms but at their foundations and their very lives. (ibid.)

This "creative destruction" he described as the "fundamental impulse that sets and keeps the capitalist engine in motion [which] comes from the new consumers' goods, the new methods of production or transportation, the new markets, the new forms of industrial organization that capitalist enterprise creates" (ibid.).

There is both irony and some loss in the fact that this insight came from Schumpeter and not from those economists who have focused on questions of antitrust policy—a subject that Schumpeter did not address. Schumpeter, who produced a major insight into the competitive process, did not develop the idea as a basis for government policy, while conservative economists have resisted, or simply ignored, the profound implications of Schumpeter's contribution.

MORE FLAWS IN THE THEORY (UNCONCEDED)

There is a sense in which all the flaws summarized here can be said to be conceded, in that not only have some economists at one time or another conceded them all, but also the truth of many of the following propositions is conceded by present-day defenders of the theory. But they rarely appear in the textbooks, and where they do they are simply recorded as other viewpoints, not assimilated into the doctrine.

Adam Smith's First Point

The first point made by Adam Smith in *The Wealth of Nations* was that the produce of every nation is affected by two factors: "first, by the skill, dexterity and judgment with which its labour is generally applied; and secondly by the proportions between the number of those who are employed in useful labour and those who are not so employed" (Smith *Wealth*: Intro. & Plan of the Work: 1). He then observed that of the two, the former seems more important, citing the example of impoverished tribes fully employed at hunting and fishing in contrast to both idle and working-class people enjoying a higher standard of living in more advanced countries (ibid., 1–2).

The difference between these two factors is in the level of technology—which depends on innovation—and the degree to which productive assets are fully employed. Economic theory concedes that innovation is beyond its competence, and the focus of the theory is on the factor that Adam Smith regarded as secondary. Stigler made this clear in his article "The Goals of Economic Policy" (1975: 284), which advocates "a two prolonged goal: (1) to employ as fully as possible . . . the resources at the society's disposal . . . and (2) to employ those resources as efficiently as possible."

Smith thus addressed at the outset of his study a question we have not yet confronted: the relative importance of innovation, which the theory does not address, and those factors which it does. The remarkable fact is that the conclusions of economists today accord with the judgment of Adam Smith. Scherer has been among the more forthright in this regard. He concedes that the whole issue of resource misallocation through less than fully competitive pricing appears statistically insignificant by every way of measuring it that has been attempted (Scherer 1980: 461–64). He also concedes the possibility that certain concentrations, and innovation, could far outstrip in productivity whatever minor gains in efficiency might be made through more competitive pricing (ibid., 22–23, 407). "On this point Joseph A. Schumpeter's cries in the wilderness have gained nearly universal acceptance" (Goldschmid 1974: 46–48).

The reaction of Scherer in particular, and economists generally, has been to focus attention on Schumpeter's additional and more controversial assertion that "large, monopolistic firms are a superior vehicle for conceiving and implementing technological innovations" (ibid., 48). This serves the convenient purpose of diverting attention from the horrendous implications of his first and more basic proposition as to the primary role of innovation itself. Schumpeter's second proposition is in some measure an overstatement—to say that large size is necessary to many kinds of innovation does not mean that it is necessary to all innovation. Schumpeter's critics have had a field day pointing out the numerous examples of innovation by small firms and entrepreneurs (Liebhafsky 1968: 581–82); and others, including Scherer, have turned to researching with crude statistical measures the correlation, if any, between size and innovation (Scherer 1980: Chap. 15). But none of this secondary controversy detracts from Schumpeter's primary point that innovation is more important than efficiency in the sense of cost minimization.

Putting aside the fact that the theory is focused on a matter of secondary importance, let us now turn to the problems it confronts on its own home ground.

The Illusory Benchmark of Perfect Competition

> "At least from the time of the physiocrats and Adam Smith," Samuelson has observed, "there has never been absent from the main body of economic literature the feeling that in some sense perfect competition represented an optimal situation."
>
> Mark Blaug (1978: 629; see also Machlup 1952: 18, 22–23)

It was noted in the section on conceded flaws in the theory that its most common criticism, that the conditions postulated for perfect competition are unrealistic, has some plausible grounds of defense. But there is a fatal objection that does not rely on unreality at all: It is that the conditions of perfect competition are not ideal; they are, in fact, undesirable. This conclusion is demonstrable by two routes: One is by the incompatibility of perfect competition with the conditions of a progressive industrial economy, and the other is by the conceptual unsoundness of an atomistic market structure as automatically self-regulating.

The first point was made by Schumpeter in the course of his thesis on creative destruction. His argument has been expanded with eloquence by John Kenneth Galbraith (1952: 88–91). The Schumpeter-Galbraith argument is that the very conditions idealized as perfect and pure competition not only do not increase productivity, they are positively harmful to it. Technical advance, and innovation generally, requires some margin of profit, a source of investment diverted from current production for the purpose of improving productivity. John Maurice Clark was another nonbeliever in the model of perfect competition as an ideal standard: "the conclusion is inescapable: this allegedly desirable condition is something nobody really wants, including the theorists whose models impliedly set it up as a desideratum" (1961: 56).

These realistic objections are based upon what a theorist can argue are special (unfortunate?) conditions associated with industrial markets. But there is a more fundamental objection, because even without the special case of capital investment and the need for innovative research, the theoretical concept of perfect competition is flawed.

Let us recall the elements of the theoretical concept. The number of both buyers and sellers is so large, and their individual contributions toward both supply and demand so small, that participation or abstention by any individual buyer or seller will have no effect on price (Stigler "Theory"1966: 87; 1957: 5; 1965: 242; McNulty 1967: 397). It is a seemingly anomalous corollary that the only variable open to discretionary adjustment by individual producers is not price but the quantity of output offered (McNulty 1968: 649 n.7).

Now let us look at the implications of this conceptual framework for what we normally think of as competition. Paul McNulty, in two clear-headed articles (1967, 1968) contrasted the theoretical construct and the idea of competition utilized by Adam Smith. Smith's concept was behavioral, the offering of goods at lower or higher prices when supply and demand were out of balance, with a resulting *effect* on price. The theoretical concept of perfect competition focuses not on competitive behavior but on market structure, and it defines that structure in such a way as to exclude all possibility of competition in the behavioral sense used by Adam Smith (McNulty 1968: 646–50; Wilson & Skinner 1976: 239).

McNulty's articles drew upon prior work by other economists who appreciated this distinction, notably Friedrich Hayek (McNulty 1968: 649 n.6; Hayek 1948: 92, 96) and Frank Knight; (Knight 1946: 102); but he stopped short of pursuing the significance of this distinction as far as others, and particularly Knight, already had. The full development of the concept of perfect competition began with Cournot in 1848, was embellished by other mathematical economists in the late nineteenth century, and was further refined around the turn of the century by J. B. Clark and Frank Knight (Stigler 1957, 1965 "Essays": 234). Knight himself, however, deplored the term "competitive" as "one of our worst misfortunes of terminology" preferring the term "atomistic" (Knight 1946: 102). McNulty noted the point, but failed to develop it, that Knight, like Marshall earlier, and many others, including Schumpeter (1942, 1950: 103–4) and Liebhafsky (1968: 579), had not considered the concept of perfect competition to represent either an ideal or a desirable condition (Knight 1921, 1957: 191–92; Chamberlin 1946: 25, 214–15; Scherer 1980:

24; Stigler 1965 "Essays": 252 n.42; 1962: 282; Marshall 1910: 548). Knight was particularly explicit: Under conditions of perfect competition there is a built-in instability with an incentive for separate agents to combine, ultimately resulting in a monopoly (Knight 1921, 1957, 1964: 191–92).

This theoretical perception has abundant empirical confirmation. One heterodox economist found exactly that tendency in a detailed case study of the U.S. sugar-refining industry (Eichner 1969). But the larger and most obvious demonstration is in agriculture. Not all agricultural markets are alike, but several effectively fulfill the conditions of perfect or pure competition; Paul Samuelson lists four: potatoes, tobacco, wheat, and cotton (Samuelson 1980: 484). It has been the universal and historical experience of such atomistically structured markets that they are not self-regulating, with the result that government intervention of the most drastic order has resulted, examples of which go back at least as far as the seventeenth century (Friedman, Lawrence 1973: 67). And if the idea of monopoly seems far fetched in agriculture, it is instructive to observe what has been happening in the United States. There is a movement of gravitational proportions absorbing U.S. agriculture into the framework of big business—"agribusiness"—not to mention an effective monopoly regime imposed through a combination of antitrust exceptions (ABA 1984: 637–40) and outright governmentally imposed control on the quantity of agricultural commodities that can be marketed (Shepard 1986).

The single, most forthright attempt to mold government policy according to the notion of perfect competition was the deconcentration proposals embodied in the Hart Bill, which fizzled in the early 1970s (Goldschmid 1974: 344–49). Its origins can be traced to a book-length academic study that expressly predicated its analysis on the "rigorous model" of perfect competition (Kaysen & Turner 1959: 7). Citing high levels of concentration in industry, it proposed legislation to break up the more concentrated firms—a policy of pulverization. The proposal was reflected in the Neal Report of a White House task force (1968), which led to the Hart Bill and hearings that buried it. The authors of the proposal ultimately recanted (Goldschmid 1974: 414).

In the ongoing debate over trucking deregulation economists urging a free market regime point with some glee to the fact that the trucking industry is so atomistically structured as to approach the conditions of perfect competition—this as proof that the industry would function efficiently on a purely competitive basis!

Does it make sense to fashion policy on a model that is a proven recipe for disaster?

The Fallacy of the U-Shaped Cost Curve and the Madness of Marginal Cost Pricing

> Marginal cost, formally defined as an increment of cost divided by the increment of product associated with the increment of cost, and

> not the more easily measured average cost (total cost divided by output) is the economist's fundamental criterion of competitive price—and of optimum price.
>
> George Stigler (1968: 11)

> The central policy prescription of microeconomics is the equation of price and marginal cost. If economic theory is to have any relevance to public utility pricing, that is the point at which the inquiry must begin.
>
> Alfred Kahn (1970: vol. 1: 65)

> He was very bright, very good to discuss things with. We tended to disagree, but we always had the happiest of discussions. He came late, having been in a printing business that failed. I afterwards said it was because he set price equal to marginal cost. [Laughter.]
>
> Ronald H. Coase (Kitch 1983: 218)

The two concepts are distinct but linked to produce one of the most absurd precepts in neoclassical theory: The U-shaped cost curve forms the predicate for the rationale for marginal cost pricing.

The concept of the U-shaped cost curve goes back to Alfred Marshall. Marshall, in turn, derived it from David Ricardo's conception of rising costs in an agricultural setting where land of decreasing fertility is brought under cultivation. Marshall explicitly stated that this same principle applied to "every other appliance of production" (*Principles*: 416). His concept of the U shape was that starting from zero units of output the average cost per unit would fall (the left leg of the U) and continue to do so with increased output until the limits of capacity were reached, at which point the declining line would level out and then turn up. (Envisaged in a more modern setting, the process may be conceived of in terms of increasing costs incurred as a plant reaches its operating capacity: increased labor costs through overtime pay, machinery breakdowns slowing production and increasing maintenance costs, premium prices for materials and extra delivery charges to expedite their shipment, etc.) This rising cost leg on the right side of the U, which represented increasing costs with further increases in production, formed the predicate for the logic of marginal cost pricing.

The principle is that under conditions of perfect or pure competition the most efficient, the most ideal price for which a commodity should sell is equal to the marginal cost of the last unit of production: P=MC. "This principle," Professor Stigler tells us,

> is easily proved. Profits are rising so long as an additional unit of output increases receipts more than costs, i.e., as long as marginal revenue is greater than marginal cost. Profits decline when an additional unit of output adds more to costs

than to receipts, i.e., when marginal cost is greater than marginal revenue. Hence profits are at a maximum—are neither rising nor falling—when marginal revenue equals marginal cost. (Stigler 1946: 259)

Before testing that proof, it is necessary to distinguish several distinct concepts that have been confused in the literature extolling the principle of marginal cost pricing.

One is the obvious case of a businessman who cannot sell his entire production at a price sufficient to recover his total costs, but who can sell some portion at a price that will cover the out-of-pocket or variable cost of those units and make some contribution to overhead. If he can do this without destroying the integrity of his normal price structure, it is obviously to his advantage to do so. Every businessperson knows this, and it has nothing to do with the price theory concept of marginal cost pricing, though the example just stated is sometimes invoked in support of that concept (Watson 1969: 82; Baumol & Blinder 1979: 497).

Second is the special case that lay at the heart of Ricardo's model: an agricultural economy in which demand so presses upon supply that it forces ever less fertile soil into production. Since the price must be sufficient to repay the cost of the most expensive land, that marginal unit will tend to set the cost for the entire market. In this case, price is raised by marginal cost, but not literally equal to it, and in circumstances where the force of demand will accept the higher price, so that cost never exceeds the market price. The mechanism of marginal cost exceeding price and thereby setting a ceiling to output therefore cannot operate.

A third distinct case is marginal price as determined in an auction market. The prices of financial securities and commodities traded on exchanges are set by the last, marginal pressure exerted by the buying or the selling side, and this final sale sets a market price for all like units. Price is thus determined at the margin, but this again is not the concept of marginal cost as it is used in the proposition that price equals marginal cost. Indeed, prices in auction markets are characteristically wholly unrelated to cost.

A fourth special case is the marginal cost analysis used to choose between alternative options. For example, an electric utility needing to expand its generating capacity can choose between several alternative measures of steam generation: oil, coal, natural gas, nuclear, and in some cases, hydro. Each type of facility will have a differing cost, and a combined facility capable of using two or more alternative fuels will provide yet other cost alternatives. The cost comparison will, however, be complicated by the varying costs of the different fuels. When all these variables have been factored in, the costs can be compared and a decision can be made based on the marginal cost advantage of the least costly alternative. This again, however, is not marginal cost pricing as that term is used in price theory, which is premised on the idea that incremental units of production will incur increasing levels of cost.

These distinct cases aside, we can now return to the theoretical concept of marginal cost pricing as explained in the extract from Stigler, premised on increasing costs incurred by increasing units of production, represented by the right leg of the U. First, the concept has a fundamental flaw—the U-shaped cost curve does not exist.

Marshall premised his concept of rising costs on Ricardo's agricultural model where the capital plant—land—is in fixed supply. Marshall reasoned that the same principle applies to every industrial appliance: Pushed to the limits of its capacity, it will eventually lose efficiency and become more costly to operate. What Marshall failed to take account of is that a machine can be replaced, and in increasing numbers. Unlike land, its supply is not fixed. A firm faced with pressure on its producing capacity will, if it foresees adequate demand, simply increase capacity, bypassing altogether the problem that Ricardo and Marshall took as the very heart of their analytical systems.

What is particularly startling about this concept in economic theory is its unquestioned acceptance in the absence of *any* empirical support for the existence of the U-shaped cost curve, and in the face of abundant evidence that there is no such thing. An English economist surveyed the massive data on U.S. corporations assembled by President Roosevelt's TNEC study of the 1930s and found that the actual cost curves of these large firms were not U shaped, but L shaped. That is, costs proceed steeply down as volume increases to a point, at which they level off and remain flat. They do not turn up again (Wiles 1961: viii, 238–62). He is not alone in this observation. Stigler (1958: 59) produced a graph simulating statistical average costs that is essentially L shaped. Scherer (1980: 86–87) acknowledges that the U-shaped cost curve may not be valid, and he sketches a curve based on empirical data in essentially the same shape as Stigler's. John Williamson (1966: 1) rejects the U shape, and William Fellner (1960: Chap. 16) places ahead of the traditional U-shaped analysis an analysis based on a level cost function premised on empirical evidence.

The economist-businessman Oswald Knauth (*infra.* "More Flaws") dismisses the idea of increasing marginal costs limiting production by the simple expedient of increasing capacity (Knauth 1948: 32, 92). Joan Robinson noted that "Pigou seemed to have reduced Marshall's *Principles* to a logical and consistent scheme" that nevertheless had one obvious defect: "The whole argument turns on 'price equals marginal cost.' This entails that the sales of an industrial firm are limited by the capacity of its equipment. . . . This was evidently absurd" (1978: ix). Much earlier

Sraffa (1926: 543) made the same point: "Businessmen, who regard themselves as being subject to competitive conditions, would consider absurd the assertion that the limit to their production is to be found in the internal conditions of production in their own firm, which do not permit of the production of a greater quantity without an increase in cost." Routh (1977: 251) is to the same effect. And yet the textbooks continue to portray this traditional U-shaped cost curve (Samuelson 1980; 428–31, 442–45; Lipsey & Steiner 1975: 282; Routh 1977: 23).

Let us turn now from the faulty foundation in the U-shaped cost curve to the concept of marginal cost pricing itself. It is obvious to any layman that a business that is forced to sell its entire production at a price that covers only variable and not fixed costs will soon go bankrupt.

This dilemma has not gone unnoticed within the profession. Three solutions have been offered. The favorite ploy invoked by defenders of the theory is to distinguish between short-term and long-term marginal costs, holding the theory to apply only to the latter. They then argue that in the long term all costs are marginal (Scherer 1980: 14; Lee 1984 ("Marginalist"): 1118–20; Areeda & Turner 1978: vol. 2: par.403c, p. 272; Blaug 1978: 631; Stigler 1949, 1969: 48). This sort of definitional manipulation has been carried to the point where economists today appear to have convinced themselves through semantic confusions that the logical dilemma of marginal cost pricing may be escaped by defining marginal cost in such a way that it equals full cost pricing (Melody 1974: 287; Kahn 1974: 301; Lee 1984 ("Whatever"): 233; 1984 ("Marginalist"): 1107). We may concede this, but at that point marginal costs by definition are equal to total costs, so that the concept of being "marginal" is meaningless.

A second solution is price discrimination: A part of the production run large enough to cover total costs is sold at a price adequate to do that, and the remainder at a price adequate to cover incremental costs (Stigler "Theory" 1966: 214). But this is cheating: The theory of perfect competition requires that all sales be made at the same price, and the *theory* of price = marginal cost calls for the sale of all units at the price that covers the cost of the last unit (Scherer 1980: 13–14; Kahn 1970: 66, 69 (par.2); Knight 1921, 1964: 82).

A third solution, which has actually been proposed in the context of public utility regulation (Liebhafsky 1968: 527–28), is, to quote George Stigler, "to charge the loss resulting from a price equal to marginal cost from the public treasury—a solution especially appealing to the buyers of the product" (Stigler "Theory" 1966: 214). This is not just George Stigler on a bad day. It is a fact that distinguished scholars for a century have supported the idea of subsidizing firms out of the public treasury for losses incurred through pricing at marginal cost (Blaug 1978: 386–87,

630–32, 701; Samuelson 1976: 503; Watson 1963: 309; Spiegal 1983: 559; Coase 1946: 169; Nordin 1947: 141; Coase 1947: 150).

Is this not madness?

Empty Boxes and Tautologies

> Though a skilled mathematician, he [Alfred Marshall] used mathematics sparingly. He saw that excessive reliance on this instrument might lead us astray in pursuit of intellectual toys, imaginary problems not conforming to the conditions of real life; and, further, might distort our sense of proportion by causing us to neglect factors that could not easily be worked up in the mathematical machine.
>
> A. C. Pigou (1925, 1966: 84)

> Mathematical logic is a powerful tool of thought, but its application in economic theory generally seems to consist merely of putting circular arguments into algebra.
>
> Joan Robinson (1981: 61)

A pervasive problem in economic theory is that it has no empirical foundation. The theory rather starts from itself; it is a fantasy world based on certain assumed economic problems in the abstract that proceeds, without facts, to manipulate these abstractions.

The lack of correspondence between these abstract conceptions and reality has long been a source of controversy within the profession. One of the more famous and colorful flare-ups occurred in the 1920s, touched off by an article by the English economist J. H. Clapham, "Of Empty Economic Boxes" (1922). The problem was rooted in the U-shaped cost curve. Alfred Marshall's concept was fashioned in the setting of individual proprietorships, not the massive capital-intensive industries that were just emerging at the time he wrote. It was obvious that the concept of increasing marginal costs did not apply where a firm had a large fixed investment with the result that its unit costs declined rather than rose with increasing volume. This led to a categorization of firms in the abstract as between those with increasing and those with decreasing cost curves. Yet even in the seemingly clear cases, firms had mixtures of increasing and decreasing costs, so that none fit clearly into one category or the other, which Clapham termed "boxes," hence the concept of empty boxes.

One recent example of the problem is the attempt to fit the oil industry into the box of decreasing or increasing costs. Traditionally, it had been viewed as a declining cost industry because costs are heavily loaded on the front end, in drilling the well, while the costs of pumping are relatively minor. Morris Adelman, in an attempt to bring the industry within the theoretical paradigm of marginal cost pricing by showing that the industry has a rising cost curve, cited the increased expenditures needed to extend a well's productive life through further investment in secondary and tertiary production methods (Adelman 1964: 33–43). But this does not put the industry squarely in the rising cost box because it still has a major, and indeed larger, declining cost component. Thus Clapham's point: The boxes are empty.

A. C. Pigou, in reply to Clapham (1922), did not fill the boxes but argued that the concept, though incomplete, described phenomena that were analytically significant. The stalemate is typical. But the concept of empty boxes is an illuminating label for a problem far more pervasive than the limited concepts of increasing and diminishing cost with which it originated; it has in fact entered the vocabulary of the profession, and it is especially descriptive of the fallacy of mathematical reasoning as a basis for deriving useful propositions from neoclassical theory. This is because these impressive-looking algebraic symbols are themselves empty boxes that for the most part cannot be filled.

The role of mathematics in economic theory has been much discussed (Stigler 1949, 1969: 37; Samuelson "Mathematics" 1967; Baumol 1966; Georgescu-Roegen 1979; Brems 1975; O'Brien 1974; Eichner 1983; Debreu 1984; Wiles & Routh 1984). Mathematics connotes the very essence of precision; but mathematics as used in most of the theoretical writing is not computational; that is, it manipulates not numbers but abstract symbols representing unknowns. Propositions stating logical interrelationships can be expressed in mathematical form; but when the content consists of unknowns, they are essentially tautologies, a criticism that has long been voiced within the profession (Leontief 1971; Robinson, Joan 1981: 15, 60–62, 99, 151; Ward 1972: 49; Hendry 1980; O'Brien 1974: 11–20; Gruchy 1973: 304–5; Rotwein 1966; Samuelson "Mathematics" 1967: vol. 2: 1751; Cochran 1930)).

That mathematics is a powerful engine of thought when properly used is indisputable. The problem lies in its misuse, and even abuse. One of the more balanced appraisals was made by George Stigler. He acknowledged the tendency within the profession, because "the mathematical method is so powerful and beautiful . . . to use it just for the sake of using it." But he also called attention to a tendency, expressed by Cournot—the first mathematical economist—who " 'put aside questions to which mathematical analysis cannot be applied' " (1949, 1969: 43). Stigler deplored this attitude as doubly wrong: first, because it tends to severely limit or contort the problem; and second, because "mathematics, for all its vast power, is dreadfully weak when alone. It cannot answer so simple a question as whether a locomotive has a higher cost of production than a toothbrush" (Stigler 1949, 1969: 43–44).

And thus we see how even the seemingly most modern and scientific tool, mathematics, serves to perpetuate two of Ricardo's most basic errors: the elevation of method over substance and the misuse of rigorous method.

The Overstated Role of Price

> In political economy the desire to simplify has occasioned an unwillingness to acknowledge the operation of more causes than one in the production of particular effects; and if one cause would account for a considerable portion of a certain class of phenomena, the whole has been ascribed to it without sufficient attention to the facts, which would not admit of its being so solved.
>
> T. R. Malthus (*Principles*: 5)

> I love a theory that explains everything.
>
> Robert Bork (*Wash. Post* 6/22/86: A16)

The central premise of price theory is that price is the universal solvent of economics, the interrelation of supply, demand, and price being a kind of gravitational law that governs all economic activity. Experience, however, has shown that price, while an important factor, does not operate with the invariable consistency of the law of gravity.

Empirical Studies. From time to time individuals or teams of economists have wandered off the reservation of pure theory and enquired empirically into how the business pricing process actually works. The results have been enlightening—and consistently inconsistent with the theory.

The first such study of note was done by two English economists, R.G. Hall and C. J. Hitch (1939). Their unqualified finding: businessmen do not set prices, either consciously or unconsciously, to equate marginal revenues with marginal cost as postulated by the theory, but rather to recover their full costs. This conclusion may seem hardly surprising to anyone but an economic theorist, but for the latter it was a very unsettling development. Perhaps the height of desperation in response to this study was reached in Fritz Machlup's attempt to salvage the idea of marginal cost pricing on the basis of the study's findings of businesspeople's sensitivity to price elasticity: "On the other hand, there is plenty of evidence in the findings that the businessmen paid much attention to demand elasticities—which to the economist is equivalent to marginal revenue considerations" (Machlup 1946: 545–47). This is pure sophistry; it does not redeem the theoretical premise that price, or marginal revenues, are equated with marginal cost.

The same conclusion permeates more recent studies: Of all the various criteria businesspeople use—and they are numerous—equating marginal cost and price or revenue is not among them (Andrews & Brunner 1975: 2–3; Weston 1972: 2–3; Wiles 1961: viii, 3, 238–62; Baumol 1967: 27 n.1,

28–29; Kaplan, Dirlam & Lanzillotti 1958; Lanzillotti 1958, 49, 669; Hollander, Stanley 1957; Backman 1953; National Bureau of Economic Research 1943). Of special interest is the Brookings study done by Kaplan, Dirlam and Lanzillotti, *Pricing in Big Business* (1958). It is instructive in several respects: first, because it sets forth through specific case studies the variety of factors that influence businesspeople in their pricing decisions; second, because it demonstrates how subordinate the pricing decision often is to other factors; third, because it shows that price changes often do not perform the automatic adjustment function posited by the theory, and for a variety of reasons; and fourth, because the study was done by economists who did not find what they expected and were admirably candid in admitting that fact. They found that the officers who were responsible for pricing decisions did not think of that function as a separate, distinct problem apart from other elements of company policy. The participants in pricing decisions included "executives from production, development engineering, accounting, finance, sales, and public relations"; and the pricing decision was "usually considered part of the strategy for achieving a broadly defined goal" (ibid., 3–4). After working their way through the body of material their investigations amassed, which showed pricing policies being dictated by a disparate variety of considerations, the authors concluded that they could find no single, unifying principle to explain the determinants of price (ibid., 289).

The determinants they did find fell into five categories: (1) pricing to achieve a target return on investment, (2) stabilization of price and margin, (3) pricing to maintain or improve market positioning, (4) pricing to meet or follow competition, and (5) pricing subordinated to product differentiation (ibid., 128).

The details of these differing objectives need not detain us. What they show is that business, as an institution, has a broader perspective than the maximization of profits by creating the fullest possible spread between cost and price, and that the particular institutional objectives vary from one market sector to another.

All of the studies cited thus far were limited case studies. More general empirical study is likewise confirmatory that price does not play the central role attributed to it by the theory. John Maurice Clark, whose work was broadly based and empirical, concluded that price does not in fact serve to allocate resources. Conceding that the concept "has a basis in truth," he rejected the idea "that it takes a change in prices to change the allocation of resources" arguing that "a moderate shift in resources, increasing the production of this and decreasing the production of that, can commonly be brought about simply by changes in the volume of sales, *without any change in price*" (1949: 119–20, emphasis in original; Stocking & Watkins 1951: 100–101, 113). Likewise, Joan

Robinson noted: "The prices of manufactures... are administered prices.... Output rises and falls with demand.... Even in a seller's market... when output is up to the limit set by capacity, firms usually prefer to lengthen delivery dates or ration customers, rather than to choke off demand by raising prices today for fear that it might be permanently lost. Movements of demand affect profits strongly, but prices hardly at all" (1969: vii-viii; see also 1981: 4–26).

The Fictional Monopolist. Price theory offers a single, simplistic view of monopoly: the restriction of output to create an artificial shortage and thereby a higher than competitive price, what the theory describes as the "deadweight loss" attributable to monopoly (Samuelson 1976: 503; Scherer 1980: 16–18, 22, 460, 464; Areeda & Turner 1978: vol. 2: par.403, p. 271; Bork 1978: 107–9; West 1978: 829, 830–31). Even at the theoretical level, however, the significance of this concept has been questioned (Weiss 1979: 1104). Both Marshall and Schumpeter questioned the presumption that a monopolist would restrict output and raise prices (Schumpeter 1954: 976–78).

One of the more striking facts in the history of antitrust experience is that the most prominent of the convicted monopolists do not conform at all to the stereotype: Standard Oil, Alcoa, and AT&T. Can any of these companies, even in the heyday of their illegal monopolistic behavior, be said to have restricted output so as to charge artificially high prices? Standard Oil did restrict output to the level of demand, which was the whole purpose of its monopoly; but it did not restrict it to the point of creating artificial shortages to inflate prices (and thereby attract unwelcome competition). Standard Oil was constantly seeking to expand its markets; its monopolistic objective was motivated by a quest for order, not exploitive profits (Chap. 3). Alcoa, too, was anxious to expand the market for its commodity, an objective that could not have been furthered by excessive prices. And AT&T, which sought monopoly for obvious reasons somewhat different from those of Rockefeller, has produced impressive technological innovation (though some critics insist it could have done more). Its main problem on that front has been, ironically, the inhibiting effects of an antitrust decree that was lifted only in connection with the consent order leading to divestiture (Peters 1985; Greene 1984; Green 1984; MacAvoy & Robinson 1983).

Joan Robinson has also observed that "the great corporations do not behave monopolistically in the sense of restricting output in order to raise prices. They continue to compete with each other, invading new markets, introducing new products, and evolving new techniques, while at the same time throwing up opportunities for new small businesses to make a start" (1981: 12; 1971: 102–3).

The point here is not to defend monopoly, which has disadvantages enough in psychological and political terms. It is, rather, that those disadvantages have nothing to do with the fictional price theory view of a monopolist who simply restricts output in order to get a higher-than-competitive price (Mayhew 1972). On the contrary, the goals of efficiency, cost, and therefore price minimization are as well if not better realized under conditions of enlightened monopoly than of unfettered market competition, a point that has been noted by more than one economist (Boulding 1945, and comments at 60 ibid. 612, 615, 619 (1946); Le Rossignol 1901: 214–19; Baumol 1977: 402; Knight 1921, 1957: 252; Quirk & Sapsonik 1968: 125–26; Machlup 1952: 182, 453–54; Goldschmid 1974: 381–82; Solo 1975: 643; Scherer 1980: 21–22, Chap. 4; Melody 1974: 299).

MORE FLAWS CONTINUED: THE NEGLECTED INSIGHTS OF OSWALD KNAUTH

We have noted the seemingly impermeable wall that separates the world of the theoretical academic economist from that of a private businessperson. It is the truly *rara avis* who knows both of these worlds at first hand (Stigler "Essays" 1965: 51) and who, even more singularly, has taken the effort to reduce the resulting insights to a coherent, written form and, even further, to train the focus of that business experience on the basic tenets of price theory. Oswald Knauth, alone, writing in the 1940s and 1950s, has done that. There have been other economists with business backgrounds, most notably David Ricardo and John Maynard Keynes. But both were speculators, not managers of business organizations. Two others, Vilfredo Pareto (Schumpeter 1951: 113–14) and Jean Baptiste Say (Routh 1977: 125–27) had business backgrounds but preferred abstract to empirical analysis. Gardner Means was an academic economist sensitive to the fact that the corporate institution is a phenomenon of independent significance, and he called for economists to pay more attention to the actual motivations of businesspeople (Means 1962: 54) but left that task to others. William Baumol is an economist with extensive consulting experience that led him to conclude that businesspeople do not, as economic theory assumes, seek to maximize profits, but rather revenues (Baumol 1967: Chap. 6; Bailey & Boyle 1977: 48, in which the authors report their "utter surprise" at their own findings). Yet Baumol's dissent from orthodoxy went no further, writing within the conventional boundaries of price theory (1967; 1977; Baumol & Blinder 1979). Herbert Simon made his field of inquiry the motivations of businesspeople but approached this inherently empirical subject in theoretical terms (Simon 1976). He did not even cite Knauth.

Knauth, trained as an economist, left academe to spend 20 years as a business executive in merchandising before giving way to an irresistible urge to return to an uninterrupted career as an economist (Knauth 1948: 7). He was conscious of the uniqueness of his experience:

> The fact that businessmen so rarely write books about their work and experience has often been deplored. But the reason is clear. The task of writing is too time consuming and exhausting to be fitted into the crannies and spare moments of an active executive life. Arriving at decisions, watching and assessing the daily process, making changes, maintaining the flow of contacts with persons and sources of information—in short, the business life—is too engrossing to leave any surplus energy for the sustained concentration of writing required in the prolonged effort of a book. Again the training and point of view of an executive is diametrically opposed to that of an analytical writer. The former makes decisions, the latter expounds. No mind can fit into both grooves at the same time. The author could not have carried through this book in its many revisions without quitting business in 1943 and giving full time devotion to the task. (ibid., 8)

Knauth, like Adam Smith, did not write as a theorist, but as an observer. He did, however, relate his observations throughout to the theory, pointing out how business reality conflicts with the basic tenets of theory. He wrote two book-length studies relevant here, *Managerial Enterprise* (1948) and *Business Practices, Trade Position, and Competition* (1956), and an article, "Monopoly Reconsidered" (1945).

His work has been neglected, overlooked, and where noticed, ignored. The reason is not difficult to fathom. For what he had to say was so fundamentally at odds with orthodox theory that it was as much welcome within the profession as an atheist at a church picnic. There is perhaps one other explanation for the lack of recognition accorded Knauth. His purpose was affirmative rather than destructive: He sought to describe the realities of the new managerially run business world, and his criticisms of the theory were only an incident of that larger purpose. He did not title any of his writings in terms of price theory, and he spoke only in general terms of "the classical theory." What Knauth did was to sketch a profile of the world of modern corporate business—not the whole economy, but that sector consisting of publicly held corporations, accounting for about two thirds of the whole (*Business*: 6 ; cf. *Managerial*: 21).

A central assumption of price theory is that the businessman's problem is to adjust the quantity of his output in response to cost and prices. But in the world of managerial enterprise that is not the sort of problem that managers have to contend with; nor can their actions be explained in terms of their unconsciously doing the sort of thing described by the theory although thinking in other terms, as Fritz Machlup has asserted (1967: 26; 1946: 534).

First, there are several reasons why the precise adjustment of output levels to costs and market price is not a realistic problem. Unlike the smooth curves drawn in the abstract by theorists, neither demand nor costs change in such neat progressions:

> The demand curve for any article cannot be determined in the abstract. It must be felt for by actual experiments. Indeed it is not a curve or at least a smooth one, but a series of steps or jumps. A lowering of price does more than stimulate existing demand gradually. It opens up new sources of demand (*Managerial*: 169)

Costs, too, tend not to vary materially over large intervals of output (ibid., Chap. 6) and so do not provide the kind of meaningful variable assumed by the theory.

More basically, cost and price do not interact as in the theory because the assumption of increasing marginal costs is mistaken. When the level of production costs presses on capacity, the simple response is to increase capacity (ibid., 32, 92; see also Wiles & Routh 1984: 39–46).

Far from the assumption of price theory that the objective of every businessperson is to maximize profits in terms of the cost-price-output paradigm, Knauth describes business managers as professionals "whose main idea is to administer the business that concerns them in the interest of continuity" (*Managerial*: 11). The "main concern" of managerial enterprise "is first to survive, and second to strengthen its trade position. Its actions are governed by long-range policies rather than by opportunism or a desire for the last cent of profit" (ibid., 20–21). Management "has no single objective that it can perceive, measure, and take pride in achieving. Its goals are multiple and are judged by criteria other than dollars and cents" (ibid., 181).

The key problem is, not production and costs, but marketing, the primary objective being to carve out some kind of trade advantage (*Managerial*: 28). It is thus, not price, but the struggle for "trade position" that characterizes modern competitive markets (*Business*: 124; 42–62).

The setting of prices has little to do with precise levels of cost and very much to do with marketing strategy, for the price set represents a judgmental exercise of discretion as to how well it will correspond to the demand (ibid., 169). Cost is an unreliable determinant of price if for no other reason than that costs in modern corporations are not capable of precise determination: the allocation of expenses for labor, material, overhead, marketing, and so on, which must be apportioned among multiple products, is necessarily somewhat arbitrary; and different allocations are made for different purposes (*Managerial*: 93).

The problem is compounded by the introduction of new products, which cannot initially sell for a price sufficient to cover their overhead and so must in effect be subsidized by the profits of other products until their own volume becomes sufficient to be profitable (*Business*: 123–24).

Knauth, in fact, envisages the accountant as playing a very different, essentially discretionary role than the popular image of the number cruncher. That function is performed by machines—and this was written in 1948! Knauth regarded the accountant as a philosopher "who ponders over the principles by which he can most correctly portray the situation" (*Business*: 39).

Prices are not set by the impersonal forces of the market place but are "administered," that is "fixed by management after a careful survey of all the factors involved—the expected demand, the cost of production and selling, the price of similar articles, the general price level, the pricing policies of the concern and its position in the trade. Management's hope is that this price will remain unchanged for a considerable period—say a season or a year" (*Managerial*: 106; "Monopoly" 565). The administered pricing decision may involve arbitrary classifications of whole classes of goods:

> Many prices are based on an average arrived at by lumping together the costs of other, quite different articles. The formula thus applied will not fit the actual cost of the specific article. In other words managers have broad classifications of goods into which they fit the specific article and the resultant price will vary according to the class to which it is assigned. (*Managerial*: 123)

Moreover, the concept of profit maximization through monopolistic pricing strategy is for the most part impractical:

> Any attempt to maximize prices in accord with monopoly theory is practically impossible. The sequence is rather that policies are formulated in the light of experience and prices are then set by the application of these policies. It would be a rare chance and difficult to prove, that a price so set maximized profits. Demand and price do not always move inversely to each other. Each is subject to many different conditions as well as to the same conditions. Experiments are conducted to isolate and analyze effects of price changes. (ibid., 134–35)

The term "administered price" as Knauth uses it should not be confused with that same term as used by Gardner Means and J. K. Galbraith to argue that corporate prices are free of competitive forces. Knauth used the term to describe the *process* whereby prices are set within the corporate institution, not as a form of *diktat* over the consumer. In fact, Knauth argued to the contrary that the consumer almost always holds the whip hand (ibid., 108). Knauth did note that there are exceptions to this general condition, citing as examples U.S. Steel and General Motors ("Monopoly": 566 n.4). Just how even the balance between seller and buyer is, is a point that could be debated endlessly. The significant point here is that Knauth's use of the term "administered price" did not carry the same connotation of arbitrary power that Means and Galbraith meant by the term. Knauth's point was that the process of setting prices in managerial enterprises is an administrative one, that is, a discretionary and judgmental one, rather than the result of an interplay of supply, demand, and cost. And discretionary though it is, the function of price setting is not a simplistic exertion of power to extract monopolistic profits; it is a judgmental decision that has as its central purpose the maximization of demand for the article or service involved (*Managerial*: 109–10, 124, 173; "Monopoly": 563, 568–69; Wiles 1961: 48; Robinson, Joan 1969: vii-viii).

Knauth recognized that the pursuit of trade advantage brings with it power that beyond a certain point is capable of abuse and becomes a subject of legitimate public concern (*Managerial*: 173–74). This recognition of the need for some form of public control, however, did not lead to an endorsement of antitrust policy, which had already come to mimic the tenets of price theory, which Knauth dismissed as completely unrealistic (ibid., 174–75).

Knauth's perception of the proper role for government involvement thus differs from the traditional assumption of antitrust policy as influenced by price theory. Monopoly was not in his view the main problem:

> Except in a few cases, there is no such thing as literal monopoly—recognizable and preventable. Rather, trade advantages of many types, of varying importance and permanence, run all through industry and commerce. . . . The degree of monopoly that grows out of an accumulation of trade advantages is constantly increasing or diminishing; it must be watched and controlled. Even cases which are adjudged monopolistic at one time may at another time be classified as competition. The long distance telephone and the air mail have together destroyed the telegraphic monopoly. Rival forms of transportation have put a crimp in certain parts of railroad monopoly. Good roads have destroyed many travel monopolies. "Monopoly": 574–75)

Noting the numerous yet indecisive measures of monopoly invoked by the courts, he identifies the problem as consisting in the occasional acquisition by sellers of excessive trade advantages (ibid., 575). Although Knauth saw such situations as tending to be transient, he acknowledged their potential for abuse (ibid., 575–77).

Knauth thus presented a balanced view, dismissing economic theory as irrelevant to the conditions of modern business and acknowledging that business does tend to acquire levels of power that are subject to abuse and is, therefore, the legitimate object of some form of government intervention.

MORE FLAWS: CONCLUDED

> In this world therefore every plain and simple doctrine as to the relations between cost of production, demand and value is neces-

> sarily false: and the greater the appearance of lucidity which is given to it by skillful exposition, the more mischievous it is.
>
> Alfred Marshall (1961: 368)

> Only when a real alternative to neoclassical theory becomes available can economists be expected to abandon it.
>
> O. Hart (Wiles & Routh 1984: 189)

A Fractured Triangle

The essence of price theory is an attempt to derive some universal law or laws from the empirical observation that prices tend to rise and fall in relation to changes in supply and demand—the base of the triangle used here to describe the elements of the theory.

The three legs of the triangle reflect three main conceptual themes in neoclassical theory: (1) the interrelation of supply-demand-price as a kind of gravitational law, a "unified field theory" of economics; (2) a presumed tendency to equilibrium in atomistically structured markets, and (3) an economic system in which the factor constraining the level of output is increasing cost of production of the last units produced. Every one of these propositions has failed empirically.

The first principle, the base of the triangle, is the only one that has not been proven wholly false. The interrelationship of supply, and demand price undoubtedly exists; the problem lies in overstatement. It is like trying to explain all of human physiology in terms of the circulatory system, as was once the vogue. Prices and output do vary in relation to shifts in demand and vice versa, but their interrelation is highly irregular and a great deal of economic activity takes place, and critical changes in its conduct and direction occur, by reason of other variables, often while supply, demand, and price remain neutral.

The second concept, atomistic equilibrium, is a will-o'-the-wisp that has preoccupied mathematically inclined economists from Walras to Debreu. It is belied by a long history of maladjustment in agriculture and by the demonstrations earlier in this chapter ("More Flaws in the Theory") that a state of "perfect competition" is in no way desirable.

The third concept, output constrained by cost, which is the lynchpin of much of the counsel professed by economic theory for antitrust policy, is an extravagance of flawed thinking. Two of its central concepts, marginal cost pricing and the U-shaped cost curve, are demonstrable absurdities. More fundamentally, it is rooted in the wholly flawed conception of David Ricardo, based on the assumption that the capital plant of agriculture, land, was fixed in supply that could not be increased. It has no application to industry, where capital plant can be expanded indefinitely to meet the level of effective demand, which is the true constraint on the level of production.

This triangle is not just flawed; it is an exploded system, one that survives only by reason of that phenomenon for which Joan Robinson found the word—mumpsimus.[1] It is a fair question why this entire analytical system should continue to be taught and written about.

The basic concept of price theory itself, the attempt to define some universal laws of economic behavior, fails. It fails because it cannot be done, because the factors that govern economic activity are affected by multiple objectives and conditions wholly apart from the attainment of equilibrium in terms of supply, demand, and price. And these are not just complications subordinate to a fundamental force; they are themselves as much and in some cases more fundamental than the price mechanism. These include innovation and the motive of continuity.

The theory, moreover, is doubly flawed: Not only does it misconceive the problem, even within its own narrowly defined context of allocating scarce resources, but the theoretical models are a prescription for chaos, not efficiency. Where the allocation of scarce resources is isolated as a singular objective, whether within a single firm or as government policy, some pattern of conscious administrative control is all but universally preferred to the random processes of the market.[2] It was suggested earlier that the theory of the firm is a virtual checkmate to the pretensions of price theory because it concedes that within the context of the firm administrative control is a more efficient means of allocating resources than market processes.

Ironically, the context in which the free market works best is in precisely those aspects of economic activity not addressed by the theory: This includes both innovation in the broad Schumpeterian sense—all forms of change in marketing and advertising as well as technological invention—and market "imperfections" such as product differentiation, nontransparency of prices, locational advantages, and other barriers that tend to preserve a viable competitive context with continuity. Conversely, it is when all the "distorting" elements are removed and market conditions approach those of the unfettered interaction of supply, demand, and price for homogenous commodities that markets lose their self-regulating tendencies and government is called upon to intervene.

Between the two major divisions of economic activity, the creation of exchangeable wealth and the efficient management of resources, microeconomic theory focuses only on the latter. And in that context the value it exalts, free markets, is one that has more relevance to the wealth-creating side of the economic process than to allocating scarce resources. The marvels the free market works in creating wealth are a false proof for the cost-minimizing focus of microeconomic theory. What the free market does best is not to minimize cost but actually to increase it—by stimulating economic activity that would not otherwise take place. (Recall Malthus's example of the idle South Americans and Irish.) Market forces do serve to control costs, but rather through providing incentives to managers to control their costs administratively than through anything resembling the chaos of atomistic markets.

In sum, the theory is a solution in search of a problem that is not the kind of problem to which either modern business or the antitrust laws are addressed; and the solution it does offer is incompetent even within the limited sphere of its own definitions.

Two Pages of History

What has been said thus far sums up the principal logical and empirical criticisms of the theory, which is somewhat complex. There is, however, a shortcut. Justice Oliver Wendell Holmes, at one point in his judicial career, was confronted with a highly technical question concerning the ancient English law of real property, which was complex, arcane, and at points incoherent. Holmes cut through the morass with the observation that on this subject a page of history could be worth a volume of logic. The same is true of economic theory.

We shall require two pages of history, the first a history of theory, and the second of fact. We have encountered them already in other contexts, but here their special significance can be highlighted.

First, the theory. Starting from the present, the theory as presented in all conventional textbooks traces back in a straight line to the English economist Alfred Marshall. He is universally recognized as the founder, or father, of present-day neoclassical theory. But the line extends beyond him, for he explicitly acknowledged his reliance on the analytical scheme of David Ricardo.

Although we have noted Ricardo's point of view on a number of issues, his lasting influence on the theory that survives to this day was in his conception of the economic system in terms of an agricultural context in which ever-increasing population pressure would lead to the cultivation of more and decreasingly fertile land. This led him to foresee a rising trend in the cost of producing food, as relentless demand pressed on a declining resource base, hence the law of diminishing returns.

Marshall accepted this analytical approach as equally applicable to industry, and the profession has accepted this lead ever since, resulting in the universal assumption of demand pressing on a declining resource base leading to an increasing cost trend.

Now, the second page of history, the factual one: The enclosure movement of the fifteenth and sixteenth centuries, described above (Chap. 2, "Transition"). The movement consisted in the consolidation of smaller landholdings into larger ones, with two dramatic results: productivity was vastly increased and the need for human labor vastly decreased, leading to a prolonged unemployment problem (Tawney 1912, 1967; Polanyi 1944, 1957: 35–39).

The contrast between this actual history and Ricardo's theoretical notion is extreme and instructive. The driving force in the real economic world was not relentless demand pressing on a declining stock of resources but excess productive capacity seeking employment while increased productivity rendered the idea of declining resources a chimera. The same process has repeated itself indefinitely, as ever-increasing productivity in all lines of business creates excess capacity that must seek employment elsewhere. What was unique about the English enclosure movement was the absence of any automatic adjustment mechanism to provide employment for those forced off the land.

It also tells us something else. Economists like to pride themselves on the idea that their discipline is a "value-free" science. Yet the contrast between Ricardo's conception and actual history shows a very strong conflict in value judgments. Ricardo's view was a subsistence view—the physical production of goods because they were needed for consumption. In this context, like that of Robinson Crusoe, maximum physical production is an unlimited good—there cannot be too much. But this is not so in a market economy where the viability of the exchange system requires an element of scarcity. The bias of neoclassical theory toward maximum physical output is as true today as it was of Ricardo. It is a value judgment, and one that is fundamentally inconsistent with the requirements of an ongoing exchange economy.

Our two pages of history thus demonstrate the fundamental wrongheadedness of neoclassical theory.

YET ANOTHER LEGACY OF CONFUSION

Chicago School Nonsense

It was noted in Chapter 6 ("The Scientific Affectation") that following the appearance of Alfred Marshall's treatise, *Principles of Economics*, in 1890, which contained a considerable formal, mathematical analysis, his successors and followers seized upon this approach more fully than even Marshall himself; and that this tendency was interrupted by the trauma of the worldwide depression of the 1930s but revived and carried to even more extreme lengths in the 1970s, continuing to this day in what has been characterized as the Formalist Revolution.

That revolution is identified with a particular academic institution, the University of Chicago, and has generated a body of ideological doctrine known as the Chicago School. Although the idea originated there, it is no longer confined to that place; it is a generic attitude with which economists everywhere can identify. Thus it was that upon their joint entries into the Reagan administration in 1981 FTC chairman James C. Miller, III, who never attended the University of Chicago, could identify himself with his contemporary, Antitrust Division chief William Baxter (who disclaims the title of economist) as fellow Chicago School economists.

There is a danger of oversimplification in the use of the term "school." It connotes a body of doctrine, a criterion that is essentially met by the concepts generally identified with the Chicago School. Yet even within this purified atmosphere there are areas of difference in individual viewpoints. A distinction has been drawn between the "Old Chicago School" and the contemporary version; and within that current version there are some distinct differences between various writers (Bronfenbrenner 1962: 72–73; Posner 1979: 932–33; Bork 1978; Kitch 1983; Reder 1982; Tollison 1980; Levi 1966; Meltzer 1966; Spiegal 1983: 641–42; Sullivan 1975; Hovenkamp 1985; Delong 1981: 317–18 n.102). These, however, are of a minor or technical sort; it is the contemporary version of the Chicago School that is focused upon here.

The essence of the Chicago School viewpoint is a mixture of laissez-faire bias and an utter devotion to pure theory (Reder 1982: 34–35; Bronfenbrenner 1982: 74–75). It is Ricardo incarnate in the twentieth century (9 *J. of Economic Issues* 585 (1975); Liebhafsky 1975: 23; Henderson 1976: 127; Bork, Bowman, Blake & Jones 1965). In its depiction of the theory Chicagoans are entirely orthodox; and as the profession in general turned increasingly to mathematical reasoning and pure theory, the gap between this group of extremists and the rest of the profession narrowed, leading to the present position in which the Chicago School is viewed as being in the ascendancy (Williamson 1979: 919; Miller 1984).

Fortune magazine featured as its cover story in the issue of May 21, 1979, an article entitled "Judges Discover the World of Economics" (Guzzardi: 58). The article describes a series of seminars for federal judges conducted by a messianic disciple of the Chicago School. The seminars featured all of the basic elements of price theory, seasoned with some Chicago School propaganda on price discrimination (ibid., 59–60).

Some of the judges, aware of the idiosyncratic reputation of the Chicago School, noted that their instructors had virtually all come from that source and suggested that others might also have been included (ibid., 66). One of the judges was quoted: "Look, I don't really believe all this propaganda. But we're on our good behavior here—nobody wants to stand up and say 'that's a lot of crap' " (ibid.).

Confronted with this and similar observations from his audience, the organizer of the seminar "[w]ith understandable sensitivity . . . strongly denies that the course has any ideological cast. He insists that the theory and the logic of economics are fundamentals that all schools agree on" (ibid.).

There is some truth in this, but it is a half truth. The theory that has been the focus of the discussion here is common ground between the Chicago School and the rest of the orthodox members of the profession. What distinguishes the Chicago School from the others has two dimensions: one is a more purist, more literal acceptance of the theory than more pragmatically oriented economists (Bronfenbrenner 1962: 74). The other is a severe laissez faire bias.

In its approach to antitrust, the Chicago School has two distinct facets: first is a deeply ingrained bias in favor of automatic, self-adjusting, that is, unfettered market processes, and therefore of laissez faire as the standard for general policy. It accepts antitrust intervention to enforce the rule against price fixing; but it is unconcerned with concentrations of power, exclusionary practices, or even with monopoly itself that results from the unfettered working of the marketplace, on the ground that the result is dictated by economic efficiency.

The second facet is the proposition, attributed to the man generally acknowledged to be the founder of the contemporary Chicago School, Aaron Director, that all questions of antitrust policy should be viewed through the lens of price theory (Posner 1979: 932).

In large measure, non-Chicago economists agree with both of these propositions; what mainly distinguishes the Chicagoans is the extremes to which they carry them. And in their extreme forms they become demonstrable nonsense.

Take, for example, the laissez faire view of Milton Friedman that the government has no legitimate function to intervene in the marketplace. Friedman argues that government intervention to prevent deceptive or misleading selling tactics is unnecessary (1975: 1, 14). This is because there will always be some portion of the public, a sophisticated 5 percent, who will catch on to the deception and cease patronizing the offending merchant. Since all businesspeople are concerned with the marginal consumer, they will modify their behavior to keep the business of this marginal 5 percent (ibid., 10).

Any streetwise shopper can see the nonsense in this. There is no patronage merchants are more willing to give up than the most discriminating 5 percent. The proof is in the newspapers every week. Any perceptive shopper can save considerably by buying only those items in different stores that are on sale, rather than to accept the convenience of buying all at one place and paying higher prices for items not on sale. If merchants could not count on the fact that most shoppers will take the latter course, they would not follow the selling strategy that they do, sacrificing patronage of the more sophisticated minority.

We see here two basic flaws in Chicago School thinking. One is a subtle semantic error. The word "marginal" has a magical significance to economists and is used by them mainly to connote the idea of the pivotal, the decisive difference. But in ordinary speech "marginal" also has a second connotation, as being expendable. Friedman was plainly using the word "marginal" in the first sense; merchants view the marginal 5 percent of customers as "marginal" in the latter sense.

The second error, and one that pervades Chicago School thinking, is to isolate only those variables that have some tendency to lead to a particular result and assume that they will therefore produce this result, without regard to whether the tendency has enough force to be effective. In the example given, this tendency is the motive of businesspeople not to lose customers; all else being equal, they will act in accordance with that tendency. But all else is not equal in the example given, and so this tendency has no effect.

This kind of thinking is clear in the "core" exam that is a prerequisite to a graduate degree in economics at the University of Chicago, which once made the front page of the *Wall Street Journal* (7/25/79: 1). The article reported the following sample question to be answered true, false, or uncertain, plus an explanation: "The higher the relative price of gasoline, the higher will be the average height of apartment buildings in the center of the city." The official answer is true, "because higher priced gasoline makes the center of the city a more convenient place to live." The realistic answer is that the price of gasoline is so remote and irrelevant a factor that it will exert no influence at all. It is a classic illustration of the Ricardian-Chicago School propensity to isolate the variables they choose to think about, ignoring others that matter in the real world.

The results of this kind of education are apparent in the thesis advanced by one Chicagoan who has served on the staff of the President's Council of Economic Advisors. He attacked government auto safety regulations prescribing mandatory seat belts, arguing that motorists adjust their driving habits to such economic factors as the cost of accident insurance and the level of their incomes, so that feeling safer by reason of their government-mandated seat belts and no longer deterred by rising insurance rates because inflation of medical costs had ceased, they will drive faster to earn more income and thereby cause more accidents (Pelzman 1975 AEI: 10–11, 17, 19–20, 27).

Are these just aberrations, taken out of context, a few instances of mere carelessness? No, they are in fact symptomatic of a mentality wholly divorced from reality, and a loose cannon when admitted to the corridors of government. William Niskannen, an admitted Chicago School extremist, resisted efforts in the early 1970s, during the height of the energy crisis, to alleviate heating oil shortages in the Northeast on the basis of a theoretical argument that there is no such thing as a "shortage" (see Chap. 4, "Potato Famine"). Niskannen also argued that the Washington subway system was unnecessary because it would be cheaper to subsidize free taxi rides.

The atmosphere of silliness thus introduced would seem a fitting transition to the contributions of Richard Posner, the Chicagoan who would have us believe that we can cast aside our traditions of law and political philosophy in favor of economics (Posner 1977). It is Posner's thesis that economics tells it all; he would have economics govern our legal system and auction babies. His philosophy recalls Adam Smith's disdain for those "many philosophers who knew only their own small art well, but were brashly eager to make it the foundation for far-fetched analysis, 'the great hinge on which everything turned' " (Chap. 4). Although Posner has written widely on antitrust (Posner 1976), he credits Bork's *The Antitrust Paradox* (1978) as "the most complete and most orthodox statement of the Chicago position" (Posner 1979: 926 n.2); and so we focus on Robert Bork.

Bork's thesis is based on two premises: that consumer welfare is the sole legitimate object of antitrust and that price theory is the only rational way of determining consumer welfare benefits.

His first premise—"the legislative history of the Sherman Act shows an intention that the courts implement only a consumer welfare policy" (Bork 1967: 245 n.5; 1978: 61; 1966: 7)—is demonstrably false. We have already noted that the preservation of freedom of business enterprise was the prime motivating factor behind antitrust legislation and that the rhetoric about consumer benefits was secondary (Chap. 4; Chap. 5). Senator Sherman's speech in explanation of his bill began with an impassioned attack on the concentration of private business power and the denial of business freedom, turning only at the end to comment that the results of monopoly were also harmful to consumers. Earlier he stated that

> the combination of labor and capital in the form of a corporation to carry on any lawful business is a proper and useful expedient . . . and ought to be encouraged and protected as tending to cheapen the cost of production, *but these rights should be open to all upon the same terms and conditions.* (21 *Cong. Rec.*: 2457 (1890); emphasis added)

This can hardly be interpreted as a statement of an exclusive purpose to enhance consumer welfare.

Bork's second premise is that "there is no body of knowledge other than conventional price theory that can serve as a guide to the effects of business behavior upon consumer welfare. To abandon economic theory is to abandon the possibility of a rational antitrust law" (1978: 117). Thus all antitrust questions are to be viewed through the lens of price theory (Bork 1978: 116–17; Posner 1979: 928, 932). This includes the cost-price-output paradigm, the absurdity of which has already been demonstrated. When applied literally to antitrust policy, the results are predictably bizarre. The theory makes two key assumptions: the businessman's universal problem is to adjust output in accordance with cost and price, and his motivation is to maximize profits in this context.

Here we see in full view the fallacy of substituting the assumptions of price theory for the actual motivations of businesspeople. Even a firm with a substantial degree of monopoly power, like Standard Oil or Alcoa, is not necessarily going to charge the highest price it could exact by virtue of its monopoly position. Standard Oil restrained its prices so as not to attract competition into the easily entered oil-refining and distribution business; and Alcoa was anxious to find new markets for its product. And as Knauth, Baumol, and others knowledgeable of the businessperson's actual motives have pointed out, maximizing revenue is a more characteristic objective of businesspeople than maximizing profits (Baumol 1959, 1967: Chap. 6; Bailey & Boyle 1977).

Almost all of Bork's book is devoted to variations on a single theme, that monopoly power cannot be extended vertically, either by merger or contractual restraint. ("Vertical" is a term used by economists to distinguish the relationships between different firms that are in the same production chain—raw material supplier, manufacturer, warehouseman, retail distributor—and so are not in competition with each other, in contrast to "horizontal" relationships, which are competing firms at the same level of the production chain, such as retail grocers, automobile dealers, and so on. The theory is that a firm that has a monopoly at any one vertical level, such as manufacturing, will extract the maximum monopoly price that can be obtained for the end product at that level, so that there is no possibility of extracting further monopoly profits at any other level, such as retailing. It is on this ground that Bork criticizes the Supreme Court decision that ruled a contract obligating purchasers of salt tablet–dispensing machines to purchase all their supplies of salt tablets from the (legal) monopoly manufacturer of the machines to be an illegal tying agreement (Bork 1978: 373; *International Salt*, 332 U.S. 392 (1947). Bork's argument is that the manufacturer would take his full monopoly profit in the price of the machine, leaving no further monopoly profit to be made on the salt tablets.

This theory is erroneous in two respects. First is the point just noted, that it does not follow from the existence of monopoly power at any vertical level that the firm will price to the full limits of its monopoly power. Second, recognizing the primary interest of businesspeople in increasing their revenue base, if the seller of the salt-dispensing machine can use the leverage of the machine to market salt, he will do so, which is indeed what led to the antitrust case from which Bork takes his example. The point is not that the seller of the machine is making a monopoly profit on the salt, but that he has obtained an additional source of revenue. Neither the machine nor the salt will be sold at a maximum monopoly price at the expense of the marketability of either.

Bork makes the same mistake in criticizing the Supreme Court's opinion in the Standard Oil case of 1911. Referring to the Court's statement that Standard had become in certain regions a monopoly buyer of crude oil, Bork argued that this was unnecessary because of the monopoly it had in refining (Bork 1978: 40). This disregards the actual motivation of Rockefeller, which was not to exact monopoly prices but to bring order into the relation of supply and demand in the industry by bringing as much of it within his control as he could. It also overlooks the major role that vertical leverage played in building the Standard monopoly. At one point Bork asks rhetorically, "Has anyone ever seen a company gain a monopoly by vertical merger?" (1978: 234). Well, how about the Standard Oil Company? True, Standard did not acquire the railroads by merger, but it gained leverage over them with the volume of its business and used this leverage to conquer its horizontal rivals in refining. We have also seen how Standard's ownership of tank cars (a vertical extension) increased its leverage over the railroads (Carr 1962). And as pipelines took over the role of transportation from the railroads, Standard moved aggressively into outright ownership and used that leverage ruthlessly in its conquest of horizontal competition (ibid., generally, and particularly pp. 24–27, 63-64). Or consider the U.S. Steel Corporation, exonerated from the charge of monopolization because it abandoned an earlier design to do exactly that, which had in pursuit of its earlier monopolistic ends made extensive vertical acquisitions in transportation and raw materials (*Columbia Steel*, 334 U.S. 495 (1948); Parsons & Ray 1975). And Alcoa, which was not exonerated, was also a vertical, highly integrated firm (148 F.2d 416). As recently as 1973 Congress reacted with alarm to the prospect that "independent" oil refiners were in danger of extinction at the hands of the vertically integrated majors. Only the forceful intervention of a regulatory regime to prevent that result deterred further action to impose limits on vertical integration itself.

These observations are not at all novel to those who focus on business reality rather than abstract theory. As early as 1904 one business manager was quoted by Moody thus:

> Competition is keener than ever to-day, but it is . . . carried on on a larger plane. Where formerly the small producer competed to reduce his costs and undersell his competitors by the ordinary means of great economy and superior efficiency, he has now gone beyond that point. . . . The advantages he now seeks are not so crude. They consist in going to the roots of things, in acquiring and dominating sources of supply and the raw material; in controlling shipping rights of

way; in securing exclusive benefits, rebates on large shipments . . ." (Moody 1904, 1968: xvii)

In other words, vertical power, so much disdained by Chicago School theory, is one of the most important components of the competitive equation.

Finally, Bork confronts the most basic problem of the theoretical approach, the role of innovation with which the theory does not and cannot deal. Any defender of the theory must find some way to dispose of this troublesome complication. Bork tries, but fails:

It is not clear how much progressiveness is desirable . . . it costs something, and no one thinks it worth paying any price, no matter how great, for faster progress. We are, therefore, necessarily ignorant of the "proper" rate of progress, and it may be wisest for that reason not to give the matter any weight in antitrust analysis. (1978: 132)

Nonsense?

The Trojan Horse of Antitrust

From the perspective of economic theory, antitrust law and policy has only one legitimate purpose, the lowering of prices to consumers and thereby presumably promoting efficiency in the allocation of resources. Efficiency being the objective, successful firms should not be penalized or prohibited from pursuing policies that promote that objective, which by definition does not include any sort of restriction on price competition.

Antitrust legislation, on the other hand, has never been primarily motivated by considerations of lowering prices and promoting efficiency (Mayhew 1972). Ritual statements adverting to these objectives have always been part of the rhetoric because they are politically simpler to explain than the primary motivation that has been directed at the *seller's* side of the market. Indeed, the political judgment has been explicit that its objective is focused on preserving a competitive structure as an end in itself even if this results in higher costs and prices than the alternative of monopoly (Rowe, Frederick 1984: 1521 n.62; *Alcoa*, 148 F.2d 416 at 429 (1945)).

We have thus come full circle. Legislation based on a political judgment that rejected the defense of the trusts for their alleged efficiencies and lower costs in favor of maintaining a competitive structure of industry as an end in itself, even at the cost of higher prices, has ultimately come under the stewardship of an ideology rooted in exactly the opposite value judgment. When Chicago School economists direct the policies of the antitrust enforcement agencies, the fox is in charge of the chicken coop.

It is one of the more fitting ironies of history that the University of Chicago was founded with a grant from John D. Rockefeller (Kirkland 1956: 84).

A Gaggle of Confusions

The first legacy of antitrust confusion was that of John D. Rockefeller, who refused to explain his perception of a market failure that was the cause of his quest for monopoly. The result was a political reaction that both overlooked the serious problem of market failure in petroleum and led to an exaggerated belief in the capacity of markets to self-adjust under conditions of unfettered competition. The prosecutor, through its single-minded belief in unfettered price competition, has contributed another. Economic theory has contributed still another legacy of confusion through the intellectual phantasy of price theory. In sum, what else than confusion can be expected of an analytical system that

1. posits as an ideal model of "perfect competition" a market condition that (a) contains no element of competition, (b) even its very expositors concede is inherently unstable with a built-in tendency toward monopoly, and (c) is demonstrably incapable of accomplishing the one object most highly attributed to free markets: self-regulation;
2. posits as the supreme quality of this "ideal" market situation that it will drive prices down to the point where they equal marginal cost—at which price any business with fixed costs will go bankrupt;
3. takes as its object the achievement of cost savings that even its advocates concede to be of minor importance and far outweighed by the positive contribution of market conditions that would be effectively banished by the strictures of the theoretical model;
4. while pretending to the status of a science, disdains the empirical study of reality in favor of abstract reasoning based on unrealistic assumptions and dismisses as not worthy of "scientific" consideration—because they cannot be measured—factors of admittedly overriding importance;
5. turns the basic policy of antitrust on its head, making with other words and symbols essentially the same arguments advanced by the apologists of monopoly in the nineteenth century.

POSTSCRIPT

> Because you are writing from the viewpoint of government policy you have every right to criticize the theory for its unreality. As an economist I don't have that right.
> (Comment by one economist to the author after reading an early draft of Chapters, 6, 7.)

> This is just a moment in the sun for neoclassic price theory, which will doubtless pass.
>
> Edmund Kitch (1983: 232)

> It is often said that one theory can be driven out only by another; the neoclassicals have a complete theory (though I am certain that it is nothing but a circular argument) and we need a better theory to supplant them. I do not agree. I think any other "complete theory" would be only another box of tricks. What we need is a different habit of mind—to eschew fudging, to respect facts and to admit ignorance of what we do not know.
>
> Joan Robinson (1981: 63)

We return to the point noted in passing at the outset of Chapter 6: The criticism here of microeconomic theory as a guide to antitrust policy is limited to that discrete theory and does not apply to the empirical contributions of economists. Within that profession there is also disagreement over the relevance of the theory to antitrust policy, and there are many economists sensitive to the actual political objectives of antitrust policy.

Most economists spend their time studying industrial facts, and to that extent they have a genuine claim to expertise. But there is a qualification. Orthodox economists have been educated in a catechism of theory that follows the value judgments of Ricardo and rejects those of Malthus, Knauth, and Keynes. This conduces to value judgments inconsistent with the political objectives of antitrust policy.

The point of this summation is thus a divided counsel. Economists should not be dismissed as a class because of the follies of their theory. Yet it should not be forgotten that their value judgments are subject to the influence of conceptual biases from a deeply flawed intellectual heritage.

NOTES

1. *Webster's Unabridged* (1976) explains: "an error or prejudice obstinately clung to; the term is supposedly taken from the story of an illiterate priest, who in his devotions, had for thirty years used *mumpsimus* for the proper Latin word *sumpsimus*, and who, on his mistake being pointed out to him, replied, 'I will not change my old *mumpsimus* for your new *sumpsimus*.' "

2. "The task of deciding how resources should be allocated is not fulfilled by the market but by the great corporations who are in charge of the finance for development" (Robinson, Joan 1981: 32).

8

Dissatisfaction with the Market

> There is no "intermediate case" of exclusion resulting from neither efficiency nor predation.
>
> Robert Bork (1978: 160, 311)

INTRODUCTION

We survey here the intermediate cases. These are the variety of instances in which the conditions of the competitive game somehow skew the process in a way that prevents the normal self-adjusting market mechanism from functioning satisfactorily. "Satisfactorily," as used here, is in the sense that when public dissatisfaction with the working of a market reaches the point that government intervention results, that is sufficient ground to pronounce the market performance unsatisfactory. That does not necessarily mean that it is *totally* unsatisfactory, only that there is a level of pathology present sufficient to warrant intervention by extra-market forces. Such forces include both original legislative responses and subsequent enforcement actions, whether governmentally or privately initiated, and they include even those unprosecuted violations that show a persisting pattern of illegal conduct.

The term "survey" is used advisedly here, for the material is vast, complex, and controversial. To attempt an in-depth study of any one of the market failings included here could easily occupy an entire volume. Aside from its impracticality, such detail would detract from the central purpose here, which is not to make an airtight case for market failure in each instance, but to sketch the overall picture of the variety of factual circumstances that constitute market malfunction. The same point is underscored by the term "market malfunction," not "market failure." Markets, like our bodies and our automobiles, can function under conditions of pathology without failing completely, and that is the kind of situation described in numerous varieties here.

The idea of pathology is also useful as an aid to understanding the nature of the problem. Physical illness and injury come in many forms and degrees of seriousness, ranging from trivial to deadly, and the appropriate remedies are equally varied. So, too, the various forms of market malfunction very widely in kind, in seriousness, and in the type of remedy appropriate.

A PREFATORY NOTE ON THE CHICAGO SCHOOL AND THE IRISH POTATO FAMINE

> Everything always turns out for the best in this best of all possible worlds.
>
> Dr. Pangloss

> Those who cannot remember the past are condemned to repeat it.
>
> Santayana

Before beginning our catalogue of market malfunctions we should confront the charge that will be leveled by economists of the Chicago School stripe, and others, that this listing shows failures, not of markets, but of the political system. Had the government not intervened, the market would eventually have sorted things out. The Chicagoans, especially, go so far as to argue that absent government intervention, there is no such thing as a shortage: Demand exists only in terms of a schedule of prices and quantities. Permit the price to rise to the point where only those willing to pay it will take the quantity available, they argue, and there will be no excess of buyers; the market clears. Those unwilling or unable to pay the price are not deprived; they simply make a decision not to buy at the market clearing price. Shortages occur only when government caps a lid on price so that there are more willing buyers at the prevailing price than there is supply available.

This is literally the policy Chicago-type economists have been urging on the government for years in the context of the energy crisis, and it became official policy when the Reagan administration announced that it would leave it to the market to deal with any future fuel shortages.

This is not the first time that such thinking has guided public policy. It has actually been implemented in the past, and the results are instructive. Let us revisit the Irish potato famine.

Between 1846 and 1851 over 21,000 people in Ireland died of starvation or related causes (Edwards & Williams 1957: 254–55). Part of the cause was natural, the potato blight, a disease that caused potatoes to rot as as soon as they were harvested. It struck an Irish farming community that lived at a subsistence level, dealt in barter for its land, and depended for its own sustenance on the yield of that land. But the shortage of food in itself need not have had such fatal consequences. Alternative foods existed and were present in Ireland. They were not, however, available to the starving farmers, and the reason for this denial was rooted in a dogmatic ideology that venerated markets and free trade.

The blight first struck in 1845, during the administration of Sir Robert Peel, whose success in meeting the partial crop failure of that year is undisputed. "He showed an initiative unusual in that era of laissez faire and undertook tasks at variance with current economic theory. The entry of the government into the market was a spectacular example of this and it gave him an effective means of price control so as to defeat monopolists" (ibid., 222).

The following year, however, brought both a worse attack of the blight, destroying the entire crop, and the new Whig government of Lord John Russell (ibid., 221–22). At two points in particular his policy clashed with Peel's. Where Peel had seen the problem as one of disaster relief that justified government intervention, Russell saw it more as a matter of poverty relief, the expense of which should be borne locally and the administration of which was consequently quite niggardly. The other significant difference was in the attitude toward public works. Because there was an adequate physical supply of food, the real problem of the farmers was to find cash to pay for it. Their subsistence and barter existence permitted them to survive when the potatoes did because they did not have to sell them as cash crops—the price of which would not have supported them. The purpose of the public works was to put cash in their hands, something the Peel administration had done forthrightly. Chancellor of the Exchequer Trevelyan, on the other hand, "suggested that the works should be unproductive so as to impose limits on the applications for the employment schemes" (ibid., 228).

A third element of free market ideology exacerbated the tragedy. Ireland at this time was exporting food, but the ideology of the time prevented diversion of this trade to prevent starvation in Ireland (ibid., 259). These inhibitions extended even to intervening to encourage imports, as Peel had done. As the crop failure worsened toward the end of 1846, the physical supply of food, not just the inability to purchase it, had become a problem. Trevelyan, however, "maintained that the supply of the home market may safely be left to the foresight of private merchants" (ibid., 223).

The particular circumstances of the Irish potato famine are unlikely to recur, but the lessons of history seldom present themselves in precisely the same form. Given the confusion of government policy over energy in the 1970s, and the still unsolved problems of the American farmer, there is ample opportunity for new disasters should the preachments of the ideologues be taken, once again, too literally.

A SAMPLER OF MARKET MALFUNCTIONS

Natural Monopoly (More or Less)

A natural monopoly typically occurs where a capital investment is required that it does not make sense to duplicate. This has normally been true of public utility systems that provide water, electricity, and natural gas. A recent addition to the list is cable TV (except in major cities). Railroads in certain areas have long been a natural monopoly. Where the monopoly is clear, some form of public regulation has almost always been imposed.

But the pure case does not define the limits of the problem. Many businesses that partake of the nature of natural monopolies have boundaries where alternative systems are possible, and in this area neither the market nor regulation has proved adequate to solve the resulting problems. Natural gas is a prime example.

A natural gas pipeline operates in a multiplicity of markets, in some of which it is an absolute monopoly—as regards natural gas—and in others where it encounters varying degrees of competition. A pipeline company is both a purchaser and seller of gas. Geographic accident determines whether, as a purchaser, it will have competition or not. If it is the only pipeline in proximity to a particular field, the owners of the field have no alternative. More typically, there are a number of pipelines converging on a producing area, which makes for some competitive alternatives. At the other end of the pipe, where it acts as seller, there are some geographic areas where no alternative pipeline is available to consumers (public utility distribution companies and some industrial users). In other areas, typically major urban centers, two or more pipelines provide alternative sources. And, of course, to the degree that consumers of natural gas can utilize alternative fuels, that adds another dimension of competitive alternatives.

Because of the considerable power the pipelines have, they have long been subject to regulation. The regulatory process, moreover, has made it a matter of conscious policy to avoid creating monopoly situations wherever possible. (See, e.g., Federal Power Commission: 7 FPC 24 at 44 (5/29/48).

Public utility companies were among the earliest violators of the common law antecedents of the Sherman Act. One of the cases cited by Senator Sherman in his speech to the Senate (Chap. 4) involved neighboring gas systems that agreed to limit their respective territories (21 *Cong. Rec.*: 2459 (3/21/1890). At the present time access to natural gas pipeline systems by owners of off-system gas has been a source of growing controversy (Tussing & Barlow 1984: 117, 171–78, 217–18; FERC Order 436, 50 Fed. Reg. p. 42, 408 (10/85).

The concept of "natural monopoly" therefore does not describe a uniform phenomenon. It represents the fact that in some circumstances it does not make economic sense to have duplicate capital investments. The degree to which this is so, however, varies from industry to industry and within a given industry itself.

The Chaos of Atomism: Agriculture and Crude Oil Production

Agriculture and crude oil production are alike in that they are atomistic markets, most nearly representing in reality the theoretical "ideal" of pure or perfect competition, but they are not self-regulating. In both cases the problem is precisely that the market is atomistic, so that no single producer may affect either the overall level of supply or price by adding or withholding his own production (Chap. 2, "Differing Markets").

In this circumstance it is to each producer's advantage to produce to the maximum of his capacity, even in conditions of general glut and falling prices. The farmer plants "fence to fence" and the crude oil producer lets his wells flow because to cut back would only decrease his revenues and not cause any improvement in the price.

We saw in the saga of Standard Oil the chaos that resulted from an unfettered free market in the Oil Regions of Pennsylvania. The breakup of the Standard Oil Company did not undo the order Rockefeller had established (Blair 1976:147–51). The divested companies were divided geographically so that they did not have to compete with each other, and their managements were all trained in the orderly philosophy of Standard Oil. This *Pax Standardis* was broken, however, by the discovery of vast new pools in the Southwest, where the Standard hegemony did not prevail. The result was a repeat of the Oil Regions chaos, only on a much larger scale (Watkins 1937; Zimmerman 1957). This time the solution was not private monopoly but government regulation, as state governments intervened to impose production limits set in accordance with estimates of market demand. This outraged many economists who followed the flawed theory of Adelman into believing that crude petroleum could be self-regulating in a free competitive market (*supra*, Chap. 7, "Empty Boxes"; Adelman 1964; 1965; Lovejoy & Homan 1967; *The Oil Import Question* 1970: par. 325, p. 88). But some economists, too, saw a valid conservation purpose to the controls in putting an end to the physical waste of petroleum (Watkins 1937; Zimmerman 1957).

Some method of extramarket control of crude oil production has remained in effect ever since, and they are worldwide (Blair 1976; Sampson 1975; Adelman 1972, 1974; Mosley 1973; Copp, E. Anthony 1976). Outside the United States, and beyond the reach of the Sherman Act, a more mature industry maintained a tight cartel such as proved impossible in the Pennsylvania Oil Regions. The cartel was the target of an abortive antitrust suit, as government policy came ultimately to recognize the futility of seeking to impose a rule of unlimited competition on the world market (Blair 1976: 71–76).

With the oil crises of the 1970s and the disappearance of excess capacity in the United States, the need for production controls disappeared; the high price of foreign oil provided a natural disincentive to import any amount in excess of market demand. But this is an accidental result of the domestic deficit condition; should excess capacity ever return, the same problems would reappear and some form of production control would be necessary (cf. Adelman 1964; *supra*, Chap. 7, "Empty Boxes").

In agriculture, the non-self-adjusting character of markets for cash crops is a matter of centuries-old experience. Production controls on tobacco were imposed in the colonies of Maryland and Virginia in the seventeenth century (Chap. 2, "Wild Card") and elsewhere (Rowe, J.W.F. 1936); and the elaborate systems of production and marketing controls in modern U.S. and European agriculture are too well known to require elaboration here.

The agricultural experience also documents the tendency of such markets, to the extent that government controls do not solve their problems, to resort to private monopoly. Farm cooperatives in the United States have been given statutory immunity from the antitrust laws, which the courts have interpreted as a blank check to the establishment of far-reaching monopoly. And there is an ongoing trend for farming to be concentrated in big business, as attested by the addition to our vocabulary of the term "agribusiness."

The case of agriculture, it should be noted, is not unmixed. The kind of conditions referred to above is most evident for commodities such as wheat, potatoes, and soybeans. The livestock market, on the other hand, presents the farmer with a different set of conditions: the size of the herd is not fixed like the acreage of a wheat farm and so can be and is adjusted to market conditions.

The same qualification has some application to industry as well. In the cases of agricultural crops and crude oil production there is another factor in addition to an atomistic structure that disrupts the self-regulating mechanisms of the market. In both cases the proportion of fixed, overhead costs to incremental costs is heavily weighted on the side of the fixed costs. Incremental costs being comparatively trivial, they are no deterrent to continued production. In the case of livestock, on the other hand, incremental costs of feeding are a larger factor, and so there is some distinction in the ability of the market to adjust production levels as between livestock and crops.

Qualifications of this kind are important to note, for the most pervasive error in U.S. competitive policy is to see all situations as black or white—free competition or total regulation. The reality is more complex, which is the primary theme of this survey of exceptions.

Homogenous Industrial Commodities and Closed-end Competition

The producer of a homogenous commodity faces market conditions fundamentally different from those faced in all other businesses. The law has long recognized that homogenous commodities have special characteristics and thus has created a special label for them: "fungible."

The special characteristic of such products is that the only factor distinguishing the product of one producer from that of another is price. A barrel of crude oil, a ton of steel, a bushel of wheat, all are interchangeable with other units of the same product.

In other lines of business differences in price can be blurred by other factors such as brand name identification, quality differences, locational advantages, and so on. These variables are actually favorable to price competition because it can be masked and is not totally decisive. In the case of homogenous commodities, aside from instances of locational advantages or other special circumstances, price is so decisive a factor that it tends to be neutralized.

The problem is compounded when the industry structure is atomistic, as in agriculture and crude oil, but the problem is distinct—the steel industry, for example, has never been atomistic.

The natural tendency in markets of this type is toward uniformity of price. In auction markets, such as those for agricultural products, this is accomplished in the manner economists most esteem, through the interaction of supply and demand. But even here the market is not self-regulating and government intervention is, in consequence, pervasive.

In other markets, price uniformity has been achieved by various forms of extramarket control. In major industrial markets the general solution has been the concentration of the industry into a tight oligopoly in which the participants, aware of the futility of open price competition, practice mutual restraint (Eichner 1969; Blair 1976).

Closely related is what may be termed the problem of closed-end competition. This occurs most typically when government agencies solicit bids for products or services that are essentially homogenous. The reaction of firms to this kind of pressure has typically been to arrange some form of bid rigging among themselves (Hay & Kelley 1974).

Public Transportation

> [I]t has been customary in England from time immemorial, and in this country from its first colonization, to regulate ferries, common carriers, hackmen... wharfingers, innkeepers, etc., and in so doing to fix a minimum of charge to be made for service rendered, accommodations furnished, and articles sold.
>
> *Munn v. Illinois*, 94 U.S. 113, 125 (1897)

Public transportation is a polyglot category, within which experience has varied, but which does admit of the general conclusion that as a rule the market has not proven to be an adequate self-regulator. Public transportation is, of course, subsidized, along two basic lines: the medium of transportation, on land, water, or by air; and as between the construction of the physical plant and the operation of the service. Problems have occurred within all of these subcategories.

Beginning with the physical plant, the most common facility is the construction of roads. There was some, largely unsuccessful, experimentation with using private capital to construct turnpikes in the United States, and a somewhat more favorable experience in England, but on the whole this function has been left to government (Hadley 1903: 26–27). The construction of canals and railroads, on the other hand, was done successfully by private companies, but in both cases some form of state intervention occurred either at the outset or later on. Canals required public franchises, and railroads needed right of way (Robertson 1973: 135–48). We have already noted the market malfunctions and government intervention in the nineteenth-century railroad industry.

Maritime transportation also has a major capital component in the construction of shipping vessels, an industry that has seen government intervention from its earliest days—a policy that received the endorsement of Adam Smith.

Turning to operation of the service we find problems dating back to postmedieval times, with antecedents in ancient history. The common law recognized problems serious enough to generate judge-made law even before the legislature intervened to regulate common carriers.

Motor carriers in the United States encountered problems of market adjustment in the 1930s, resulting in federal regulation in 1935. The status of this industry is presently in controversy, for partial deregulation has had the predictable effect of increasing concentration to cope with the irregularities of an atomistic market (ABA 1984: 686–89; *Forbes* 12/25/78: 41–43; *Business Week* 8/25/80: 33–34).

Most controversial of all is the case of the airlines. (See, generally, Doganis 1985; Harlan 1979; Bk Rev. Hrgs. 48 *Am. Econ. Rev.* 732 (1958).) Here, uniquely, there is no prior history of market performance because the industry was regulated from the outset. Therefore, until the advent of deregulation in the 1970s and 1980s we are without empirical evidence as to how satisfactorily this industry can function in an unfettered competitive market.

The railroads, too, have been targeted in the current vogue of deregulation. Here, as in the case of the airlines, the dominant current trend is to consolidation as mergers lead to increased levels of concentration in response to the vagaries of the marketplace.

The Compounding of Power

In addition to the identification of particular markets that are not adequately self-regulating, the political process has identified a variety of conditions that can infect normally healthy competitive markets in ways that impair or even destroy the competitive environment. The most apparent of such conditions is a tendency for market power to compound itself. This takes a variety of forms.

The classic case was Rockefeller's use of sheer size to negotiate advantageous rates with the railroads, on the basis of which he was able to persuade other refiners to sell out to him, thus compounding his power. Not only in oil but in other industries as well the railroads singled out larger firms for special treatment, thereby eliminating sources of competition.

There was on the face of this relationship between the railroads and their favored customers a perfectly rational business judgment. Larger shippers by virtue of their size alone had meaningful advantages for the railroads. Rockefeller's logic that shippers were entitled to some recompense for the savings they brought to the railroads cannot be faulted on principle.

Similarly, the huge buying power of retail chain stores gave them leverage to negotiate favorable prices that enabled them to undercut their smaller rivals, leading to the Clayton and Robinson-Patman Acts barring price discrimination when the effect is anticompetitive.

Another major factor that tends to a compounding of power is the differing ability of large and small firms to obtain credit. The way the banking system works is inherently prejudicial to the small borrower, which has led to the establishment of an alternative government source of financing through the Small Business Administration (SBA).

The tendency to the compounding of power also appears when vertically integrated companies are able to squeeze or eliminate their nonintegrated competitors (*Alcoa*, 148 F.2d at 438 (1945); Scherer 1980: 90).

The fundamental nature of the compounding problem is clearly illustrated by an especially pure case. Professional athletic leagues survive and prosper by providing entertainment in the form of competition. The continuation of the competitive process is essential to their survival. Yet to assure the continuity of the competition they have almost universally placed limits on the freedom of the individual competitors. The familiar device of the player draft, which favors the teams that were less successful and disfavors the winners, is a clear recognition that without such a handicap system the winners' success would tend to compound itself and destroy the vital competitive balance. Indeed, the propensity of power to compound itself is a key form of market malfunction.

INTERNATIONAL TRADE

Here we encounter one of the most controversial and thoroughly debated areas of economic policy. That ground will not be replowed here. Our narrow focus here is on the fact that when competition takes place across national boundaries, rather than within them, a number of additional factors enter the picture that are sources of dissatisfaction with the unfettered working of the marketplace. We put aside the perennial debate over the merits of free trade in the abstract with the observation that as a matter of objective political fact there is a general consensus that free trade is desirable except where it leads to serious political pain. Once that threshold is reached, the criterion applied here has been satisfied, and the market is to that extent not performing satisfactorily. What should be done about it, and for how long, is another question. We will confront that latter question at the end of this study in the course of sketching "The Elements of a Competition Policy." Here, the purpose is to identify the source and nature of the problems.

There are, unfortunately, at least six distinct respects in which competition that occurs across national boundaries differs from that within them.

First, in internal commerce both buyer and seller are constituents of the same government, which tends to be neutral as between them; whereas in international commerce each government has only one party as a constituent, which it therefore has an incentive to favor.

Second, international trade involves different currency systems, and the fact that the government itself has a stake in defending its balance of payments position gives it a distinct incentive for favoring its own nationals, both in terms of exports and imports.

Third, the fact that national markets are typically isolated from one another makes practical geographical price discriminations that would not be practical in domestic commerce. Thus, a company with a well-protected price structure in its home market, which enables it to recover its overhead costs, may choose to compete vigorously on price in foreign markets without affecting its domestic price structure, thus forcing its foreign competitors to operate under severe competitive stress. The practice has been labeled dumping, and it is commonplace, though with by no means uniform effects. (See, generally, Viner 1923, 1966). The political complaints press the allegations to the point of asserting a monopolistic purpose—sales in the foreign country being at less than cost to drive out the competition. This has occurred in the context of international cartels purposely seeking to destroy noncooperating competitors (Chapman 1973: 423–38), but it is rare. The more normal practice is to shade the export price enough to compensate for the handicap of being a nondomestic supplier, but to otherwise realize as good a price as is obtainable. Even so, the practice remains a source of concern, and because of the artificial limiting effect of the separate national markets, it cannot be said to represent a freely competitive market situation.

Fourth, specific development and subsidy programs to favor a nation's exporters or the development of home industry can create competitive distortions. This is a problem of increasing contemporary importance that has produced an unusually vigorous corrective response within the European Common Market (Chap. 9).

Fifth, national security interests in food self-sufficiency, energy supplies, the preservation of a viable merchant marine—even Adam Smith conceded an exception for this (Smith 1776, 1976: Vol. I, Bk. IV, Chap. II, p. 484)—and control over the export of strategic materials or sensitive technology are long-established grounds for exceptions to free trade.

Sixth, we cannot avoid mention of the most troublesome ground for exceptions to free trade: imbalance between the level of economic development between different countries. Economists reject the legitimacy of this ground emphatically, arguing that the low-wage countries lack the productivity to seriously threaten more advanced countries, and that the performance of low-cost labor is more efficiently done by them than in higher-wage countries. The argument is plausible but not conclusive, for a variety of other factors are likely to merit consideration. In any event, this factor has been an undeniable element in causing the imposition of restrictions on free trade.

Another application of this same concept is the familiar infant industry rationale for import restraints. Whatever the objections in principle, the fact remains that two of the most powerful free world economies spent their adolescent years of growth behind extremely protective import barriers—the United States and Japan.

Before leaving the subject of international trade, several observations of principle should be recorded. One is that there are no absolutes in this area. Whatever benefits the U.S. economy derived from a protectionist policy in the nineteenth century must be qualified by the disastrous effects of a highly protectionist policy in the early years of the twentieth century.

Second, in terms of principle, the differing rationales of Malthus and Ricardo for freedom of international trade were noted above (Chap. 6), Malthus arguing that it increased wealth by expanding the opportunities for profitable exchanges, and Ricardo, rather, that it reduced costs by efficient specialization. Also noted was the fallacy of Ricardo's classic "proof" of the gains from such specialization, that is, that it measured the gain strictly in terms of physical output without regard to value. To this defect we may now add the observations made here: For all the advantages of international trade, which surely does expand markets, the one effect that generates the most controversy is specialization that involves discontinuing the production of a product in one country. This not only creates political pain but also may have serious economic disadvantages in terms of dependency and national security. Of all the advantages from international trade, the one that has long been regarded by economists as the chief and most easily demonstrated is in fact the least and of even doubtful validity—for imported wines, caviar, fashions, and prestige automobiles are hardly cost-minimizing purchases. What is distinctly important about international trade is not whether it is an unlimited good or a menace, but that it introduces special factors capable of producing dissatisfaction with the unfettered working of free markets.

A SPECTRUM OF MARKETS

The concept ventured here is admittedly hazardous, and all the more so if one attempts to be overly precise. And so the painting here will be with an extremely broad brush. The point is to contrast two widely varying conceptual approaches to the classification of markets. The idea of a spectrum of markets in the economic literature dates back at least as far as Cournot in 1848 and continues unaltered to the present day. It is a gradation based on the degree of concentration versus atomism, with monopoly at one end and atomistic ("perfect competition") at the other, with a clear preference for the latter. The disagreement with the second of these propositions here has already been made clear.

Is there an alternative? Yes, seemingly scandalous in orthodox terms, but entitled to at least a fair hearing. The criterion is political—spelled with a small *p*. The standard is whether a particular market causes irritation at the political/governmental level sufficient to provoke governmental intervention. Intervention may take the form of legislation, government prosecution, or court decision, but in any of these cases it represents an expression of public dissatisfaction with what is happening in the marketplace.

To apply such a criterion produces a curious contrast with what is customarily associated with the spectrum of economic theory. On the political spectrum next to private monopoly as a source of public irritation are markets such as those for agricultural commodities, which approach the conditions of "perfect competition." At the opposite end of the spectrum, among many defensible candidates, let us propose the urban restaurant. This line of business, aside from its public health aspects, has not been a significant source of government intervention (franchising cases being an admitted exception). There is a wide variety of product and service competition, differing levels and a blurring of price competition, significant locational advantages, and ease of entry—and exit. In short, there are no significant public competition problems despite the fact that most of the principles of economic theory do not prevail in this line of business.

In between, contrast the position of firms disdained as "oligopolists," firms that in fact engage in substantial competitive behavior, and precisely because they do have some degree of control over the distinguishable products they place upon the market and are capable of adjusting their volume of production to the effective level of market demand. In short, some degree of market power and some blurring of price competition are conducive to self-regulating competitive markets, whereas an atomistic structure and pure price competition are not.

9

Reflections from Abroad

CONVENTIONAL UNWISDOM

"Reflections" as used here is a shameless *double entendre*. On the one hand an American antitrust lawyer viewing the rash of post–World War II "antitrust" legislation abroad will see reflected much in the way of basic principles that have been taken over from the U.S. law. On the other hand, a closer view of the leading European laws discloses a more thoughtful, balanced, and sophisticated approach than that of the U.S. law. The suggestion will be made here that the more thoughtful European laws might reflect back on the United States to the benefit of our own law.

Three of the foreign systems are cited here as sources of potentially useful ideas not present in the existing U.S. law: those of Britain, the Federal Republic of Germany, and the European Economic Community. They are taken up in this order, not to indicate any preference as to their relative importance, but for ease of explanation. The British system is the least complex and affords a very clear conceptual contrast to the U.S. pattern. The German law is more ambitious and more complex, while the EEC competition policy, because it is implemented in a supranational context, has some unique features that are significant in the area of international trade.

The reaction of the typical American antitrust lawyer to the suggestion that foreign laws can be a source of ideas for improving U.S. antitrust law may be likened to that of a French vintner being told that he could learn something from U.S. viticulture. Those who know something of the history of wine, however, will recall that U.S. vineyards once salvaged the European vineyards when a blight threatened to destroy the European vines. The U.S. vines, which were resistant to the blight, were imported, and the superior European varieties were grafted onto their roots (Rahl 1971: 766). It is in much the same sense that U.S. antitrust law stands to benefit from the European legislation—not on the premise that the European laws, in their own jurisdictions, work better than our own, but as a source of ideas that could be usefully transplanted here. Just as the U.S. roots contributed to superior wines in the more propitious conditions of Europe, so there are concepts, both of substance and administration, in European antitrust legislation that in the favorable political climate of the United States could provide substantial improvements in the effectiveness and workability of our own system.

The traditional attitude of U.S. antitrust lawyers toward the post–World War II legislation in Europe is understandable. The U.S. law has long been noted for its rigor, its firm rules not admitting of exceptions, and its outright ban on monopoly. The European laws, on the other hand, are not so firm; they permit exceptions, and they do not even ban monopolization.

This point of view, however, fails to take into account that the European legislation was conceived in the light of half a century of U.S. experience to draw on, but without the historical accidents and the emotional reaction to them that occurred in the United States in the late nineteenth and early twentieth centuries that have so clouded U.S. thinking on these problems. The Europeans entertain no illusions about self-regulating free markets and frankly recognize that the true need for state intervention is rooted in the tendency of competitive markets in various circumstances to self-destruct rather than to be self-regulating.

The European approach is a conscious intervention in the marketplace to promote a variety of public policy objectives, primarily the preservation of a competitive context. There are no criminal penalties. Although the courts play an important role, the primary emphasis is on administrative policy making. Most fundamentally, the Europeans do not pretend to prevent the existence of powerful private market power—as the United States does not despite its pretensions in that regard—but to limit its behavior where it does exist.

THE MODERATE BRITISH

> It would also seem wrong in view of the independence of the judiciary to entrust matters of great controversy to it. Controversy is

> the meat of politics, not the law. Politically controversial issues should be decided by politically responsible bodies, and not by courts of law.
>
> I. A. Macdonald (1965: 368)

> The final decision is based upon an elaborate case by case approach to decide whether a particular monopoly situation or a particular restrictive practice by agreement situation is meritorious in the sense of being on the whole, on balance, in favour of the public interest, or whether it is not. This approach we use to a much greater extent than you do, I think, by employing lay members of the various bodies which exist to deal with these matters.
>
> Lord Shawcross (1971: 1009)

The British post–World War II "antitrust" legislation provides a useful transition from the U.S. policy structure to the European, serving as something of an intermediate point between the U.S. and the continental policies of West Germany and the European Economic Community (EEC).

The most salient characteristic of the British legislation, in contrast to the U.S., is its moderation. The problem of monopoly is treated, not as a crime, but as a political problem, with the key decision-making process vested squarely in the legislature. The approach to the problem of concerted actions between two or more firms also contains no criminal penalties and is dealt with by a specialized administrative tribunal.

Mention should also be made of a factor that is fundamental to the British approach, even though there is nothing in the legislation itself that makes it obvious. That is the awareness that in their "antitrust" literature the British show the fundamental inadequacy of economic theory to serve as a guide to policy. A. D. Neale, in his popular one-volume work *The Antitrust Laws of the U.S.A.*, sums up the more well known criticisms of the theory and comments that "All of these points have been made many times before" (1970: 481). The authors of another work on the law of the U.K. and the EEC make the suggestion that economists contribute more by "the detailed analysis of how specific firms or industries actually operate and detailed study of the workings of particular structures of the economy [rather than macroeconomics or] the delights of mathematical analysis and model building" (Kenneth & Joll 1975: 2). Another British lawyer dismisses the theoretical economic analysis as "radically defective" (Richardson 1965: 435).

The British legislation has evolved in stages, the details of which are fully described elsewhere (von Kalinowski 1986; 1987; Korah 1982; Rhinelander 1971; Wilberforce, Campbell and Ellis 1966) and need not be recounted here. What is of interest to the present study is the structure as it is presently in place. A point of fundamental difference between the British and American laws is the clear-cut distinction in the British law between the problems of loose combination (concerted practices between separate firms) and tight combination (single-firm behavior, monopolization). In contrast to the Sherman Act, which links both together in Sections 1 and 2, the British law treats them as two distinctly different kinds of problems, subject to two separate legal regimes. The problem of concerted practices is dealt with by a specialized agency that is something of a blend between a court and an administrative agency, in which the administrative element dominates. The problem of monopoly is treated separately as essentially a political problem, addressed first by a study commission, with the power of decision left to the legislature.

Let us turn first to the problem of loose combination and the agency created to deal with it, the Restrictive Practices Court.

The Restrictive Practices Court

The Restrictive Practices Court is divided into panels, in each of which only one member is a judge, the other two being laymen (Rhinelander 1971: 827–28). In a further departure from judicial tradition, the court is given a broad range of discretionary authority not available to U.S. courts. The legislation itself spells out a general prohibition of what roughly corresponds to the same offenses that the U.S. Supreme Court has declared to be per se violations: fixing prices or other terms of sale, limitations on quantities to be produced, the processes to be used, and the persons or places from which supplies may be obtained (ibid., 828, 838).

The discretionary element enters through two qualifications that are attached to these prohibitions. An agreement that otherwise violates one of these prohibitions may nevertheless be approved by the court if the parties can establish any of eight "gateways" that provide grounds for exception. These are available for restrictions that can be shown to be

1. reasonably necessary to protect the public against injury;
2. of specific and substantial benefit to the public;
3. reasonably necessary to counteract measures taken by a third party that are restrictive of competition;
4. reasonably necessary to enable the parties to negotiate fair terms of sale from a third party who controls a predominant part of such business;
5. preventing a serious and persistent adverse effect on the general level of unemployment in an area in which a substantial proportion of the industry is situated;
6. a substantial aid to exports;
7. required for purposes connected with any other restriction that is not contrary to the public interest; or

8. not directly or indirectly discouraging to competition to any material degree in any relevant trade or industry. (Rhinelander 1971: 838–39; Edwards 1966: 455–56)

Establishing the existence of a "gateway" is not sufficient to obtain an exemption. Once a gateway has been shown, the "tailpiece" of the statute, which requires the court to make a balancing judgment comes into play. The exception is to be allowed only if the benefits shown outweigh the harm of allowing the restriction.

To traditional U.S. antitrust thinking this discretionary authority is an element of weakness in the policy, as well as a source of much potential mischief. Sensibly applied, however, it can avoid many of the dilemmas that the rigidities of our system place on businesspeople—they are not put to the choice of violating the law or going to Congress when they see no alternative to a particular practice—and tend to force the assertions of need for exceptions to be proved on their own merits. The British have, in fact, been quite stringent in allowing exceptions. Price fixing, for example, has been rejected on most occasions but allowed on a few others, notably to assist firms to compete more effectively in export markets (Sutherland 1965: 427–31; *In re Water-tube Manufacturers' Agreement*, L.R., 2 R.P. 50 (1960), and by nut-and-bolt manufacturers to save small-lot purchasers the trouble of shopping around—after a finding that the prices fixed were reasonable (Scherer 1980: 505–6).

The mixed composition of the Restrictive Practices Court, being partly judicial and partly administrative, is one of the features of the British law that make it a halfway point between the U.S. and the continental regimes, the former being rooted in the judicial system and the latter in administrative bodies. This schizophrenic nature of the British system has brought its share of criticism. One English lawyer has commented: "It would seem wrong in view of the independence of the judiciary to entrust matters of great controversy to it. Controversy is the meat of politics, not the law. Politically controversial issues should be decided by politically responsible bodies, and not by courts of law" (MacDonald 1965: 368, fn omitted). And further:

> Yet the matters entrusted to the Restrictive Practices Court are very often controversial, and its decisions are likely to come in conflict with those of other decision-making bodies, unless a high degree of coordination can be provided. This . . . is absent in the case of the Restrictive Practices Court. (ibid.)

Recognition of the policy-making nature of the law is, of course, reflected in the predominant role of laymen on the court. So, too, is it reflected in the role played by the executive branch.

The Executive Role

The Restrictive Practices Court is only one of three constitutional players in the British antitrust scheme. The executive, the enforcement arm, was originally the registrar, with whom all restrictive agreements are required to be registered, who reports them all and takes up with the court those he finds objectionable and which cannot be resolved through negotiation—which many are. Under a 1976 amendment, this office was superseded by a director of fair trading, who in addition to the function formerly performed by the registrar has responsibilities relating to monopolies and mergers as well as consumer protection (von Kalinowski 1987: sec. 1.02[6]).

The Special Treatment of Monopolies

With respect to tight combinations—monopoly and merger—the British have an entirely distinct regime, which does not involve the Restrictive Practices Court. The approach is jointly executive, administrative, and legislative, but with no involvement by the judiciary. Two different agencies are responsible for this aspect of policy: the Board of Trade within the Department of Trade and Industry, an executive department with authority to impose obligations on private firms, and the Monopolies Commission, which serves as an advisory body to the board. The board is empowered to refer to the commission for its recommendation situations where a monopoly is thought to exist and to require reports on practices that "distort competition" in goods, services, or exports. "Monopoly" is defined by the statute to exist whenever a third or more of the supply of goods is controlled by one person or by two or more people acting together so as to restrict competition. The commission may be asked if a monopoly exists or also, if it does, to determine whether it operates against the public interest.

The Board of Trade may issue an order to carry out recommendations, but that order must itself be approved by an affirmative vote of each house of Parliament. There have been very few such orders, most cases being resolved through negotiation with the private parties (Rhinelander 1971: 834).

Both the Monopolies Commission and the Board of Trade have a broader range of policy-making discretion in the merger area then is afforded to their counterparts in the United States. This was illustrated by the proposed conglomerate acquisition of the De La Rue Company by the Rank Organization. Both were diversified companies, and De La Rue was not engaged in any of the same businesses as Rank; but the Monopolies Commission concluded that the merger would operate "against the public interest." There was active opposition to the takeover by De La Rue's management, which threatened a loss of key personnel that could have jeopardized the company's exports. The Board of Trade issued an order prohibiting the acquisition (ibid., 836–37).

An Exemplary Administration

Another interesting feature of the British law is the expedition of its process. The Restrictive Practices Court requires parties to exchange written statements of their proofs in advance, which has eliminated the need for them to present their entire testimony orally before the court. After a brief statement affirming the contents of his written statement, the witness is ready for cross-examination (ibid., 828–29). This has made it possible "to record all the evidence and arguments for a case in from 6 to 35 hearing days" (Scherer 1980: 506)—a brevity almost unheard of in the United States. Even more momentous savings are realized in monopoly and merger cases. The commission has on occasion taken years to submit a report on a particularly complex matter, but the time is usually much shorter. And because the question of monopoly is viewed as a question of policy rather than as a moral offense, there is nothing like the monster monopoly cases that arise in the United States.

THE LOGICAL GERMANS

> Where no effective legislation to protect competition exists, there is a tendency for the decentralized market system to destroy itself.
>
> Eberhard Günther (1977: 1)

The West German Law against Restraints of Competition, created in the aftermath of World War II, is now the most sophisticated competition policy in the world—the United States included. The law of the European Communities is understandably given wider attention because of its greater geographic application, but as a competition policy its design is affected by the larger political objectives of the EEC. This is not to suggest that there is anything undesirable about these broader considerations, just that from the perspective of competition policy alone, the German law presents a purer case.

A Legislated Policy

The German Law against Restraints of Competition (*GWB*) has much in common with U.S. antitrust law (Kirchner 1980).[1] There is a basic prohibition against agreements or concerted practices that restrain competition, anticompetitive mergers are prohibited, and there is a premerger notification requirement.

But here the resemblance ends. The German law differs from U.S. law in part as to the details of what things it permits or prohibits, but more basically in its philosophy and approach to the problem. In contrast to the cryptic legislative standards of U.S. antitrust law, the German law is a carefully constructed fabric of legislation developed through numerous revisions since it was first enacted in 1957. This difference is reflected in the greater specificity and precision of the German law, but more importantly in its balance. Germany has approached the problem from the outset as one of competing values, including both consumers and the concern of businesspeople for stability, each of which has been treated as respectable.

The Theory

The moving force behind the adoption of the German law was the strong-minded champion of free markets and competition, the economics minister Ludwig Erhard. His views were not altogether welcome in the conservative German business community, which was sensitive to the pressures of the U.S. government during the occupation regime to impose an antitrust law in Germany, which had no prior significant policy of that kind. Erhard's political task required that his proposals be identified as German rather than as U.S. hand-me-downs, and he was at pains to emphasize the differences:

> The draft which was finally passed by the Federal Government contradicted the principles of American law in its basic construction. The principle of outright prohibition is strictly enforced in North America; the alternative of making administrative exceptions, which characterizes the German law, is foreign to American law. (Erhard 1960: 121)

Erhard saw the problem in terms of both the buyers' and sellers' sides of the market, the welfare of consumers (Erhard 1960: 123–25) as well as the individual businessperson's right to compete: "No individual citizen must be powerful enough to suppress individual freedom, or, in the name of false freedom, to be able to limit it" (ibid., 3).

Erhard saw the threats to free competition, not in the U.S. tendency to look for villains, but as arising in part from the workings of the market itself and from government policies encouraging tendencies toward monopoly (ibid., 124). Erhard's idea of competition was not laissez faire. He saw a need for state intervention on the basis that complete competition was not possible or that what competition existed needed help (ibid., 123, 128). This enthusiastic champion of free markets and competition thus conceded that the market, left to itself, will not always function satisfactorily, and thus it creates a need for intervention by the state, not to displace competition, but to shore it up as much as possible.

Erhard was greatly assisted in his drive for a procompetitive policy by the collaboration of Dr. Eberhard Günther, the principal author of the legislation, and president of the Federal Cartel Office from its inception in 1958 until his retirement in 1976. Dr. Günther has described the objective of the law as "the decentralization of economic power. This mechanism curbs the area of action of the individual market participant so that it cannot be unduly extended at the expense of others" (1977: 1). It is recognized that though power positions tend to be eroded over time by competitive processes, these processes work slowly; and structural factors such as capital requirements, technological knowledge, patents, and access to raw materials limit access to markets (ibid.). The competitive process, far from being viewed as ideal, tends on occasion toward self-destruction.

Basically two courses are open to public policy: the one structural, the other regulatory. The structural approach focuses on such variables as the number of suppliers and customers, product differentiation, producer goodwill, barriers to market access, and the like. The regulatory approach—using "regulatory" in the European antitrust sense rather than as it is customarily thought of in the United States—"tolerates existing power positions and the formation of new positions either by external or internal growth of enterprises or restrictive or collusive practices" (ibid., 3). The theory is that it is "not the existence of economic power but its abuses that cause the public policy makers to take corrective steps" (ibid.).

The Concept of the Market-Dominating Enterprise

A "market-dominating enterprise" is defined by Section 22 of the GWB in the alternative, the basic criteria focusing on lack of competitors, the second on the company's overall financial and market strength.

Under the first criterion a firm is market-dominating if as a seller or buyer of goods or services it "does not have competitors or is not subject to any substantial competition." A further basis for finding a lack of competition applies to "two or more enterprises . . . if for factual reasons substantial competition for a particular type of goods or commercial services generally or in particular markets does not exist between or among them and if they together" do not have competitors or are not subject to any substantial competition.

The absence of substantial competition is given some helpful specificity by two statutory presumptions. It is presumed that a firm is market-dominating "if it has a market share of at least one-third for a particular type of goods or commercial services," but not if the enterprise had sales of less than DM 250 million (<$125 million) during the preceding fiscal year. A second presumption as to the absence of substantial competition applies when (a) three or fewer enterprises have a combined share of 50 percent or more or (b) five or fewer enterprises have a combined market share of two thirds or more. There is also a minimum requirement that the enterprises involved had sales of at least DM 100 million (<$50 million) during the preceding fiscal year.

The alternative concept based on overall market power was added by amendment in 1973 as a result of dissatisfaction with the original concept of the market-dominating enterprise. That idea is limited, as the U.S. law of monopolies and mergers, by the boundaries of what constitutes a market. The argument was made by Günther and others that the effective power of a firm is adequately measured, not by its market share alone, but by its overall "power" including assured sources of supply, financial strength, total size, and the like. Thus, a new alternative test was added to classify a firm as market-dominating if it has a market position in relation to its competitors that may be roughly expressed in English as one of overall or predominant power. (The German word is *überragende*, which is literally translated as "paramount, overriding." It has been variously translated in this context as "paramount" (Günther 1977: 9; von Kalinowski 1987: vol. B5: W.GERGA1–14), "superior" (Riesenkampff & Gres 1980: 31), and "commanding" (CCH *Doing Business in Europe* par. 36–670, p.37,552). This new concept adds to the presumptions based on market share the criterion that "its financial strength, its access to supply and sale markets, its corporate ties to other enterprises, as well as to legal or factual barriers to market access by other enterprises shall in particular be taken into account" (Sec. 22(1) 2; translation based on slightly different versions in von Kalinowski and Riesenkampff, cited above in this paragraph.)

What consequences follow from a finding that a firm has a market-dominating position? The concept has three distinct applications, only one of which may lead to the breaking up of a firm on the ground that it has such a position. All involve a variation on the principle that firms above a certain threshold of market power must play by a somewhat different set of rules (Hoppmann 1972; Klaue et al. 1971; Günther 1970; Stahl 1980; Edwards 1977: 17–18). There is a general prohibition against the abuse of a market-dominating position (Sec. 22, par.5) and a specific prohibition against price discrimination (Secs. 25, 26), and the concept is used as a test for the permissibility of mergers (Sec. 24). The latter is the one element of structural control in the German law, barring mergers that either create a new or strengthen an existing market-dominating position (Hoppmann 1972; Klaue et al. 1971; Günther 1970; Stahl 1980). The Cartel Authority may order divestiture to break up an unlawful merger.

The Concept of Abuse

The major innovation of the market domination concept is in its linkage with the idea of abuse of such a position. Whenever the Cartel Authority finds an abuse of a dominant position to have occurred, it has authority to prohibit the abuse and declare related agreements ineffective (Sec. 22(5)). This broad authority, and the vagueness of the concept of market domination, are mitigated by the fact that the abuse is not in itself a violation of law and by a requirement that the Cartel Authority first seek a voluntary termination. Legal consequences attach only prospectively.

What amounts to an abuse? An abuse can occur in the dominated market, in vertically related (buyers and sellers) markets, or in third markets. The statute was amended in 1980 (Sec. 22(4)) to provide criteria that include behavior that impairs the competitive opportunities of other firms in the absence of facts justifying such behavior; demands terms different from those that would likely result under effective competition, taking into account practices of firms in comparable markets; or demands more onerous terms than those exacted from similar firms in comparable markets.

Examples of specific types of contracts listed by Dr. Günther are classified into three categories: (1) abuses within the dominated market itself, (2) abuses with respect to firms that deal with the dominating firm as suppliers or resellers, and (3) abuses in third markets.

Examples in the first category include exclusive dealing contracts, restrictions on product use, certain types of restrictive patent-licensing agreements, "blocking purchases" to prevent a competitor from meeting his requirements, and basing point systems (Günther 1977: 20–21).

This category of abuse within the dominated market also reaches cases of excessive prices harming consumers, and it was this provision that provided Germany with its antitrust alternative to a Federal Energy Administration during the oil crisis of 1973–1974. Among the more obvious ways a market-dominating position may be abused is through exploitive, excessive pricing in times of emergency (OLG in *WuW/E* 8/74: 549 (*in re British Petroleum*). When the embargo crisis broke in October 1973, the German government made a decisive choice: "better poor and warm than rich and cold" ("Ludwig II," *Capital Köln* (Cologne): Capital-Redaktion, 2/74: 7–10). The oil companies were told to go where they had to and pay what they must, but be sure that the supply was adequate. This they did, and the resulting prices were spectacular enough to be a problem; indeed, they were far more severe in Germany than elsewhere in Europe. The one lever of control the government had against exploitation by the oil companies was the abuse principle.

A formal investigation was launched at the behest of the administration, for the Federal Cartel Office anticipated the problem and had found very skimpy grounds on which to challenge the oil companies. The Office found itself in a difficult position, since the proof of abuse or exploitation in a situation where there is every legitimate reason for prices to not only rise but explode is a highly subjective matter, and the decisions of the Federal Cartel Office are subject to judicial review. The investigation nonetheless went forward, and hearings were conducted amidst vast publicity in the glare of television lights, all of which made the oil companies even more uncomfortable than the Federal Cartel Office. The publicity and the possibility of government action led the oil companies to moderate their prices enough to leave the Federal Cartel Office with no substantial ground of complaint, and thus the political pressure was defused.[2]

The problem of abuse through excessive prices presents an inherently difficult problem for the reasons so apparent in the oil crisis. Since exploitation occurs almost by definition under market conditions that justify some increase in prices, what standard can be applied? The practical solution adopted by the Federal Cartel Office is the concept of the comparable market: "The allegedly abusive price is compared with the price charged in a market which except for its greater competitive intensity is otherwise comparable" (Günther 1977; 25).

The far-reaching potential of the abuse concept, however, is more apparent in the second of the three listed categories, which concerns the relation of the dominating firm to its suppliers and resellers. Several years after the oil crisis of 1973, in reaction to a crisis not of supply shortage but of sharply rising import prices that wiped out the margin of middle-sized firms and threatened their existence, the Federal Cartel Office developed a principle under Section 26(2) that in critical market periods suppliers are obliged to continue supplying their traditional customers (FCO 1981: 44–45).

The third category, relating to third markets, includes discriminatory pricing arrangements, loyalty rebates, refusals to supply or purchase on a discriminatory basis, reciprocal dealing, tying agreements, customer allocations, and arrangements designed to circumvent the ban of resale price maintenance (Günther 1977: 21).

Discrimination by Market-Dominating Enterprises

Market-dominating enterprises are prohibited from price discrimination both under the abuse principle and by a specific prohibition in Section 26. The latter prohibition, however, goes farther than just price discrimination, requiring that such an enterprise

not directly or indirectly hinder another enterprise in business activities which are usually open to similar enterprises, nor, in the absence of facts justifying such differentiation, treat such enterprise, directly or indirectly, in a manner different from the treatment accorded to similar enterprises. . . . They must not use their market power to induce other enterprises to grant them special benefits in the absence of facts justifying such differentiation. (Sec. 26(2), (3) as amended in 1980. Riesenkampff & Gres 1980: 65)

A simple refusal to deal would thus be banned by this section if the market-dominating enterprise sells to similar firms on terms that the buyer in question is willing to meet.

The Concept of Dependence

In addition to the constraint on market-dominating enterprises to avoid discrimination in selecting with whom they will deal as well as on what terms, the German law imposes that same obligation on all firms, regardless of their market power otherwise, to deal with firms that can show a special dependence on them as suppliers. The provision applicable to market-dominating enterprises by Article 26(2) is also made applicable to "enterprises and associations of enterprises insofar as suppliers or sellers of particular types of goods or commercial services depend upon them to such extent that sufficient and reasonable possibilities to switch to other enterprises do not exist."

This principle has been liberally applied, even to include businesses not previously served by a supplier when it can be shown that the would-be buyers could not otherwise *enter* a business. This was the holding of a case involving BASF, which had refused to supply two minor firms with certain polyester raw materials in which BASF had a market-dominating position, because the two firms were dependent on these materials. "The Court held Section 26(2) is also designed to protect enterprises which had not formerly been active . . . in a particular line of business" (Günther 1977: 13, fn omitted).

The dependence principle was an obvious resort for companies seeking critically short supplies during the oil embargo crisis. The Federal Cartel Office concluded that there was a duty on the part of a major oil firm to partition its supplies between its own dealers and others "because of the public interest in maintaining independent . . . [gasoline] stations as a factor in competition, and the specific threat to the survival of the firms" (ibid., 31). The Berlin Court of Appeals, however, overruled the Federal Cartel Office because the supplier in this case would have endangered its own survival had it continued to supply independent stations (ibid.). Absent that concern, a different result could be expected, as indicated by the court's comments on the obligation of market-dominating firms to allocate supply in times of shortages: "The fact that a product is in short supply, so that not all deliveries can be made as requested, does not entitle the market-dominating enterprise to give similar enterprises different treatment. Even in this particular situation it is not allowed to satisfy the needs of only part of the buyers, while excluding other similar firms from the purchase of scarce products. Rather, it is obliged to meet the demand proportionately" (ibid.).

Mergers

The new merger control provision grants the Cartel Authority power to prohibit a merger that "will result in or strengthen a position of market domination" (Secs. 23, 24a; Hoppmann 1972; Klaue et al. 1971; Günther 1970; Raisch, Solter & Kartte 1970). There is a reporting requirement with criteria based on the size of the merger; and if at least two of the participating enterprises have total sales of DM 1 billion (<$500 million) each there must be prior notification (Secs. 23, 24a; Riesenkampff & Gres 1977: 79–93, 105–9). In all other cases the report is regarded as timely filed if it is made within three months after the merger is consumated (Sec. 23; Riesenkampff & Gres 1977: 87).

The 1980 amendments added some new presumptions that make easier the satisfaction of the criteria for blocking mergers. A new section 23a provides that it is presumed that a merger will result in or strengthen a market-dominating position if the combined firms exceed certain size limits (von Kalinowski 1987: vol. B5: W.GERGAl–20–1; Riesenkampff & Gres 1980: 43–45). The amendment thus injects a wholly new kind of presumption based on the sheer size of the firms, a provision that has been termed the "marriage of elephants law."

There are two levels, however, at which a merger may be upheld even if it would create or strengthen a market-dominating position. Before the Cartel Authority the parties have the opportunity to "prove that the merger will also result in improvements of competitive conditions and that such improvements outweigh the detrimental effects of the market domination" (Sec. 24(1)). This criterion is not satisfied by a showing of "merely economic and financial improvements" such as "improvements by virtue of rationalization and of efficiency of the participating enterprises"; it is rather satisfied by such improvements as "the loosening of an existing oligopoly by entrance of a strong offeror . . . or that it led to a greater number of offerors" (Riesenkampff & Gres 1977: 101). Repeal of this balancing test was recommended in a report of an advisory committee to the minister of economics on the ground that it is not practically possible to quantify gradations in the intensity of competition (*WuW* 1987: 297).

If the merger is disapproved by the Cartel Authority, it may be appealed to the federal minister of economics, who is directed to approve the merger if the restraint of competition is balanced by the overall economic advantages of the merger or by an overriding public interest. The permission may contain restrictions and requirements, but not such as to amount to continuous control (Sec. 24(3). Appeals to the minister must be made within one month, and he must decide within four (Sec. 24(4); Bartran 1979).

There is here a more detailed and meaningful legislative guide to policy than the U.S. Clayton Act's cryptic standard: "where in any line of commerce in any section of the country the effect of . . . [a merger] may be substantially to lessen competition, or to tend to create a monopoly." The German formulation also expressly takes account of the international context in which much competition takes place.

Exceptions

A major barrier to U.S. understanding of the German law is its open tolerance of the label "cartel." The Federal Cartel Office is something of a cross between the Antitrust Division of the Department of Justice and what the FTC was imagined to be, but the label makes it sound to Americans like some agency designed to promote cartels. This impression is furthered by the designation of several species of cartels that are legally permissible under the German law.

But a deeper look, behind the labels, shows what is actually a quite logical approach to the question of when exceptions should be permitted, and one that is in some respects much tougher than the U.S. system. How so? In the United States the enforcement officials have no power to make exceptions to the law; they vaunt their single-minded toughness—and that of the law—by directing all requests for exceptions to the Congress. But Congress is a representative body. What forum could be more sympathetic to the pleadings of any special interest group—and has been? In Germany, as in Britain, those who seek exceptions must make their case, not to sympathetic politicians, but to the antitrust enforcement officials. And the arguments they most typically parade before the politicians have been transformed from theoretical into hard questions: Are conditions in an industry truly depressed? Is there a genuine need for rationalization? Is cooperation in exporting really necessary? This is the real significance of the cartel exceptions in the German law—a few limited categories in which the arguments for exceptions are conceded a limited legitimacy. Some plainly allow practices that would be illegal under U.S. law, but others amount to no more than what we permit under the label of "trade association" activity. There are eight categories of permissible cartels, plus a catchall general authority given to the federal minister of economics to grant exemptions on an *ad hoc* basis (Sec. 8(1)). The eight types permitted are (1) terms of sale cartels, (2) discount cartels, (3) structural crisis cartels, (4) rationalization cartels, (5) specialization cartels, (6) rationalization through cooperation for small and medium-sized enterprises, (7) export cartels, and (8) import cartels (Secs. 4, 5(2), 6(2), 7, 8, 9; Edwards 1966: 168–69).

Finally, there is a general exemption provision. If none of the foregoing conditions can be satisfied, "the Federal Minister of Economics may, upon application, permit an agreement or resolution if, exceptionally, the restraint of competition is necessary for predominant reasons relating to the economy as a whole and the public interest" (Sec. 8(1); Riesenkampff & Gres 1977: 39). Resort to this authority is limited by a requirement that "if there is imminent danger to the continued existence of the enterprises within a particular business section," it may be used "only if other legislation or economic measures cannot be taken or cannot to taken in time, and if the restraint of competition is likely to avert such danger." This extraordinary authority "may be granted only in particularly serious individual cases" (Sec. 8; Riesenkampff & Gres 1977: 39; Friedrich 1979).

These exceptions have not been widely used, particularly those that have the greater anticompetitive impact. Their availability, however, provides German businesspeople with an alternative to the dilemma faced by U.S. businesspeople who believe they must deliberately violate the antitrust laws to survive. And the extensive oversight and discretionary powers given to the Cartel Authority afford some assurance that the public interest will be protected.

Penalties

There are no criminal sanctions in the German antitrust law. A proposal to add such was made by the Federal Ministry of Justice but was rejected by the Federal Ministry of Economics, citing among other reasons a belief that the social harm from restraints of competition is not comparable to that of the existing criminal offenses and that the numerous clauses of the *GWB* that are in need of interpretation could create legal uncertainty (Riesenkampff & Gres 1977: 9). How noteworthy, this difference of viewpoint between the prosecutor and the economic policy maker!

As to civil penalties, the U.S. pattern is reversed, but with a novel twist. Private parties may recover compensatory damages only (Sec. 35); whereas the government may sue for three times, not damages, but the amount of the illegal gain, in addition to fines of up to DM 100,000 (<$50,000) (Sec. 38(4)).

In theory, this liability for the entire illegal gain should pose a greater deterrent than the U.S. fixed fines, since the calculus of profit to be gained from violation, if caught, would never be favorable, as it often is in the United States. Dr. Günther has criticized this provision as unworkable in practice, however, because the amount of gain is too difficult to prove. He proposes instead the use of annual sales as a basis for calculation (Günther 1977: 43).

The Machinery

The careful reader may have noticed that the terms "Cartel Authority" and "Federal Cartel Office" have both been used alternatively to describe the German government's antitrust agency. This is because Germany, like the United States, has both state and federal governments; though unlike the United States, the federal government has legislative jurisdiction at the state level as well. The same law is thus administered by both federal and state officials, depending on whether the case is intrastate or interstate. Each state organizes its own administrative operation, which is the "Cartel Authority" for that state; the Federal Cartel Office is the "Cartel Authority" for the federal government (Sec. 44).

The Federal Cartel Office is an administrative body subject to the supervision of the minister of economics, of whose ministry it is a part. Alleged violations of the law are tried in the nine Decision Divisions of the FCO (divided along industry and commodity lines (Blake 1969: vol. 3: 159; eight at that time, one added since), in quasi-judicial proceedings (Günther 1977: 38–39). The Cartel Authority is the competent authority in all proceedings regarding fines (Sec. 81), and proceedings may be initiated by the Cartel Authority on its own initiative or upon application (Sec. 51). District courts are given exclusive jurisdiction over civil litigation under the *GWB* and cartel agreements or cartel resolutions (Sec. 87).

Decisions of the Cartel Authority may be appealed to the court of appeal having jurisdiction at the seat of the Cartel Authority (Sec. 62), and the appellate court decides issues of fact as well as of law from the entire record (Secs. 68(1), 70(1)). Appeals on points of law only may be taken to the Federal Supreme Court (Sec. 73).

To American eyes, the idea of judicial review of so discretionary a decision by a high-ranking political official seems incongruous, and it does in fact reflect a tension within the German system between the legal and economic perspectives. Despite the fact that the Federal Cartel Office was organized outside the court system, within the Ministry of Economics, and given a basically economic policy making function, the lawyers, representing conservative interests, maintained a tight control in the administration of the law.

In addition to appeals available through the courts, the quasi-judicial proceedings within the Federal Cartel Office are made up of three-man panels, each member of which must be qualified to serve as a judge

(Sec. 48(4)). Even the staffing of the administrative side of the office was complicated by a remarkable law that bars an economist under 35 from being a public official![3]

The attempt to build a more or less balanced representation of viewpoints into the enforcement machinery is especially clear in another innovation added by the 1973 amendment. A Monopoly Commission was created as an adjunct to the new merger control provisions as an ongoing study group to evaluate developments and recommend any changes it deems desirable (Sec. 24b). Its membership, appointed by the president of the Republic, consists of five members "who must have special knowledge and experience in the field of economics, business administration, social policy, technology or business law" (ibid.). The commission is required to report every two years.

Overall, the machinery that administers the German law includes a blend of economic policy and legal institutions, as well as a built-in, diverse advisory body with a mandate to carry on a continuing oversight of the law. The economic policy making function is explicitly recognized and given distinct institutional form through the administrative responsibilities of the Federal Cartel Office and the supervisory role of the federal minister of economics. The minister's role, too, despite its subjection to judicial review, is a frank concession to the existence of a political ingredient in competition policy, a healthy safety valve that is conspicuously missing from the U.S. system. The German system, by separating the litigation and policy-making functions, and by dividing the latter into two stages—the one at the technical, career civil servant level, the other plainly political—gives a healthy freedom for each of these different institutional perspectives to express itself without inhibition by the other.

Interface

We saw in Chapter 8 the various market malfunctions that have led to separate regulatory agencies and occasional conflicts with antitrust policy. The German law gives explicit legislative recognition to these separate areas—primarily in transportation, utilities, banking, insurance, agriculture, and fisheries—but incorporates them into the overall competition policy, with a formal advisory role for the antitrust enforcement authorities (Secs. 99–104).

An interesting feature of the German response to the interface problem is in its patent legislation. Here, unlike the United States, Germany gives recognition within the patent system itself to competitive values. Fees are charged for the patent protection, there is a provision for compulsory licensing, and the fees rise toward the end of the patent term, which typically leads to early abandonment (Blake 1969: vol. 3: 46–47).

The broader mandate and capacity that the Federal Cartel Office has as an economic policy maker than the prosecutorial Antitrust Division contributes to greater coherence of German policy than is found in the United States. The Federal Cartel Office issues a biennial report that deals more coherently with issues of competition policy across the entire economy than can be readily gleaned from a summary of the Antitrust Division's prosecutions and a miscellany of speeches by its top officials. Thus, the more explicit policy role of the German law contributes to a consistency of government policy in the interface between the market and regulated or exempt areas of the economy.

The Ongoing Dialogue

A persistent theme running through the foregoing highlights of the German competition policy is its capacity for growth and change. In addition to the legislative changes is another dimension of dialogue, spawned by the legislation already in place, that provides a refreshing contrast to the dreary tone that currently prevails in U.S. antitrust circles. Because the German law admits the consideration of many issues precluded by the narrow rigidity of U.S. law, the ongoing dialogue in the Federal Cartel Office, in the courts, and in the literature is much richer in content than anything that is now to be found in the United States—and unconfused by the known but unaccepted preachments of the Chicago School.[4]

In both its substantive and administrative ideas, the German competition policy offers a rich supply of new vines that might be profitably cultivated in U.S. soil.

COMPETITION POLICY ON AN INTERNATIONAL SCALE: THE EUROPEAN COMMUNITIES

The Context and the Concept

The European communities have created something truly unique: an "antitrust law" through international treaty. They did so on two different occasions, first with the establishment of the European Coal and Steel Community (ECSC) in 1951, and second in the treaty of Rome establishing the European Economic Community in 1957. The specific content of the competition rules in the two treaties differs. They are essentially alike in their treatment of agreements and concerted practices, but the Coal and Steel Treaty is more detailed and more in the nature of a quasi-regulatory regime than an antitrust law. Our focus here will be on the EEC.[5]

Superficially, the EEC treaty provisions suggest an amalgam of the

Sherman Act and the German law. The substantive provisions, like the Sherman Act, are set forth in two sections, Articles 85 and 86 of the treaty, the first dealing with concerted action by two or more firms, the second with single-firm behavior. Article 85, however, is much more specific than the Sherman Act, including much of what is separately covered in U.S. law by the Clayton Act. The second provision, Article 86, is directed to single-firm concentration; but unlike the Sherman Act and like the German law, deals with it through the concept of abuse control, and there is no prohibition of monopolization.

One of the most remarkable points of comparison between the EEC and the U.S. law is the distinctly different perspectives from which they approached the subject. The overriding object of the EEC was to provide the continent of Europe with something the U.S. Constitution did for most of the North American continent in 1787: a unified, free, continentwide market.

The nations on the continent of Europe had for centuries functioned as isolated economies, thereby denying themselves the economies of scale available to nationwide firms in the United States. The post–World War II European focus was on freeing its industries to grow and cross national boundaries. They were not concerned about monopoly, their purpose being to encourage the building of larger firms, not break them up (Joliet 1970: 16; Hallstein 1979: 141, 153).

Why, then, include an antitrust policy at all? The drafters of the Rome Treaty saw a competition policy as a means to the market integration they were seeking, and one of the dominant themes of the EEC's enforcement history has been to prohibit restrictive arrangements that limit market boundaries in line with national boundaries (Hawk, *Guide*: 118–21; Toepke, *EEC*: Sec. 222.3, p. 39–43).

There was also, however, a consciousness of the role that cartels and other combines had played in support of the Fascist powers during the war, as well as a desire to prevent a rebirth of that sort of power. There was, in addition, a substantial missionary campaign by the U.S. government urging the adoption of antitrust legislation. Further, the awesome performance of the U.S. economy during World War II led some Europeans to see a cause-and-effect relationship between a competitive economy and superior performance (Edwards 1967: 1–13; Hallstein 1979: 136–61).

But the size of national markets was not the only cause of difference in outlook between the U.S. and European governments. The Industrial Revolution had led to combinations and monopolies in Europe, too, but without producing the same public backlash. The reason was rooted in a different cultural background. Business in Europe developed, or rather evolved, out of a medieval economy. That economy embraced the guild tradition, and prevailing moral views about the ethical conduct of business induced self-restraint that had no counterpart in the United States. Such spectacular abuses as the Standard Oil Company's war on the Pennsylvania Railroad and the extravagances of the "Robber Barons" did not happen in Europe and create an impression of criminal behavior. Also, the guild tradition was rooted in perceptions of market breakdowns and imperfections. Restraint and discipline, not freedom and excess, marked the European attitude toward business (Edwards 1967: 15–23; Rahl 1971: 771).

The postwar political context is perhaps best summed up by Corwin Edwards, who saw a general recognition, even among socialists, that large parts of the economy would inevitably "be privately administered through market mechanisms" and that "Policies based upon competition tended to occupy a middleground between extremes of collectivization and cartelization. They became politically viable and sometimes even expedient" (Edwards 1967: 12). Europeans thus approached the question of public control over business behavior as an issue of economic policy, not morality.

These differences of perspective are reflected in the major differences between the EEC and U.S. versions of antitrust law: (1) the absence of any criminal penalites in the European system; (2) an enforcement system that is primarily administrative rather than court directed, though there is judicial supervision; (3) specific authority conferred on administrative authorities to grant exceptions to the rules, which are also set forth with a greater specificity than in the U.S. law; (4) control of single-firm power through a supervisory policy of abuse control rather than the prohibition of monopolization; and (5) some express level 3 rules that go farther than the U.S. legislation of 1914 in granting rights to individual businesspeople.

More fundamentally, there is a clearer concept of the direction of policy than in the United States. We have noted in Chapter 5 the schizophrenic personality of U.S. antitrust policy, divided between the purists who believe the policy begins and ends with the one word "competition" and those who see an element of artificiality in the process, as reflected in the legislation of 1914. In Europe no such conflict exists because no one accepts the purest point of view. The EEC Commission has stated its philosophy very clearly:

> It is an established fact that competition carries within it the seeds of its own destruction. An excessive concentration of economic, financial and commercial power can produce such far-reaching structural changes that free competition is no longer able to fulfill its role as an effective regulator of economic activity. . . . The desire to maintain a competitive structure dictates the Commission's constant vigilance over abuses by dominant firms and over mergers which result

in abrupt and substantial increases in the market shares of such firms. (*Ninth Report*: 9–11; Hawk, *Guide*: 15)

In line with this policy the EEC Commission has adopted an affirmative policy to assist and protect small and medium-sized firms:

[O]ne of the Commission's main concerns in the competition policy area was its concern to strengthen and preserve small and medium-sized enterprises (SMEs) as an essential element in a healthy and competitive environment. The Commission remains convinced that such businesses form one of the basic foundations of the European economy because of the contribution they make to the competitive structure of the market, their flexibility and their dynamism. (*Seventeenth Report*: par.23, p. 29)

Together, these statements make clear a policy to preserve a competitive context as an end in itself.

There is another important feature of the EEC Treaty that stems from the fact that the EEC is an international institution rather than a single nation. The treaty addresses directly a problem that can only be dealt with effectively by international agreement: the problem of subsidies, grants, and other government-conferred favors that give some businesses an unfair advantage over their competitors. It is a violation of the treaty for member states to take such actions, and the enforcement of these rules has proven to be one of the most active areas of enforcement activity.

Before turning to the specifics of these innovations, let us look first to the institutions that administer them.

The Institutional Architecture

The EEC was originally formed in 1957 as one of three separate communities, The institutions of which have since been merged, the other being the European Coal and Steel Community and EURATOM. Their founders had a much more ambitious concept of creating another United States of America than what has thus far emerged; those ambitions are no longer regarded as realistic. The institutional structure of the European Communities, while lacking the comprehensive powers of the U.S. federal government, possess some innovative features that the U.S. government does not have, particularly in the area of "antitrust."

The Rome Treaties play generally the same role as the U.S. Constitution. They created several councils of ministers that have since been merged into a single body, which has a legislative role comparable to the U.S. Congress, though with executive powers as well. Beneath the Council of Ministers is the European Commission, which has no precise counterpart in the U.S. government. It may be roughly described as a cross between an independent regulatory agency and the President's cabinet, as it indeed functions in both of these respects. The European Commission deals with the same full range of political issues as the members of the U.S. cabinet, but it does so as an organic institution, which the president's cabinet is not. The Commission both formulates political and legislative proposals for action by the Council of Ministers and takes administrative actions on its own, which are subject to review variously by the Council of Ministers or the Court of Justice, created by the treaties to play a role comparable to that of the U.S. Supreme Court (Hawk, *Guide*: 13, 29–30).

The Commission is empowered to issue regulations that add specificity to the general language of the treaties, just as the U.S. Federal Trade Commission is empowered to do under its own statute (but not the Sherman Act). The European Commission is also empowered to make exceptions to the treaty rules, according to criteria, but essentially in its own discretion, an option that does not exist in the United States under the Sherman Act.

The Court of Justice has broad powers of review over the decisions of the Commission, even to overrule the Commission's denial of a discretionary decision not to grant an exception to the rules (*Kali* 1975 E.C.R. 499, CCH par.8284; Hawk *Guide*: 198–99). The Court of Justice normally acts in this reviewing capacity over decisions initially taken by the Commission, rather than as the tribunal of first instance, as happens under U.S. law in Sherman Act cases. The European national courts, however, are occasionally confronted with issues involving the EEC's competition rules in deciding cases brought before them. They have the option of making their own decision, thereafter subject to review by the Court of Justice, or of referring the question directly to the Court (EEC Treaty Art. 177; Hawk, *Guide*: 30–35).

There is one facet of the Commission's procedural structure that has been criticized by both European and U.S. lawyers. The administrative apparatus that decides to bring cases also decides them, a violation of the separation-of-powers principle—an objection that also applies to the U.S. Federal Trade Commission (Kirkpatrick 1989: 35). Some procedural changes were made in 1982 that enlarge the independence of the European Commission staff, but which do not entirely remove the objection (Hawk, *Guide*: 25–27).

The Competition Rules

The competition rules are concerned primarily with the problems of loose combination, that is, agreed and other forms of concerted behavior between independent business firms. The general thrust of Article 85 is like Section 1 of the Sherman Act, but is much more specific than the latter's general prohibition of "restraints of trade," covering much the same ground as the U.S. Clayton Act. Article 85 prohibits

> agreements . . . and concerted practices . . . which have as their object or effect the prevention, restriction or distortion of competition within the common market, and in particular those which:
>
> (a) directly or indirectly fix purchase or selling prices or any other trading conditions;
>
> (b) limit or control production, markets, technical development, or investment;
>
> (c) share markets or sources of supply;
>
> (d) apply dissimilar conditions to equivalent transactions with other trading parties, thereby placing them at a competitive disadvantage;
>
> (e) make the conclusion of contracts subject to the acceptance by the other parties of supplementary obligations which, by their nature or according to commercial usage, have no connection with the subject of such contracts.

The first three subparagraphs spell out specific forms of prohibited behavior that the U.S. Supreme Court has found objectionable here in the legislation itself. The second two subparagraphs cover all the trade practices addressed by the Clayton Act, but with a generality of concept that makes much more clear what is objected to than the bland formulation "substantially to lessen competition or tend to create a monopoly." If the practice "distorts" competition that is enough, without the need to make a quantitative judgment as to whether it substantially lessens competition, let alone whether it tends toward monopoly. The prohibitions of subparagraphs (d) and (e) reach all forms of distorting discrimination, whether in terms of price or trade conditions. There is a much clearer focus on setting the rules of the game, unobsessed with the hobgoblin of monopoly.

It is the third paragraph of Article 85 that most clearly distinguishes the European from the U.S. policy, for it grants express authority to administrative officials to grant exceptions for agreements in admitted violation of paragraph 1 if they meet certain public interest criteria. This authority has been invoked to approve even so unthinkable an idea to U.S. antitrust partisans as "crisis cartels" (Hawk, *Guide*: 143–50; Toepke, *EEC*: Sec. 224, pp. 56–62).

Three points should be noted concerning this exception authority: First is that the authority has been very strictly construed, not an open doorway to undermining the basic policy of paragraph 1 (Hawk, *Guide*: 103–12). This is in no small measure a consequence of the fact that the decision makers are the same people who are responsible for affirmative enforcement of the law, not the political representatives of those whose interests lie elsewhere.

One example is the case of export commerce, where there is some case to be made for flexibility in the rules. The U.S. Congress responded by making a wholesale exemption (the Webb-Pomerene Act), which has been turned into a vehicle for the most blatant of anticompetitive activities, to the prejudice of some of the very small businesses it was intended to benefit (Chapman 1973: 426–32). The EEC, too, has recognized that export markets merit special treatment, but the extent of the exemption is carefully limited to the dimensions of the problem and controlled by the discretion of enforcement officials (ibid., 412–13).

The second point is that this is not just weakness or softness in the law; there are in fact meritorious reasons for exceptions. As noted earlier, the British and U.S. common law courts recognized this; it is only the turn-of-the-century confusion of the U.S. Supreme Court in its mishandling of the Sherman Act that has impressed upon that law the mindless rigidity that has characterized it for half a century.

The third point is that the policy roots of antitrust—or rather "competition"—policy are not exclusively economic or "efficiency" related. The Common Market treaty provision gives full scope to this insight in the criteria it establishes for exempting any agreement that

> contributes to improving the production or distribution of goods or to promoting technical or economic progress, while allowing consumers a fair share of the resulting benefit, and which does not:
> (a) impose on the undertaking concerned restrictions which are not indispensable to the attainment of these objectives;
> (b) afford such undertakings the possibility of eliminating competition in respect of a substantial part of the products in question.[6]

This authority has generated a vast amount of work for the Commission. A procedure was established whereby firms could notify agreements to the Commission for a determination of their legality or grant of an exemption, and the volume of applications was massive (Hawk, *Guide*: 112–13; Rahl 1971: 770). This may be criticized for the volume of bureaucratic paperwork it created, but there is something to be said for a system that tells businesspeople in advance whether what they propose to do is legal rather than taking their chances on what a court may decide after the fact. Moreover, extending the point made above that when exceptions are made by the enforcement agency there is less pressure for broad legislative exceptions, this sort of system allows for many more discrete judgments based on individual cases, both in granting and denying requests for exceptions.

One device the European Commission has used to deal with the vast flood of paper has been to grant block exemptions for whole categories of agreements (Hawk, *Guide*: 112–13). The Commission also issues "nonbinding 'communications' or 'notices' setting forth the Commission position with respect to certain issues" (Hawk, *Guide*: 89).

The exception policy of Article 85(3) stands in especially sharp contrast to U.S. antitrust law in the Commission's policy to approve so-called crisis cartels under carefully limited circumstances (Hawk, *Guide*: 143–50; Toepke, *EEC*: Sec. 224, pp. 56–62). The single rationale applied thus far for this purpose is to eliminate excess capacity on an industrywide basis.

The model situation is one in which some change in circumstance has left a number of firms with excess plant, typically of varying efficiency. Ideally, the least efficient plants should be shut down; but if a company acts unilaterally, it opens an opportunity for others to market their own excess production. If done on the basis of a controlled multilateral agreement, however, it is possible to make a rational cutback focused on the least efficient plant, resulting in a healthier industry without eliminating firms and increasing concentration.

The Commission announced the criteria for granting such exemptions in its *Twelfth Report on Competition Policy* of 1982. The general policy is to permit restraints for the purpose of correcting structural problems, "provided that they are aimed solely at achieving a coordinated reduction of overcapacity and do not restrict free decision-making by the firms involved" (Hawk, *Guide*: 146–47). To assure this result the Commission announced four criteria it would apply:

1. The reductions in capacity are likely in the long run to increase profitability and restore competitiveness, and if coordination of closures helps to mitigate their impact on employment.
2. Consumers will enjoy a share of the benefits on the ground that at the end of the agreement there is a competitive and healthy supply structure in the Community, without consumers having been deprived, during the period in which the agreement is in effect, of their freedom of choice or the benefit of performance competition.
3. The agreement is indispensable to achieving the needed reduction of capacity, and is limited in time to a period required for that purpose.
4. The agreement will not afford the possibility of eliminating substantial competition in that (a) eliminating excess capacity is only one dimension of competitive performance, all others remaining unaffected; (b) non-participating firms and imports remain as competitive elements; and (c) because the agreement is limited in time, participants will have to be prepared to survive in a competitive market upon its termination. (ibid., 147)

This policy has been sparingly and strictly applied, and in cases where the factual premises on which it is based are clearly present. The most significant example to date is the exemption approved in 1984 involving the synthetic fiber industry (ibid., 144–46). The industry had accumulated enormous overcapacity, attributed by the Commission to technological advances and a stagnant demand trend. Losses industrywide in 1981 had reached DM 1,200,000,000. The parties held market shares in a variety of product lines ranging from 54.6 percent to 77.6 percent in Western Europe.

The Commission insisted on deletion of clauses, among others, that would have banned investment leading to capacity increases without consent of all parties, and another clause that would have created a presumption that a plant operating at over 95 percent of capacity had an incorrect capacity rating. According to the agreement, each party undertook to reduce its capacity pursuant to a general plan; provision was made for an independent body of trustees to resolve factual details; retraining and deployment of displaced workers was provided for; and reports were required to be made to the Commission.

This policy has been criticized on the ground that competition should be left to sort out which are the more efficient firms and let the others perish (ibid., 149). But we have seen in Chapter 4 ("A Plague of Trusts") that competition did not work in the nineteenth-century experience with excess capacity. That experience with unrestricted competition and widespread overcapacity was a tendency toward monopoly. By allowing limited restraints in these kinds of circumstances, the European law works better to preserve the policy object of a competitive context than does its rigid U.S. counterpart.

One of the prime characteristics of the use of the exception authority provided by Article 85(3) is the opening it has provided for the consideration of social and political factors—such as effects on employment—that have no recognized place in U.S. antitrust policy. There has been a conscious evolution in this direction in the interpretation of the competition rules of the treaty. In the early years the emphasis in the application of Article 85 was on its purpose to prevent private restrictions from replacing governmental ones as barriers between the member states. But over time the Court of Justice has followed the lead of the European Commission in coming to think of Article 85 in terms of economic policy. J. Mertens Wilmars, former president of the Court of Justice, in a recent conference on developments in the community competition law, described a three-stage evolution in this direction, concluding that

> the most important step was made later in a third period. As the Commission was aware of the impact on the progress of integration arising from the economic crisis and technology development, it was urging the Court to take a more dynamic view of Article 85. The Court accepted this view and interpreted Article 85(1) and 85(3) no longer as a rule and an exception, but Article 85(1) as an economic model of workable competition with a certain degree of flexibility and Article 85(3) as an instrument in the hands of the Commission in order to pursue

economic policy—in matters such as unemployment—in order to correct the imperfections of the market. (Fordham 1987: 636–37)

Abuse Control

The term "monopoly," "monopolize," or "monopolization" appears nowhere in the prohibitions of the competition policy provisions of the EEC Treaty. Does this mean that the European Community policy is much weaker than the U.S., the foundation of which is the prohibition of monopolization? Not at all. Any conceivable offense that would violate Section 2 of the Sherman Act would assuredly constitute an abuse of a market-dominating position, but the reverse is not true. There is much that can be reached through an abuse control provision that would not approach the level of illegal monopolization under Section 2 of the Sherman Act.

The abuse control provision of the EEC treaty is contained in Article 86 of the treaty, which provides:

Any abuse by one or more enterprises of a dominant position within the common market or in a substantial part of it shall be prohibited as incompatible with the common market insofar as it may affect trade between Member States. Such abuse may, in particular, consist in:

(a) directly or indirectly imposing unfair purchase or selling prices or other unfair trading conditions;

(b) limiting production, markets or technical development to the prejudice of consumers;

(c) applying dissimilar conditions to equivalent transactions with other trading parties, thereby placing them at a competitive disadvantage;

(d) making the conclusion of contracts subject to the acceptance by the other parties of supplementary obligations which, by their nature or according to commercial usage, have no connection with the subject of such contracts.

An obvious, and significant, feature of this article is that it expressly embraces both dimensions of the policy: protection of business interests from harm by other businesspeople and protection of consumers. In the latter respect it is also noteworthy that businesspeople are protected in their role as buyers as well as sellers.

The key concept, as under the German law, is abuse by a "market-dominating enterprise." The much greater flexibility of this concept than that of monopolizing is clear in the following elaboration of the concept by the European Commission:

Undertakings are in a dominant position when they have the power to behave independently without taking into account, to any substantial extent, their competitors, purchasers and suppliers. Such is the case where an undertaking's market share, either in itself or when combined with its knowhow, access to raw materials, capital or other major advantage such as trademark ownership, enables it to determine the prices or to control the production or distribution of a significant part of the relevant goods. It is not necessary for the undertaking to have total dominance such as would deprive all other market participants of their commercial freedom, as long as it is strong enough in general terms to devise its own strategy as it wishes, even if there are differences in the extent to which it dominates individual submarkets. (*Re United Brands*. 19 *O.J. Eur. Comm.* (No. L 95) 11 (1976), 1976–78 Transfer Binder, *CCH Comm. Mkt Reptr.*, par.9800)

(See, generally, Hawk, *Guide*: Chap. 12: 525–658.1; Korah 1982: Chap. 10: 219–29; (1978); Temple Lang 1979: "Abuse" and "Some Aspects": Fox 1984.) In the early applications of this article there was a tendency to emphasize its role as a check on pricing abuses by large firms, but increasingly the concept of abuse has been applied to practices that distort the competitive process itself (Adams, G. B. 1985: 4–6; Korah 1974: 256–57).

As under Article 85, the European Commission and the Court of Justice consider the whole range of government policy considerations in applying Article 86, including social policy and employment (EEC Commission 1988: 14, 29–30; Hawk, *Guide*: 9–10, 131, 143–50, 167–78). This perspective is reflected particularly in the application of Article 86 to reach refusals to deal, a point of sharp contrast with U.S. law.[7]

The Commission has been particularly aggressive in such cases (Adams, G. B. 1985; Hawk, *Guide*: 608–21), and although the Court of Justice has occasionally overruled the commission on other technical grounds, it has not disapproved, and expressly affirmed, the Commission's policy in principle.[8] On one occasion during the oil crisis of 1973–1974 the Commission found an abuse under Article 86 when a major refiner refused to sell to an independent distributor on the ground that this constituted discriminatory treatment in comparison to the refiner's continued dealings with other distributors.[9] The Court of Justice reversed on the factual ground that the distributor in question had been only an "occasional" customer of the refiner, so that "BP cannot be accused of having applied to it during the crisis less favorable treatment than that which it reserved for its traditional customers."[10]

Perhaps the singularly most interesting case to date in the application of Article 86 is the decision known by the short name *Commercial Solvents*.[11] What makes its especially interesting is its clear reflection of the philosophical premise underlying the European competition policy, which is what has been described here as the preservation of a competitive context as an end in itself. The decision has been criticized for lack of rigor in terms of traditional antitrust analysis, but it is precisely in the avoidance of entanglement in such technicalities that both the Court of Justice and the European Commission showed the superior insight of the European competition policy compared to traditional antitrust analysis.

The facts of the case, which include a number of mind-boggling chemical names, may be simplified by substituting letters. The defendants were a U.S. manufacturer, Commercial Solvents (CSC), and its European subsidiary, Instituto. For years CSC had manufactured chemical products—(A)—that were incorporated into an end product—(B)—that competed with other end products—(C). The complainant, Zoja, had for years purchased (A) from Instituto, which it used to manufacture (B). Then CSC decided that it wanted to integrate forward, manufacturing the end product rather than just the raw material. Pursuant to this policy it decided to discontinue sales of (A) as a raw material. The problem this posed for Zoja was that it had no other source of supply, which would have left CSC without a competitor for the end product, (B).

Commercial Solvents's defense was that its decision to integrate forward was a legitimate one, and that there was no relevant market for (A) because it was only a component of an end product (B) that had plenty of competition from other products (C). The Court's answer was succinct and portentous:

> However, an undertaking being in a dominant position as regards the production of raw material and therefore able to control the supply to manufacturers of derivatives, cannot, just because it decides to start manufacturing these derivatives (in competition with its former customers) act in such a way as to eliminate their competition which in the case in question, would amount to eliminating one of the principal manufacturers of . . . [B] in the Common Market.[12]

Two things are troublesome about this decision to those accustomed to thinking in terms of the conventional wisdom of U.S. antitrust doctrine (Hawk, *Guide*: 610–11). One is the attitude injected by economic theory that anything that can be characterized as vertical presents no problem for competitive policy. This case, like that of Standard Oil, is a clear example to the contrary: Vertical power is here being used effectively to eliminate competition. The second problem from the U.S. perspective is the thinking habits that have grown out of having to deal with the clumsy term "monopolize." Because product (B) had plenty of competition from other products (C), there could be no claim of monopolization. But that is precisely the advantage of the abuse criterion. A competition policy with the clear-sighted objective of preserving a competitive context as an end in itself sees a proper policy objective in preventing the arbitrary elimination of an important competitor.

Another use that has been made of the abuse control principle merits passing notice. The EEC Treaty contained no merger control provision, a reflection of the purpose noted above to encourage the building of larger firms, not break them up (Joliet 1970: 16; Hallstein 1979: 153). This was all the more remarkable because the earlier Coal and Steel Treaty did provide for merger control (Hawk, *Guide*: 659). The contrast was not contradictory, however, because in Coal and Steel there was a purpose to prevent the buildup of excessive power positions—which was indeed the main purpose of the treaty (Kapteyn & von Themaat 1973: 5).

The European Commission was provoked to act on the merger front when a U.S. company pursued a persistent policy of acquisitions in the canning-packaging "industry." The Commission argued that building up a dominant position through mergers was itself an abuse, and the Court of Justice agreed in principle, though rejecting the Commission's complaint in that case for want of a relevant market.[13] The case established the principle that Article 86 could be used as an effective merger control device, and this has developed into a significant area of the EEC competition policy.[14] This facet of the EEC policy need not be elaborated here because an explicit merger control provision, such as that in the German law, provides a more useful model. It is noteworthy, however, that the German law concerning mergers does so in terms of a market-dominating position, essentially the EEC concept.

Rules on Trial

As a supranational organization the EEC has contributed an innovation in the policing of international trading conditions that is without meaningful precedent. We have noted earlier the basic game-like nature of modern business, in which both the course and the outcome of competition are highly influenced by the rules, many of which are within the discrete control of government (Chap. 2) as well as the peculiar nature of international trade, where competitors in different countries are subject to different governmental regimes, the policies of which can distort the competitive balance between them (Chap. 8).

The authors of the Rome treaties were acutely aware of this problem and addressed it in several far-reaching provisions. (The discussion here will be limited to the EEC provisions, which are sufficient to illustrate the principle.) The policy is comprehensive, extending to the many varieties of aid forms, and to all forms of especially privileged positions conferred by action of public authorities. When the European Commission or the Court of Justice finds that a particular form of aid violates the treaty rules, the Commission has authority to order the subsidy to be repaid (EEC Commission 1988: 139).

The treaty addresses three distinct forms of state intervention. One, addressed in Article 90, deals with state-owned enterprises, state-established monopolies, and specially privileged firms (Temple Lang 1985). Second is all forms of subsidization that have a distorting effect on competition as between the member states, known as state aids, covered by Articles 92 and 93 of the treaty. These two problem areas, and particularly the latter, have been a central concern of the Commission's enforcement efforts on competition policy (Caspari 1984: 1). Third is a prohibition against member states using their authority to cloak violations of the articles on competition policy through official acts (Joliet 1989). Some measure of just how important such problems are to the Commission may be seen from its annual reports on competition policy. The *Seventeenth Report* (1988) devotes 48 percent of its 259 pages to this subject matter; and the commission has displayed an impressive sophistication in dealing with this problem, which provides a rich source of study in the problems of market malfunction.

The Integration of Policy

One of the most singularly distinguishing features of the European approach to "antitrust" policy in contrast to that of the United States is the Europeans' much greater breadth of vision. It was noted at the outset of this section that the competition policy of the EEC is administered by the same officials responsible for the full range of economic and political issues that confront the European Community. In contrast to the United States, where no single agency presides over all of even antitrust policy, the EEC competition policy is administered by the same officials who deal with trade, agricultural, transportation, energy, fiscal, tax, and other broad areas of policy.

The European Commission every year produces a *Report on Competition Policy,* which reports broadly on not only enforcement actions of an antitrust nature but also trade issues, support for small and medium-sized enterprises, and Community economic policy generally. Paragraph 2 of its report for the year 1987 begins with the following statement: "The overall economic policy of the Community has the threefold aim of promoting a cooperative strategy for the creation of employment, of strengthening economic aid and social cohesion and of achieving an internal market by the now widely publicized deadline of 1992" (fn. omitted). Each year the Commission's *Report on Competition Policy* is the subject of an extensive commentary by the European Parliament (EEC Commission 1988: 260–65).

That antitrust and trade issues are part of a common subject matter is attested by their increasing linkage in both government policy and the scholarly literature. Beginning in the early 1970s the Antitrust Division of the Department of Justice began intervening in dumping and other types of trade proceedings. The annual Fordham Corporate Institute conducted by Prof. Barry Hawk produces a collection of papers by a mixture of distinguished European and American speakers that range interchangeably over both U.S. and European antitrust and trade issues (Fordham). During the oral discussions at these sessions American lawyers continue to suggest that there are lessons in U.S. antitrust law for Europe, to which the Europeans have come to retort, "No, there are not. The objectives of antitrust law in Europe are broader than they are in the United States." And so they are.

NOTES

The author gratefully acknowledges the assistance of Heinz Diehlman, a West German lawyer, in providing much of the German language research materials for this chapter.

1. The *Gesetz gegen Wettbewerbsbeschränkungen* (*GWB*) appears in parallel German and English texts in Riesenkampff & Gres 1977, supplemented in a separate volume of the 1980 amendments (1980). An extended treatise that also contains an English translation of the law is in the *World Law of Competition* (von Kalinowksi 1987: vol. B5).

2. Author's interview with Dr. Günther, Washington, D.C., 1979. The report of the Federal Cartel Office was inconclusive, finding the suspicions of abuse neither confirmed nor disapproved, a result it attributed to the limited capacity of a single nation to oversee the activities of multinational firms; and it referred its findings to the EEC Commission (*WuW* 1974: 324–26; *Der Spiegel* 12/3/73: 41).

3. Informal remarks by Eberhard Günther, note 2 *supra*.

4. See, e.g., *WuW* 1987: 130, 218–19, 289, 441, 452–53, 646–47.

5. The leading comparative treatise on U.S. and EEC antitrust law, Hawk, Barry, *United States, Common Market and International Antitrust: A Comparative Guide*, 4 vols. (2d ed. 1987), is cited here as "Hawk, *Guide*," without reference to the volume because all citations are to the second volume unless otherwise indicated. Another treatise that covers only the EEC, Toepke, Utz, *EEC Competition Law* (loose leaf), is cited here as "Toepke, *EEC*." Citations to decisions of the Court of Justice are first to the official reports, "E.C.R.," and to the CCH *Common Market Reporter*, as "CCH." Reports of decisions by the European Commission are to the *Official Journal* of the European Community, cited as "O.J."

6. EEC Treaty Art. 85(3). The word "enterprise" is the appropriate American English translation of the French *entrepris* and the German *Unternehmen*," both of which can translate literally as "undertaking." In British English, however, the usage for what Americans call "enterprise" is "undertaking," which makes the standard English translation of the EEC Treaty in this respect awkward to American ears.

7. The one area in which U.S. law provides relief against refusals to deal is when a lawful monopolist controls an essential facility (*Terminal Railroad*, 224 U.S. 383 (1912); *AT&T*, 524 F. Supp. 1331, 1352–53 (1981). Aside from some fringe applications of this doctrine, the rule in the United States is that a seller has a right to refuse to deal, even where there are obvious anticompetitive effects (Adams, G. B. 1985; Zito 1981; Collin 1981).

8. *Hugin/Liptons*, O.J. L 22/23 (Jan. 27, (1978), CCH par. 10,007,*rev'd on other grounds, sub nom. Hugin v. Comm.*, 1979 E.C.R. 1869, CCH par.8524.

9. *ABG-oil companies operating in the Netherlands*, or *BP*, O.J. L 117/1 (May 9, 1977), CCH par.9944, *rev'd sub nom. BP v. Comm.*, 1978 E.C.R. 1513, CCH par.8465.

10. *BP v. Comm.*, 1978 E.C.R. 1513, pars.28–35, 39–42, CCH par.8465; Hawk, *Guide*: 616.

11. *Instituto Chemioterapico Italiano and Commercial Solvents v. Comm.*, 1974 E.C.R. 223, CCH par.8209.

12. Ibid., pars.23–26, CCH at 8819–20; Hawk, *Guide*: 610–610.1.

13. *Europemballage & Continental Can v. Comm.*, 1973 E.C.R. 215, CCH par.8171: Hawk, *Guide*: 660–62.

14. Hawk, *Guide*: Chap. 13; Toepke, *EEC*, Chap. 33; Banks, "Mergers and Partial Mergers under EEC Law," *1987 Fordham Corporate Law Institute*: Chap. 17; Korah, "Joint Ventures (Exemption or Clearance) Merger and Partial Merger," ibid.: Chap. 18; Panel Discussion, ibid., 453; Adler & Belman, "Antimerger Enforcement in Europe—Trends and Prospects," 8 *Int'l Law & Economics* 31 (1973).

10

The Elements of a Competition Policy

WHAT SHOULD GOVERNMENT DO?

Some Reflections On Medieval Medicine and Twentieth-Century Government

The emotional reaction to trusts in the nineteenth century was fueled by a combination of several factors: the novelty of big business, aggravated by the monopolistic image of railroads, and corporations generally, and compounded by the shift of farming from a subsistence economy to the sale of cash crops in a market that was inherently not self-regulating.

World War I changed the public attitude toward large business organizations, and by the end of World War II young people had come to identify with them (Hofstadter 1964). Railroads were no longer the dominant force they once were; and despite the failures of some major antitrust prosecutions, the tendency among those near monopolies that survived legal attack, such as sugar, whisky, and steel, has been to atrophy over the course of time.

Policy has come full circle. As the irritations of the nineteenth century have been largely put to rest as a result of the legal inhibitions placed on large organizations, it has been the irritations caused by these inhibitions themselves that has attracted the main focus of recent public attention, reflected in the current vogue for deregulation and dampening of antitrust enforcement. It is a tempting conclusion to draw from the variety of regulatory follies and antitrust excesses in the decades between World War II and the 1970s that government should simply withdraw from the scene, which is the clear drift of current policy.

But let us put the question in historical perspective. It would have been easier to make a case for banishing the practice of medicine in the nineteenth century than banning the Interstate Commerce Commission (ICC) in the twentieth. Not until the latter nineteenth century did truly scientific medicine as we now know it emerge; before then all manner of useless and dangerous remedies were purveyed in the name of medicine. Adam Smith in the eighteenth century wrote disdainfully of "the absurd prescriptions of the doctors" (*Wealth*: Bk. II, Chap. 3: 364). From the Middle Ages through most of the nineteenth century, the case remains persuasive: "As late as 1860, 'bleed and purge' remained the most common prescription for the treatment of serious disease" (Higgs 1971: 38).

Given that the highly varied, complex, and difficult problems of market malfunction emerged in force only as recently as the latter half of the nineteenth century, and that the governmental response to them was fashioned only around the turn of the century and is essentially all that we have to work with today, the state of the art may fairly be compared to medical practice in medieval times. The mistakes that government has made do not mean that government cannot act effectively, any more than the incompetent remedies of early medicine were proof that medical practice was unneeded or impossible.

History has revealed many governmental mistakes; yet it has also demonstrated many market malfunctions, perception of which has been obscured by exaggerated ideological faith in self-adjusting markets. The oil crisis of 1973 was a vivid demonstration that our conceptual and institutional tools for dealing with market malfunctions are inadequate.

A Competitive Context as an End in Itself

> [A] word is not a crystal, transparent and unchanged, it is the skin of a living thought and may vary greatly in color and content according to the circumstances and the time in which it is used.
> Oliver Wendell Holmes (*Towne* v. *Eisner*, 245 U.S. 418, 425 (1918))

One of the most fundamental sources of confusion in antitrust policy is to take the word "competition" as an objective too literally. This tendency is undiluted in the policy views of the Antitrust Division and in Robert Bork's *Antitrust Paradox*. The paradox Bork posits is that antitrust is supposedly a policy favoring competition and yet the law at points restrains competition by such rules as those against price discrimination and efficiency-creating mergers. Yet even the Sherman Act was never intended as a declaration in favor of competition in this single-minded sense.

Senator Sherman's own views on this point were most explicit in the context of the railroad problem. In the face of strong sentiment to outlaw pooling agreements (which ultimately prevailed), Senator Sherman argued against this, stressing the destructive nature of cutthroat competition (Chap. 2). Senator Sherman's own philosophy did not embrace the extreme view of competition as an unlimited good.

There is in fact a tendency on the part of the most radical antitrust partisans to envision a kind of consumer Valhalla in which businesspeople are forced by severe competition to practically give away their goods and services free. This attitude is nothing new. Senator Platt of Connecticut, who made the decisive speech that sent Sherman's bill to the Judiciary Committee, had earlier attacked this point of view head on, again in the context of the railroad debates:

> [T]here is a class of people in this country who hold that any competition between the railroads is for the public interest. . . . There are shippers who would rejoice to get secret rates . . . and they welcome all competition which puts down prices to unremunerative points. Such individuals gain by such competition, but it is to the . . . demoralization of all business. (Schwartz 1973: vol. 1: 332)

It is no objection to these remarks that they were made in support of a losing cause and in the context of the railroad problem, not the antitrust laws. These same senators were prominent players in both of these debates (Kerr 1908; Coolidge 1910), and what they said in the context of railroads was as much an expression of their personal philosophy toward competition as anything that was said specifically in the context of antitrust legislation. Senator Platt continued:

> I want to look this bugbear of so-called free competition, which it is claimed must not be limited, in the eyes for a few minutes. . . . I have heard much talk of the so-called law of nature and social life and economic life, 'the law of competition and the survival of the fittest.' In the sense in which they are invoked I deny and repudiate them both. (ibid.)

The central purpose of antitrust policy is to set limits to the acquisition and use of private business power. This describes the political philosophy behind both the Sherman Act and the legislation of 1914, as well as behind the leading foreign systems summarized here. It is not a concept of moral wrongdoing punished by criminal sanctions, or an idealized notion of an optimally efficient theoretical system, nor primarily rooted in notions of consumer welfare. Its object is to maintain balance and continuity in the game of business as an end in itself. Competition is valued, but in moderation, not as an absolutist value judgment. As Europeans have long recognized, a competitive context requires some artificial propping, which in some respects involves restraints on competition itself—and that is the proper object of antitrust or, better, of competition policy.

A Competent Assertion of the Public Interest

The word "competent" is used here in the sense not just of personal qualifications, but of a policy mandate broad enough to effectuate a coherent public policy. The major weakness in this respect has been in the specialized regulatory agencies.

It is a typically frustrating experience in government to observe the many occasions on which wise counsel is neglected. Quoted above in the context of "The Railroad Problem" (Chap. 2) were the prescient remarks of Representative Reagan that the proposed railroad commission would never become the prestigious body its creators envisaged because of its very specialized function. The same experience has been repeated in all of the regulated industries. Regulatory agencies with jurisdiction over only one industry are captured by the industry. The result is that the regulators, instead of operating from a strong public interest orientation, tend to become dependent on the specialized expertise of the industry they are supposed to be regulating.

The antitrust agencies do not suffer from this problem, in large measure because of the great breadth of their jurisdiction over an almost complete spectrum of industries. It is also true that the professional staffs of the Antitrust Division and the FTC are highly competent in a professional sense. But even within these agencies, their capacity to effectuate a coherent public policy approach is severely constrained—and distorted—by the narrowness of their mandates. The Antitrust Division, in particular, for all of its professional competence, has its vision skewed by its cowboy enforcement mentality, compounded by the doctrinaire views of economic theory that have taken command in recent years. When this bizarre combination of mandates is directed at complex questions of rearranging corporate and market structures, the process suggests something like approaching the repair of a complex machine equipped only with a bludgeon and a book of charms. The Division's perspective is also skewed by its tunnel vision, as noted earlier. It thinks only in primitive Sherman Act terms, disdainful of much of the 1914 legislation and unconstrained by the political judgments of market malfunction that have led to the establishment of the various regulatory agencies.

In addition to these problems is what might be termed Amateur Hour: Deregulation by an Article of Faith. The current vogue for deregulation is in large measure reflective of the doctrinal notions of economists who accept the idea of self-regulating free markets as an article of faith. The focus of economists' arguments has been on the foibles of the regulatory agencies (MacAvoy 1970; Stigler 1975 (*Citizen*)—and not on the market malfunctions that gave rise to them. That self-regulation can be relied upon in markets that have a history of unsatisfactory performance has never been demonstrated, and what experience we have in that regard is not favorable (Kristol 1978: 107–11).

The solution to this fragmented confusion is to eliminate the specialized agencies and centralize the regulatory function in a single agency with the broadest of mandates, including antitrust, or rather competition, policy. This brings us to the starting point for a restructuring of policy: the institutional framework.

STRUCTURING POLICY

A Focal Point for Competition Policy: Companion to the Federal Reserve

It has been the experience of history in the United States and other leading capitalist economies that a free market system requires at least two pillars of discipline to keep it on track: (1) control over the money supply and banking system and (2) some restraint on the uses of private business power.

The first of these the United States has addressed through the Federal Reserve system, and few would quarrel with the proposition that the Federal Reserve Board has been the most successful and prestigious of the economic regulatory agencies in the nation's history. This vital function is centered in a single, independent agency with a broad base of representation and an organization conducive to the formulation and carrying out of a coherent policy.

The existing institutional structure that addresses the companion problem of maintaining discipline over market power, in contrast, is so scattered about as to make coherent policy all but impossible. The formal responsibility is divided among the courts, the FTC, and the Department of Justice, not to mention the roles played by the various agencies having responsibilities for international trade issues such as dumping, countervailing duties, and special relief from import competition.

If the proposition argued for here and already accepted in the leading European systems is accepted, that is, that the substance of antitrust policy is an economic policy question and not a moral issue, the predominant role that has been left to the courts in our system is inappropriate.

This is not to say that the present system does not have its advantages, and any thought of restructuring it along administrative lines should take account of the most important point made by its defenders. Because a major part of our antitrust legislation, the Sherman Act, is a criminal as well as a civil statute, its enforcement enjoys a degree of independence that purely administrative agencies, with the exception of the Federal Reserve, ordinarily do not. Even a strong-willed president inclined to intervene in antitrust policy is to some degree limited by the special status of a prosecuting official, and this carries over even in purely civil matters. The resistance of even highly loyal top officials in the Justice Department to President Nixon's intervention in regard to International Telephone and Telegraph (ITT) is a classic example of this.

In contrast, the FTC, which is nominally independent, and is indeed beyond the control of the executive branch, is so completely controlled by the legislative branch that it is totally subject to the political whims of the moment. It does not follow, however, that criminal penalties should be imposed on behavior that is not criminal for the purpose of protecting the independence of government agencies.

The fact that the FTC exists is a recognition of the inherent economic policy nature of antitrust. The fact that the president and Congress alike in 1914 wanted to leave the Sherman Act untouched reflected a survival of the moralistic reaction to the era of the trusts. Now that that attitude has largely faded and we have the experience of half a century since 1914, including that of the European systems, it should not seem a radical idea to suggest that the legislation of that year did not go far enough in the direction it took. The example of the Federal Reserve demonstrates that it is possible to create an administrative agency with a degree of independence that the FTC does not possess. Indeed, the further examples of the EEC and West German governments in vesting "antitrust" policy in administrative agencies that exercise policy-making authority over a much broader range of economic issues than the U.S. antitrust agencies shows that a comparable agency in the United States would be both feasible and better suited to present needs.

Should the Federal Trade Commission be strengthened by giving it authority to interpret and enforce the Sherman Act and exercise the additional powers just proposed? The answer must be no, the objective of restructuring should not be impaired by pouring new wine into this old bottle. The independence needed to make an administrative system effective would be rendered suspect by the political history of the FTC. An entirely new agency should be created, with authority over all substantive "antitrust" as well as trade and (economic) regulatory legislation, and the FTC abolished, with certain of its functions transferred to another executive branch agency, as proposed below.

The composition of the agency should also be more carefully structured than the FTC. It needs to be a collegial body to assure an adequate diversity of representation. This can be done by requiring, as Congress has done on many occasions, that a minimum number of seats be filled by persons chosen as representative of specific disciplines or interest groups. Economists there must be, but what has been said on that subject here leads to a recommendation that criteria be included to assure that more than one point of view is represented. Experienced businesspeople should be included, as they have been on the British Restrictive Practices Court, and in sufficient numbers to reflect the diverse nature of business problems. Lawyers, too, should be included for their skills as generalists and problem solvers. (It is interesting to note that an economist many years ago, in fashioning a similar proposal, placed lawyers at the head of his list (Burns, Arthur R. 1936: 574). A chairman, of course, would be needed and should be given sufficient power to lend an element of coherence to this collegial body. The agency, like the Federal Reserve, should be independent of both the executive branch and Congress, though, as suggested below, the president should have a power to override its decisions.

The structures of the EEC and West German systems thus provide useful models for an institutional framework. The role of the new agency proposed here would be essentially the same as these European bodies, its administrative decisions being subject to both judicial review and an executive override.

An important advantage of vesting the decision-making function in an independent agency is that it leaves the executive free to appear as a policy advocate before the agency and Congress, just as the Justice Department has done for years, while the agency retains the responsibility to weigh the executive policy in terms of its own mandate. Routine allegations of error would be subject to judicial review just like decisions of the present FTC. In cases where private damage awards are deemed appropriate, the agency should be given authority to make a finding to that effect, which would be made the basis for a suit to recover in court, allowing the court the usual powers of judicial review over administrative agency decisions.

Separating the Functions of Advocacy and Decision Making

There is, however, one respect in which the examples of the EEC and West Germany, as well as the U.S. FTC, should not be followed. All three violate the separation-of-powers principle by placing within the same chain of command those who play an advocacy role and those who make the decision. This form of organization is unhealthy in at least two respects. One is that the decision to institute a prosecutive action is taken by the same tribunal that makes the final decision—an obvious temptation to prejudice. The other is that those playing an advocacy role within the agency are arguing before decision makers who are also their employers—a circumstance that can inhibit freedom of advocacy on the part of the subordinate. It has been argued in support of the "unity of function" that such conflicts are extremely rare and are also avoided by the professionalism of the participants. This is no excuse for structuring the system in a way that invites conflict of interest. The principal argument for this type of structure is that an agency with a policy-making mandate should have the enforcement means to implement its policy. This same logic would justify giving Congress the enforcement function that the Constitution vests in the executive branch. The executive agency proposed here should provide an adequate enforcement mechanism for policies devised by this independent agency just as the Justice Department enforces regulations imposed by other executive agencies.

The role of the independent agency proposed here should therefore be limited to decision making and policy formulation, including the promulgation of regulations. The advocacy function, where the government is involved, should be performed by a newly formed executive branch agency with a mandate to bring enforcement actions under the governing legislation and regulations, and additionally to act as an advocate for competitive policies generally, including a specific responsibility to further the legitimate interests of consumers and small business. It should be formed in part by an amalgamation of the staffs of the FTC, the Antitrust Division of the Department of Justice, and the Small Business Administration. The overlapping interests of these three different agencies has been lost sight of in their separate institutional incarnations. Their consolidation would be an impetus to coherence of policy.

Another point of fundamental importance is that individuals should have free access to file complaints before the agency. A major objective of this restructuring being to shift the function of policy making from the courts to a centralized administrative agency, private parties should not be deprived of their right of access to redress by a concept such as governs the Federal Trade Commission, that is, that only the agency can initiate a complaint—a thoroughly bad idea.

This shifting of the focal point of decision making from the courts to the agency will of course make for a substantial volume of litigative activity. To accommodate this, a page may be lifted from the example of the British Restrictive Practices Court, a mixed body including both lawyers and businesspeople. And one hopes, as has been the British experience, the procedures of such a body would be designed to act much more expeditiously than the court system. There would need to be not just one such body, but a diversity of panels, geographically dispersed, with all subject to appeals to the governing body of the agency.

Altogether, such a structure should contribute to coherence, expedition, and integrity of the policy. The unified administrative structure would provide coherence and its administrative focus, expedition; while the independent freedom of advocacy by both the proposed executive agency and private parties would be reinforced by the option of a forthright presidential override. As in the German system, where the minister of economics has the power to overrule the Federal Cartel Office, the agency is left free to call its own shots, undistorted by political considerations, which are nonetheless free to be given effect in their own separate and legitimate mode.

Integrating Antitrust, Regulatory, Trade, and Tax Policy

The new independent agency should also be vested with the powers presently lodged in the variety of agencies that administer competitive rules specifically applicable to international trade, as well as what survives of the powers of the independent regulatory agencies. This would give the agency both an added dimension of coherence and a broader perspective, comparable to that of the EEC Commission. Although the area of tax policy is much too broad to be consigned to this agency, considerations of tax policy that affect competitive conditions should be a part of the agency's role as an advocate of competition policy. The Antitrust Division of the Department of Justice, despite its broad role as an advocate of competitive policies, has traditionally made a unilateral decision to abstain from commenting on tax issues, thus leaving a void in one of the more important areas of government policy that affects the competitive process.

Spelling Out the Rules

A very large portion of existing U.S. antitrust law has been invented by the courts under the Delphic standards of the Sherman Act. The Clayton Act adds some specificity but lacks the comprehensive coverage, in particular, of the German legislation. That legislation leaves much leeway for administrative discretion, but it also provides much more guidance to decision makers than the hodgepodge structure of U.S. antitrust law and related legislation. A comprehensive rewriting of the legislation, including broad rule-making authority in the new independent agency, should provide the foundation for a modern "competition policy."

Handling Exceptions Within the System

The independent agency should have both rule-making authority and the authority to permit exceptions from even legislated rules, just as the

EEC Commission is permitted to do under Article 85(3), and the German Federal Cartel Office under a variety of legislative provisions.

A Political Safety Valve

In addition to the independent agency's authority to grant routine exceptions as permitted by Article 85(3) of the EEC Treaty, there should be an express provision for presidential override, comparable to that given the German minister of economics. This would avoid pressures to contort the law when political pressures warrant exceptions; and by vesting the authority in the president, its use would be exceptional and subject to the balancing process of the White House staffing system.

An Institutional Gadfly

One of the innovations in the West German legislation is the formal establishment of a group of nongovernment experts to make periodic recommendations on competition policy. There is real merit to having such a mechanism, for not only pressures of politics generally but also internal institutional pressures within government often lead to the suppression of ideas that are potentially in the public interest. An independent study group of outsiders to comment and make recommendations on the national competition policy could be a useful addition to the policy-making apparatus.

THE TOOLS OF POLICY: DISCARDS AND ADDITIONS

Let us begin the discards with the Sherman Act. The idea may at first seem unthinkable. The act has acquired an enormous prestige; it has become a part of our culture. Years of enforcement activity have brought it home to the business community, and there is an immense body of jurisprudence lending specificity to its broad and general language.

Yet it is just this mind-set and encrustation that we need to be rid of. The Sherman Act has been transmogrified by the Supreme Court into something quite unlike what its legislative authors had in mind, and the vast accumulation of jurisprudence is rather an accidental series of reactions to an incoherent policy framework that has distorted and at times even perverted policy. To the extent that the jurisprudence has developed useful, undistorted principles, these can be codified through new legislation.

Beyond the distortions attributable to what the courts have done with it, the act itself is something of an unnatural creature that has to bear much of the responsibility for what the courts have done. Its most fundamental flaw was to link the common law concept of contracts in restraint of trade with the idea of criminality. When one recalls the extravagant behavior of the Standard Oil Company in its war with the Pennsylvania Railroad, and other nineteenth-century abuses, it is easy to understand why such behavior was branded criminal. But such behavior, to the extent that it is criminal, can be reached under other laws protecting property and business rights. The rules that are unique to antitrust are rules of policy, not criminality.

The first and most essential step toward the creation of a realistic competition policy is to dispense with the idea that the subject matter is simply one of law enforcement. It is not. It is pure policy, an artificial intervention by government into the marketplace for the purpose of preserving political/economic values, and it should be recognized for just that.

With the elimination of the Sherman Act, and all notions of criminality, our next discard is the Justice Department, as already indicated above in the proposed institutional restructuring. This is not altogether a happy choice because the element of professionalism that this strong legal institution has brought to antitrust policy has been one of the more positive features of the existing antitrust regime. But competent lawyers can be employed by other institutions as well, and the criminal enforcement mentality of the Justice Department is a distorting and confusing element that should be eliminated.

Another beneficial discard that goes with the Sherman Act is the confusing term "monopolize." It was a very appropriate term to deal with the phenomenon of the Standard Oil Company, but little else since. Its main disadvantage is that it describes an extreme case, one rarely encountered in the real economic world. Although the Supreme Court and Judge Learned Hand have taken a commendably flexible approach to the meaning of "monopolize," which has prevented it from becoming the dead letter that a literalist interpretation would have ensured, the concept of monopoly is still too narrow to describe the real problems that stem from the existence of market power. Lower court judges, in particular, tend to get hung up by the concept of "monopoly," seeing no problem, no violation of the law, when there is something less than 100 percent monopoly. The term represents something that was genuinely feared to be a realistic threat in the early stages of industrial development in the nineteenth century, but that specter has become obsolete in the closing decades of the twentieth. The concept of monopoly in the United States has been the source of much confusion, its presence in the law appearing to provide a broad safeguard while actually masking the problems of abusive uses of market power in circumstances not extreme enough to be branded monopolization.

The reliance of the law on the concept of monopoly has had another, and fundamentally distorting, effect. When the only test a court has to apply is that of monopoly, it is naturally led to ask the question, Just what is being monopolized? hence, injects the concept of the relevant market. But the boundaries between markets tend to be fuzzy, and the existence and abuse of economic power can take place without regard to an artificial definition of market boundaries. This factor has been given explicit recognition in the German law concept of a firm with *überragende* power, a term that does not translate precisely into English but includes the concepts of power stemming from large financial resources, a prestigious trade position, and the like. The concept of the relevant market is also used in defining the European concept of a market-dominating enterprise, though the influence that the U.S. law has had on the formation of European concepts gives rise to the suspicion that it is something of a U.S. import.

There is thus much to be gained through the avoidance of confusion by discarding the concept of monopoly from the law. Since the concept of abuse control reaches everything that the concept of monopolizing does—and much more as well—nothing is lost by discarding it. The EEC and West German laws do not use it at all as a legislative standard, relying instead on the principle of abuse control. The British law, which does use it, is careful to separate it from the normal law enforcement system, treating it as a political problem.

Although logically unnecessary, it may be conceded that the concept of monopolization has such a powerful hold on U.S. political traditions that its complete discard may be unrealistic. Preservation of the concept itself would do no real harm so long as it is relegated to being just one cumulative tool in a revised system that incorporates the principle of abuse control.

Another discard already indicated by the proposed institutional restructuring is the Federal Trade Commission. Not only has it failed to become the dominating policy-forming body envisaged by its legislative creators; it also projects an illusory appearance of independence that is belied by its total subordinance to the whims of Congress. Its functions, as proposed earlier, should be transferred and divided between the proposed independent agency (the decision-making function, including the promulgation of rules and regulations) and the proposed new executive agency (the prosecutorial function).

Turning to additions, an obvious point of departure is to substitute for the Sherman Act's vague prohibition of contracts in restraint of trade a more detailed codification of what is prohibited and what is not, as in the German law, along with an express power in the administrative authorities to make exceptions, as is done in Article 85 of the EEC Treaty and somewhat more complexly under the German law.

Second is the addition of an abuse control concept. The idea that preventing concentrations of private business power is the central purpose of antitrust policy is obsolete. The idea is not totally irrelevant, however, particularly in the context of mergers. But the fictional notion so long indulged by the Antitrust Division, that the solution to the problem is the prevention of concentrated business power, should be recognized for what it is—a mirage. There is a point beyond the level of business concentration that can be identified as unjustified in terms of business practicalities, but even this does not suffice to prevent substantial, defensible concentrations of business power. Both the prevention of excessive concentrations of business control and the containment of defensible concentrations can be addressed through the concept of abuse control, as it has been in both the German and EEC approaches to merger control and abuse control in general. As to mergers, the EEC/German test of whether a merger would create or strengthen a market-dominating position provides a more comprehensible standard than the Clayton Act test of a substantial lessening of competition.

Another useful addition would be meaningful monetary penalties. The traditional limited fines give a firm considerable leeway to calculate that the profit from a violation may far exceed any monetary fines imposed. The German law expressly provides for the disgorging of illegal gains. Although as noted in Chapter 9 this has led to problems of proof, there are various ways in which the concept may be implemented, and it is highly desirable in principle.

Somewhere between the categories of discards and additions is the mixed case of treble damages. The concept serves a very valid social purpose in enabling a damaged small firm to obtain legal representation when by reason of its very injury it lacks the financial resources to pay customary legal fees. The conversion proposed here of a judicially oriented to an administratively based system should permit speedy remedies in some cases that will preclude the incursion of damages in the first place; of course, there will be a remainder of cases in which the damage has occurred and needs to be recompensed. At the other end of the spectrum are such incongruous cases as that of a foreign government recovering three times the damages alleged to result from a multimillion-dollar price-fixing case. An intermediate solution is to adopt a sliding scale (e.g., trebling of damages up to $1 million, doubling for up to $2 million, and single damages thereafter).

THE INTERNATIONAL DIMENSION

The sorest subject concerning the application of U.S. antitrust law in an international context has been the extraterritorial enforcement of the law. Foreign countries have been particularly offended by the fact that the U.S. law attaches criminal penalties to business behavior that is not so regarded in other countries and that in many instances is not even viewed as illegal. To this aggravation has been added the burdensome intrusion of U.S. discovery practice. The result has been a widespread adoption of so-called blocking legislation (Atwood 1986: 327; ABA 1984: 527–80). The problem has in recent years been somewhat mitigated by the willingness of the courts and the enforcement agencies to follow the principle of comity, though the problem still exists (ABA, ibid.).

Jurisdictional problems aside, there remains an issue of conflicting legal standards, a problem dealt with by the courts under that branch of the law known as conflict of laws or private international law. While a number of principles have been developed for resolving such conflicts, one of the most universally accepted solutions is to compare the two legal standards and, if they are essentially the same, to apply that standard without making a choice of law. If the U.S. law were redesigned as proposed here, eliminating criminal penalties and shifting the enforcement emphasis to an administrative agency rather than the courts, the substantive regime on both sides of the Atlantic would be substantially the same. This would provide an avenue of solution that courts and arbitral tribunals have both favored: When the substantive law in both jurisdictions is the same, there is no need to choose between them; the common principle is applied (Lipstein 1942: 151).

Moreover, by creating the new agency proposed here with broad authority to deal with trade as well as antitrust issues, U.S. officials would be able to deal with the more broadly oriented officials of the European Community on a much more common basis than is presently possible. If the issues are seen by both sides as matters of economic policy rather than law enforcement, much conflict could be avoided and a more rational policy dialogue would be made possible. A common outlook that blends antitrust and trade policies into the same spectrum should make for a more rational and mutually acceptable framework for the governance of international trade. Upon such a foundation there might some day be a sufficient consensus to create an international regime by treaty (Timberg 1953).

QUESTIONS FOR POLICY

Having put aside the major shibboleths of the confused U.S. antitrust tradition—excessive faith in the concept of self-regulating free markets, the view of competition as an unlimited good, the notion of consumer welfare through cost minimization as the objective of antitrust policy, the false value judgment that takes a maximization of physical output as a touchstone of policy, the rationale for free international trade proceeding from this same premise through the concept of relative advantage, and the view of antitrust as a moral, criminal issue—a whole series of new questions opens up. In Europe, where "antitrust" policy has operated free of these confusions, the dialogue in both litigated cases and policy forums is much richer than in the United States. More questions are open to discussion; thought is not frozen by invariable per se rules, and a more genuine Rule of Reason is applied than at any time in the United States since the *Trenton Potteries* decision of 1927.

Is there such a thing as a business firm getting just too big? The consistent answer in the United States has been no; but the German law has opened up this question with its "marriage of elephants law" and the experience of the split-up of the Standard Oil Company and AT&T in the United States with resulting gains in dynamism suggests that there may in fact be such a problem.

Does a tax policy that permits a corporation to deduct interest payments but not dividends create an artificial incentive to excessive corporate accumulations?

In cases where size is not deemed excessive but creates substantial market or business power is there not a potential for abuse that should be subject to some kind of government supervision, short of outright regulation?

Should firms with established trade names whose merchandise is vital to individual retailers be permitted to refuse to sell arbitrarily, as they are presently permitted in the United States but not in Europe?

Does it make sense in times of distress brought on by industrywide overcapacity to allow some kind of government-supervised cooperative plan to preserve the existence of multiple firms rather than forcing them into a cutthroat competition from which only one or a few can survive?

Are there some businesses that by reason of the circumstances in which they operate—crude oil production, agriculture, highway construction contracting, and so on—cannot be expected to compete in the same way as most other businesses and thus should be allowed specially tailored variations in the rules?

Does it make sense in the context of business to impose some restraints on competitive freedom for the sake of preserving and fostering a continued, balanced competitive context such as is done in professional league sports?

And if there are legitimate reasons for allowing such restraints within the domestic economy, should not the same logic be applied to international trade?

And so on. The list is endless. Once dogma is put aside, the problems of administering a competition policy do not admit of the kind of simplistic assumptions that have so characterized traditional U.S. antitrust policy. That policy is overdue to go through a molting process, to cast off its outgrown rigid shell, broaden its horizons, ask meaningful questions, and base policy on market realities rather than ideology—or mumpsimus.

11

Epilogue: A Final Consultation with Our Friendly Cynic

Fair is fair. We have subjected the existing antitrust regime to the acid test of criticism by one of a cynical persuasion. It is only fair to yield up this manuscript to the same kind of scrutiny.

Oliver: So, you have purported to address this subject from the perspective of a government staff person. Yet, having made an elaborate argument for change in the law, you have not provided a draft of proposed legislation. Isn't this incomplete staff work?

Author: You have a point. But it is bad luck. Recall the Kaysen-Turner book of 1959 that made an ambitious proposal for revision of the antitrust laws and included a draft of proposed legislation. That proposal is now six feet under. More basically, there are many different versions of specific legislation that would be compatible with the basic philosophy expressed here. A specific legislative proposal would tend to preempt the basic argument. There is much room for design flexibility, as exhibited by the European models cited here. There is no one ideal system, and it would create a misleading impression to propose something pretending to be that.

Oliver: I am not sure I believe that, but let it pass. There is a more basic problem. You make the same mistake as your predecessors whom you criticize: You assume that the government can control the situation. The reality of the present-day world economy is a new form of feudalism. Multinational corporations have an infinite capacity to circumvent any control measures that national governments—which are as limited as the state governments whose limitations Senator Sherman pointed out—can possibly impose. The West German antitrust regime, which you praise so highly for its performance in the oil crisis of 1973, thereafter threw up its hands after being unable to sort out the facts of the multinational oil companies' pricing practices, passing the buck to the EEC Commission, which did nothing. Governments the world over are tugged this way and that by competing interests. Corporations, in contrast, have single-minded managements clearly focused on whatever they want to achieve. The contest between the modern corporation and any government is a mismatch; the corporation has all the options at its disposal; the government, bounded by all manner of special interests, is the proverbial pitiful, helpless giant.

Author: Excuse me, the phone is ringing.

Bibliography

ABA, Antitrust Section. *Antitrust Law Developments*. 2d ed. Chicago: ABA Press, 1984.

Abels, Jules. *The Rockfeller Billions*. New York: Macmillan, 1965.

Adams, Charles F. "The Granger Movement." 120 *North American Review* 394 (1875).

Adams, G. B. "Antitrust Constraints on Single Firm Refusals to Deal by Monopolists in the European Economic Community and in the United States." 20 *Texas Int'l. L. J.* 1 (1985).

Adams, John (ed.). *Institutional Economics: Contributions to the Development of Holisitic Economics*. Boston: Martinus Nijhoff, 1980.

Adams, Walter (ed.). *The Structure of American Industry*. 5th ed. New York: Macmillan Publishing Co.; London: Collier Macmillan Publishers, 1977.

Adelman, M. A. "Efficiency of Resource Use in Crude Petroleum." 31 *Southern Economic Journal* 101 (1965).

———. "The World Oil Outlook," in Clawson, Marion (ed.). *National Resources and International Development*: 27–126. Baltimore: Johns Hopkins Univ. Press, 1964.

———. *The World Petroleum Market*. Baltimore: Johns Hopkins Univ. Press, 1972; 2d printing, 1974.

Adler, Howard J. & Belman, Murray J. "Antimerger Enforcement in Europe—Trends and Prospects." 8 *J. Int'l. L. & Econ.* 31(1973).

Andrews, Phillip W. S. *On Competition in Economic Theory*. London: Macmillan; New York: St. Martin's Press, 1965.

Andrews, Phillip W. S. & Brunner, Elizabeth. *Studies in Pricing*. London: Macmillan Press, 1975.

Areeda, Phillip & Turner, Donald. *Antitrust Law*. Boston: Little, Brown & Co., 1978.

Armentano, D. T. *The Myths of Antitrust: Economic Theory and Legal Cases*. New Rochelle, N.Y.: Arlington House, 1972.

Arnold, Thurman. *The Folklore of Capitalism*. New Haven, Conn.: Yale Univ. Press, 1937.

Atwood, James. "Blocking Statutes and Foreign Sovereign Compulsion: Recent Developments and the Proposed Restatement," in Hawk, Barry (ed.). *1985 Fordham Corporate Law Institute*. New York: Matthew Bender, 1986.

Backman, Jules. *Price Practices and Price Policies*. New York: Ronald Press, 1953.

Bailey, Duncan & Boyle, Stanley. "Sales Revenue Maximization: An Empirical Vindication." 5 *Indus. Org. Rev.* 46 (1977).

Baker, Donald. "Antitrust and Deregulated Communications." 28 *Antitrust Bulletin* 1 (1983) (with Beverly Baker).

———. "The Antitrust Division, Department of Justice: The Role of Competition in Regulated Industries." 11 *Boston College Industrial & Commercial L. Rev.* 571 (1970).

———. "Antitrust Remedies against Government-inspired Boycotts, Shortages, and Squeezes: Wandering on the Road to Mecca." 61 *Cornell L. Rev.* 911 (1976).

———. "Competition and Regulation: Charles River Bridge Recrossed." 60 *Cornell L. Rev.* 159 (1975).

———. "Does Antitrust Law Preclude the Need for Geographic Constraints on Banking?" 93 *Banking L.J.* 1005 (1976).

Baldwin, William. "The Motives of Managers, Environmental Restraints, and the Theory of Managerial Enterprise." 78 *Qtrly J. of Economics* 238 (1964).

Balogh, Thomas. *The Irrelevance of Conventional Economics*. New York: Liveright Pub. Co. (W. W. Norton), 1982.

Banks, Karen. "Mergers and Partial Mergers under EEC law," 1987 *Fordam Corporate Law Institute* 373. New York: Matthew Bender, 1988.

Barber, William J. *A History of Economic Thought*. New York: Penguin Books, 1967.

Bartram, Dirk. "Zur Problematik der 'Ministererlaubnis,' " *WuW* 1979: 372.

Baumol, William J. *Business Behavior, Value and Growth*, Rev. ed. 1959. New York: Harcourt, Brace & World, 1967.

———. "Economic Models and Mathematics," in Krupp, S R. (ed.). *The Structure of Economic Science*: 88 (1966).

———. *Economic Theory and Operations Analysis*. 4th ed. Englewood Cliffs, N.J.: Prentice-Hall, 1977.

Baumol, William J. & Blinder, Alan S. *Economic Principles and Policy*. New York: Harcourt Brace, 1979.

Baxter, William F. "Interview." 51 *Antitrust L.J.* 23 (1982).

———. "Interview." 52 *Antitrust L.J.* 23 (1983).

———. See also Tollison, *infra*.

Benson, Lee. *Merchants, Farmers, and Railroads: Railroads and New York Politics, 1850–1887*. Cambridge, Mass.: Harvard Univ. Press, 1955.

Bezanson, Anne. *Wholesale Prices in Philadelphia, 1852–1896*. Philadelphia: Univ. of Pennsylvania Press, 1954.

Bittlingmayer, George. "Decreasing Average Cost and Competition: A New Look at the Addyston Case." 25 *J. of L. & Econ.* 201 (1982).

Blair, John. *The Control of Oil*. New York: Pantheon Books, 1976.

Blaisdell, Thomas L. *The Federal Trade Commission*. New York: Columbia Univ. Press, 1932.

Blake, Harlan (ed.). *Business Regulation in the Common Market Nations: West Germany*. 3 vols. New York: McGraw-Hill, 1969.

Blaug, Mark. Book review. 56 *Am. Econ. Rev.* 203 (1966).

———. *Economic Theory in Retrospect*. 3d ed. Cambridge (Eng.); New York: Cambridge Univ. Press, 1978.

———. *Ricardian Economics*. New Haven, Conn.: Yale Univ. Press, 1958.

Bok, Derek. "Section 7 of the Clayton Act and the Merging of Law and Economics." 74 *Harv. L. Rev.* 226 (1960).

Bonar, James. *Letters of David Ricardo to Thomas Robert Malthus*. Oxford: Clarendon Press, 1887.

———. *Philosophy and Political Economy in Some of Their Historical Relations*. 3d ed. 1893; 2d impr. 1922. London: Allen & Unwin; New York: Humanities Press, 1967.

———. *The Tables Turned*. London: P. S. King & Son, 1931; 1970 repr.

Bonar, James & Hollander, J. H. *Letters of David Ricardo to Hutches Trower and Others, 1811–1823*. Oxford: Clarendon Press, 1899.

Bork, Robert H. *The Antitrust Paradox: A Policy at War with Itself*. New York: Basic Books, 1978.

———. "The Goals of Antitrust Policy." 57 *Am. Econ. Rev. (Proceedings)* 242 (1967).

———. "Legislative Intent and the Policy of the Sherman Act, 9 *J. of Law & Economics* 7 (1966).

Bork, Robert, Bowman, Ward, Harlan, Blake & Jones, William. "The Goals of Antitrust: A Dialogue on Policy." 65 *Columbia L. Rev.* 363 (1965).

Boulding, Kenneth E. "In Defense of Monopoly." 59 *Qtrly J. of Economics* 524 (1945).

———. "The Economics of Knowledge and the Knowledge of Economics." 56 *Am. Econ. Rev. (Proceedings)* 1 (1966).

———. "A New Look at Institutionalism." 47 *Am. Econ. Rev. (Proceedings)* 1 (1957).

———. *Religious Perspectives of College Teaching in Economics*. New Haven, Conn.: Edward W. Hazen Foundation, 1951.

Boyer, Allen. "Form as Substance: A Comparison of Antitrust Regulation by Consent Decrees in the USA, Reports of the Monopolies and Mergers Commission in the UK, and Grants of Clearance by the European Commission." 32 *Int'l. Comp. L. Qtrly* 904 (1983).

Brems, Hans. "Marshall on Mathematics." 18 *J. of Law & Economics* 583 (1975).

Bronfenbrenner, M. "Observations on the Chicago School(s)." 70 *J. of Political Economy* 72 (1962).

Brozen, Yale. "The Antitrust Task Force Deconcentration Recommendation." 13 *J. of Law & Economics* 279 (1970).

Brown, Dee. *Hear That Lonesome Whistle Blow*. New York: Holt, Rinehart & Winston, 1977.

Bureau of Corporations (U.S. Dept. Cmrce). *Report of the Commissioner of Corporations on the Petroleum Industry*. Washington, D.C.: G.P.O., 1907.

Burns, Arthur R. *The Decline of Competition*. New York: McGraw-Hill, 1936.

Cabinet Task Force in Oil Import Control. *The Oil Import Question*. Washington, D.C.: G.P.O., 1970.

Carnegie, Andrew. *Empire of Business*. New York: Doubleday, Page, 1902, 1933 (repr. of article in 148 *No. Am. Econ. Rev.* (1889).

Carr, Albert. *John D. Rockefeller's Secret Weapon*. New York: McGraw-Hill, 1962.

Caspari, Manfred. "State Aids in the EEC." in Hawk, Barry (ed.). *1983 Fordham Corporate Law Institute: Antitrust and Trade Policies of the European Economic Community*. 1 New York: Matthew Bender, 1984.

Chamberlin, Edward. *The Theory of Monopolistic Competition*. 5th ed. Cambridge, Mass.: Harvard Univ. Press, 1946.

Chandler, Alfred D., Jr. *The Changing Economic Order*. New York: Harcourt, Brace & World, 1968.

———. *The Visible Hand: The Managerial Revolution in America*. Cambridge, Mass.: Harvard Univ. Press, 1977.

Chapman, Dudley. "Exports and Antitrust: Must Competition Stop at the Water's Edge?" 6 *Vanderbilt J. of Transnational Law* 399 (1973).

Chicago School of Economics. Symposium issue on the institutionalist perspective. 9 *J. of Economic Issues* 585 (1975).

Clapham J. H. "Of Empty Economic Boxes." 32 *The Economic Journal* 305 (1922), repr. in Stigler, George & Boulding, Kenneth. (eds.). *Readings in Price Theory*: 119. Homewood, Ill.: Richard D. Irwin, 1952.

Clark, J. B. & Clark, J. M. *The Control of Trusts*. 1914, Rev. ed. New York: Augustus M. Kelley, 1971 repr.

Clark, J. M. *Competition as a Dynamic Process*. Washington, D.C.: The Brookings Institution, 1961.

———. *Guideposts in Times of Change*. New York: Harper & Bros., 1949.

———. "Toward a Concept of Workable Competition." 30 (1) *Am. Econ. Rev.* No. 2, Pt. 1, p. 241 (1940).

Clark, John M., Douglas, Paul, Hollander, Jacob, Morrow, Melchior, Palyi & Viner, Jacob *Adam Smith, 1776–1926*. 1926. New York: Augustus M. Kelley, 1966 repr.

Clark, Victor. *History of Manufacturers in the United States, 1607–1860*. Washington, D.C.: Carnegie Institute of Washington, 1916, 1929 ed.

Coase, R. H. "The Marginal Cost Controversy." 13 *Economica, N.S.* 169 (1946).

———. "The Marginal Cost Controversy: Some Further Comments." 14 *Economica, N.S.* 150 (1947).

———. "Marshall on Method." 18 *J. of Law & Economics* 25 (1975).

———. "The Nature of the Firm." 4 *Economica* 386 (1937), repr. in Stigler, George & Boulding, Kenneth (eds.). *Readings in Price Theory*: 331. Homewood, Ill.: Richard D. Irwin, 1952.

Coats, A. W. "The First Two Decades of the American Economic Association." 50 *Am. Econ. Rev.* 555 (1960).

Cochran, Thomas. "The First Ricardian Mathematical Model." 2 *History of Political Economy* 419 (1970).
Cochran, Thomas & Miller, William. *The Age of Enterprise*. Rev. ed. New York: Harper & Row, 1961.
Collin, Thomas. "Refusals to Deal by Monopolists—Recent Decisions." 14 *Akron L. Rev.* 549 (1981).
Commons, John R. *The Legal Foundations of Capitalism*. Madison: Univ. of Wisconsin Press, 1932, 1957.
Coolidge, Louis. *An Old Fashioned Senator: Orville H. Platt of Connecticut*. 1910. Port Washington, N.Y.: Kennikat Press, 1971.
Copp, E. Anthony. *Regulating Competition in Oil: Government Intervention in the U.S. Refining Industry*. College Station: Texas A&M Univ. Press, 1976.
Copp, John S. 40 *ABA Antitrust L. J.* 991 (1971).
Cournot, Augustin. *Researches into the Mathematical Principles of Wealth*. 1838. New York: Augustus M. Kelley, 1960 trans. and repr.
Cramer, Clarence. *American Enterprise: Free and Not So Free*. Boston: Little, Brown & Co., 1972.
Crew, Eugene. "The Chicago School Teaches the Supreme Court a Dubious Lesson." 1 *Antitrust* 11 (1986).
Cullom Report. Schwartz, Bernard (ed.). *The Economic Regulation of Business and Industry: A Legislative History of U.S. Regulatory Agencies*. New York: Chelsea House Publishers, 1973.
Dawson, John P. *The Oracles of the Law*. Ann Arbor: Univ. of Michigan Press, 1968.
Deane, Phyllis. *The Evolution of Economic Ideas*. Cambridge: Cambridge Univ. Press, 1978.
Debreu, Gerard. "Economic Theory in the Mathematical Mode." 74 *Am. Econ. Rev.* 267 (1984).
———. *Theory of Value*. New York: Wiley & Sons; London: Chapman & Hall, 1959.
———. *New York Times* 10/23/83: F15; *Washington Post* 10/18/83: A18b and 10/19/83: B3a.
Delong, James. "The Role, If Any, of Economic Analysis in Antitrust Litigation." 12 *Southwestern Univ. L. Rev.* 298 (1981).
Deringer, Arved. *The Competition Law of the European Economic Community*. New York: Commerce Clearing House, 1968.
Dession, George. "The Trial of Economic and Technological Issues of Fact II." 58 *Yale L. J.* 1242 (1949).
Destler, Chester M. *Roger Sherman and the Independent Oil Men*. Ithaca, N.Y.: Cornell Univ. Press, 1967.
Dewey, Donald. "The Economic Theory of Antitrust: Science or Religion?" 50 *Virginia L. Rev.* 413 (1964).
———. *The Theory of Imperfect Competition: A Radical Reconstruction*. New York: Columbia Univ. Press, 1969.
Diamond, Sigmund (ed.). *The Nation Transformed*. New York: George Braziller, 1963.
Doganis, Rigas. *Flying Off Course*. London: Allen & Unwin, 1985.

Drucker, Peter F. *The Concept of the Corporation*. New York: John Day Co., 1946, 1964.

Dudden, Arthur P. *Antimonopolism, 1865–1890: The Historical Background and the Intellectual Origins of the Antitrust Movement in the United States*. Ph.D. Thesis. Ann Arbor, Michigan: Univ. Microfilms, 1950.

———. "Men against Monopoly." 18 *J. of the History of Ideas* 587 (1957).

Eads, George. "Airline Capacity Limitation Controls: Public Vice or Public Virtue?" 64 *Am. Econ. Rev.* 365 (1974).

Ebel, Hans-Rudolf. "Vierte Kartellrechtsnovelle in Kraft Getreten." *Der Betrieb* 1105 (1980).

Edwards, Corwin. "American and German Policy toward Conduct by Powerful Enterprises: A Comparison." 8 *J. of Reprints for Antitrust Law & Economics* 193 (1977); also at 23 *Antitrust Bulletin* 83 (1978).

———. *Control of Cartels and Monopolies*. Dobbs Ferry, N.Y.: Oceana Publications, 1967.

———. "Policy toward Big Business: What Lessons after Forty Years?" 9 *J. of Economic Issues* 343 (1975).

———. *Trade Regulations Overseas: The National Laws*. Dobbs Ferry, N.Y.: Oceana Publications, 1966.

Edwards, Dudley R. & Williams, T. Desmond (eds.). *The Great Famine*. New York: New York Univ. Press, 1957.

EEC Commission. *Ninth Report on Competition Policy*, 1980.

———. *Seventeenth Report on Competition Policy*. Brussels: Luxembourg Office for Official Publications of the European Communities, 1988.

———. *Sixteenth Report on Competition Policy*. Ibid. 1987.

Eichner, Alfred S. *The Emergence of Oligopoly: Sugar Refining as a Case Study*. Baltimore: Johns Hopkins Univ. Press, 1969.

———. (ed.). *Why Economics Is Not Yet a Science*. New York: M. E. Sharpe, 1983.

———. "Why Economics Is Not Yet a Science." 17 *J. of Economic Issues* 507 (1983).

Ekelund, Robert & Hebert, Robert. *A History of Economic Theory and Method*. 2d ed. New York: McGraw-Hill, 1983.

Elzinga, Kenneth. "The Goals of Antitrust: Other than Competition and Efficiency, What Else Counts?" 125 *Univ. of Pa. L. Rev.* 1191 (1977).

———. "Predatory Pricing: The Case of the Gunpowder Trust." 13 *J. of Law & Economics* 223 (1970).

Emmerich, Volker. *Das Wirtschaftsrecht der Öffentlichen Unternehmen*. Bad Homburg v.d.H/Berlin/Zürich: Verlag Gehlen, 1969.

Erhard, Ludwig. *Prosperity through Competition*, 3d ed. London: Thames & Hudson, 1960.

Faulkner, Harold. *American Economic History*. 8th ed. New York: Harper & Brothers, 1960.

Federal Cartel Office (*Bundeskartellamt*). *Bericht des Bundeskartellamtes über seine Tätigkeit in den Jahren 1979/1980 sowie über Lage und Entwicklung auf seinem Aufgabensgebiet (Sec. 50 GWB)*. (*Drucksache* 9/565, 1981).

Fellner, William. *Emergence and Content of Economic Analysis*. New York: McGraw-Hill, 1960.

Fetter, F. W. "The Rise and Decline of Ricardian Economics." 1 *History of Political Economy* 67 (1969).

Flynn, J. T. *God's Gold: The Story of Rockefeller and His Times*. Westport, Conn.: Greenwood Press, 1982.
Foley, Vernard. *The Social Physics of Adam Smith*. West Lafayette, Ind.: Purdue Univ. Press, 1976.
Fordham Corporate Law Institute. Hawk, Barry (ed.). New York: Matthew Bender, 1988 (and earlier annual volumes, cited by year).
Fox, Eleanor. "Abuse of a Dominant Position under the Treaty of Rome—A Comparison with U.S. Law." in Hawk, Barry (ed.). *1983 Fordham Corporate Law Institute*: 367. New York: Matthew Bender, 1984.
Fox, Eleanor & Halverson, James (eds.). *Antitrust Policy in Transition: The Convergence of Law & Economics*. Chicago: ABA Press, 1984.
Frederick, John. *The Development of American Commerce*. New York: D. Appleton & Co., 1932.
Friedman, Lawrence M. *A History of American Law*. New York: Simon & Schuster, 1973.
Friedman, Milton. *Price Theory*. Chicago: Aldive Press, 1976.
Friedrich, Manfred. "Zur Auslegung des Secs. 8 Abs. 1 GWB," 1979 *WuW* 85.
———. *There's No Such Thing as a Free Lunch*. LaSalle, Ill.: Open Court, 1975.
Galbraith, John K. *American Capitalism*. Boston: Houghton Mifflin, 1952.
Garraty, John. *The New Commonweath, 1877–1890*. New York: Harper & Row, 1968.
Georgescu-Roegen, Nicholas. *The Entropy Law and the Economic Process*. Cambridge, Mass.: Harvard Univ. Press, 1971.
Gilchrist, D. T. "Albert Fink and the Pooling System." 34 *Business History Rev.* 24 (1960).
Goldschmid, Harvey. J., Mann, Michael & J. Fred Weston (eds.). *Industrial Concentration: The New Learning*. Boston: Little, Brown & Co., 1974.
Gordon, Wendell. *Institutional Economics*. Austin: Univ. of Texas Press, 1980.
Gramm, Warren. "The Selective Interpretation of Adam Smith." 14 *J. of Economic Issues* 119 (1980).
Green, Celilliane. "The 1982 AT&T Consent Decree—Strengthening the Antitrust Procedures and Penalties Act." 27 *How. L. J.* 1611 (1984).
Greene, H. H. "AT&T Divesture and Consumers." 5 *Univ. of Bridgeport L. Rev.* 251 (1984).
Gressley, Gene (ed.). *Voltaire and the Cowboy: The Letters of Thurman Arnold*. Boulder: Colorado Associated Univ. Press, 1977.
Gruchy, Allan G. *Contemporary Economic Thought: The Contribution of Neo-Institutional Economics*. Clifton, N.J.: Augustus M. Kelley, 1972; London: Macmillan, 1973.
———. "Neoinstitutionalism and the Economics of Dissent." 3 *J. of Economic Issues* 3 (1969).
Günther, Eberhard. "German Policy toward the Market Conduct of Powerful Enterprises." 8 *J. of Reprints for Antitrust Law and Economics* 135 (1977).
———. *Probleme der Fusionskontrolle*. Köln: Carl Heymanns Verlag, 1970.
———. "Die Regelung des Wettbewerbes im Vertrag zur Grundung der Europäischen Wirtschaftsgemeinschaft." *WuW* 1957: 275.
Guzzardi, Walter. "Judges Discover the World of Economics." *Fortune* 5/21/79: 58.

Hadley, Arthur. *Railroad Transportation: Its History and Its Laws.* 1903 ed. New York: G. P. Putnam's Sons, 1903.

Hall, R. G. & Hitch, C. J. "Price Theory and Business Behaviour." 2 *Oxford Economic Papers* 12 (1939).

Hallstein, Walter. *Die Europäische Gemeinschaft.* Dusseldorf: Econ Verlag, 1979.

Handlin, Oscar & Handlin, Mary. *Commonwealth, A Study of the Role of Government in the American Economy: Massachusetts, 1744–1861.* New York: New York Univ. Press, 1947.

Harlan, Glen. "Airline Deregulation: Antitrust and Safety Considerations." 14 *The Forum* 1001 (1979).

Hawk, Barry. *United States, Common Market and International Antitrust: A Comparative Guide.* 2d ed. Englewood Cliffs, N.J.: Prentice-Hall Law & Business, 1987.

Hay, George & Daniel Kelley. "An Empirical Survey of Price Fixing Conspiracies." 17 *J. of Law & Economics* 13 (1974).

Hayek, F. A. *Individualism and Economic Order.* Chicago: Univ. of Chicago Press 1948.

Heilbroner, Robert L. *Economic Relevance: A Second Look.* Pacific Palisades, Calif.: Goodyear Publishing Co., 1976.

———. *The Economic Transformation of America.* New York: Harcourt Brace Jovanovich, 1977.

———. *The Worldly Philosophers.* Rev. ed. New York: Simon & Schuster, 1961.

Henderson, John. "The History of Thought in the Development of the Chicago Paradigm." 10 *J. of Economic Issues* 127 (1976).

Hendry, David. "Econometrics—Alchemy or Science?" 47 *Economica* 387 (1980).

Hicks, John. "The Birth of the Populist Party." IX *Minnesota History* 219 (1928).

Hidy, R. W. & M. E. Hidy. *Pioneering in Big Business, 1882–1911: History of the Standard Oil Company (New Jersey).* New York: Harper & Row, 1955.

Higgs, Robert. *The Transformation of the American Economy, 1865–1914: An Essay in Interpretation.* New York: John Wiley, 1971.

Hilton, Boyd. *Corn, Cash, Commerce.* Oxford: Oxford Univ. Press, 1977.

Hirsch, Eva & Abraham Hirsch. "The Heterodox Methodology of Two Chicago Economists." 9 *J. of Economic Issues* 645 (1975).

Hobsbawm, E. J. *The Age of Capital, 1848–1875.* New York: Charles Scribner's Sons, 1975.

Hofstadter, Richard. *The Age of Reform.* New York: Random House, 1955.

———. "What Happened to the Antitrust Movement?" in Cheit, Earl (ed.). *The Business Establishment.* New York: John Wiley, 1964.

Hollander, Jacob A. *David Ricardo, A Centenary Estimate.* 1910. New York: Augustus M. Kelley, 1968 repr.

———. "The Dawn of a Science," in Clark, John M. and Paul Douglas, Jacob Hollander, Glenn Morrow, Melchior Palyi, and Jacob Viner. *Adam Smith, 1776–1916.* 1926; New York: Augustus M. Kelley, 1966 repr.

———. "The Development of Ricardo's Theory of Value." 18 *Qtrly J. of Economics* 455 (1904).

Hollander, Samuel. *The Economics of David Ricardo.* Toronto: Univ. of Toronto Press, 1979.

———. "The Reception of Ricardian Economics." 29 *Oxford Economic Papers* 221 (1977).

Hollander, Stanley. "Theoretical Implications of Empirical Research on Retail Pricing." 47 *Am. Econ. Rev. (Proceedings)* 252 (1957).

Hoppmann, Erich. *Fusionskontrolle*. Tübingen: Mohr, 1972.

Hovenkamp, Herbert. "Antitrust Policy after Chicago." 84 *Mich. L. Rev.* 213 (1985).

Howey, R. S. *The Rise of the Marginal Utility School, 1870–1889*. Lawrence, Kans.: Univ. of Kansas Press, 1960.

Huber, Ernst R. *Wirtschaftsverwaltungsrecht*. Band I Tübingen: Mohr, 1953.

Hughes, Jonathon. *The Governmental Habit: Economic Controls from Colonial Times to the Present*. New York: Basic Books, 1977.

Isenbergh, Maxwell & Seymour Rubin. "Antitrust Enforcement through Consent Decrees." 53 *Harv. L. Rev.* 386 (1940).

Jackson, John. *World Trade and the Law of Gatt*. New York: Bobbs Merrill Co., 1969.

Jenks, Jeremiah. "The Development of the Whisky Trust." 4 *Political Science Qtrly* 297 (1889).

Joliet, Rene. *Monopolization and Abuse of Dominant Position*. The Hague: Martinus Nijhoff, 1970.

———. "National Anticompetitive Legislation and Community Law." in Hawk, Barry (ed.). *1988 Fordham Corporate Law Institute: European/American Antitrust and Trade Law*: 16–1. New York: Matthew Bender, 1989.

Josephson, Matthew. *The Politicos*. New York: Harcourt, Brace & World, 1938, 1966.

———. *The Robber Barons*. New York: Harcourt, Brace & World, 1934, 1962.

Kahn, Alfred. *The Economics of Regulation: Principles and Institutions*. New York: John Wiley, 1970.

———. "Economic Theory as a Guideline for Government Intervention and Control." 8 *J. of Economic Issues* 301 (1974).

Kaldor, Nicholas. "What Is Wrong with Economic Theory?" 89 *Qtrly J. of Economics* 347 (1975).

Kalodner, Andrea. "Consent Decrees as an Enforcement Device." 23 *Antitrust Bulletin* 277 (1978).

Kaplan, A.D.H., Joel Dirlam & Robert Lanzilloti. *Pricing in Big Business*. Washington, D.C.: The Brookings Institution, 1958.

Kapteyn, Paul & Verloven von Themaat. *Introduction to the Law of the European Communities*. London: Sweet & Maxwell, 1973.

Kauder, Emil. *A History of Marginal Utility Theory*. London: Oxford Univ. Press, 1965.

Kauper, Thomas. "Competition Policy and the Institutions of Antitrust." 23 *So. Dakota L. Rev.* 1 (1978).

———. "The 'Warren Court' and the Antitrust Laws: Of Economics, Populism and Cynicism." 67 *Mich. L. Rev.* 325 (1968).

Kaysen, Carl & Donald Turner. *Antitrust Policy*. Cambridge, Mass.: Harvard Univ. Press, 1959.

Kenneth, George & Joll, Caroline (eds.). *Competition Policy in the U.K. and the EEC*. Cambridge: Cambridge Univ. Press, 1975.

Kerr, Winfield. *John Sherman, His Life and Public Service*. Boston: Sherman French & Co., 1908.

Keynes, John M. *Essays in Biography*. London: Rupert Hart-Davis, 1951.

———. *The General Theory of Employment, Interest, and Money*. New York: Harcourt, Brace & World, 1935; 1964 ed.

Kintner, Earl W. (ed.). *The Legislative History of the Federal Antitrust Laws and Related Statutes*. New York: Chelsea House Publishers; London: Clark, Boardman, Company, 1978, 1980, 1982.

Kirchner, Christian. "Ökonomische Analyse des Rechts und Recht der Wettbewerbsbeschränkungen (Antitrust Law and Economics) Die americanische Discussion und Folgerungen für das deutsche Recht." 144 *Zeitschrift für die gesamte Handels-und Wirtschaftsrecht* 563 (1980).

Kirkland, Edward C. *Dream and Thought in the American Business Community, 1860–1900*. Chicago: I. Dee, 1956.

Kirkpatrick, Miles. *Report of the ABA Commission to Study the Federal Trade Commission*. Chicago: ABA Press, 1969.

———. *Report of the American Bar Association Section of Antitrust Law Special Committee to Study the Role of the Federal Trade Commission*. Washington, D.C.: Bureau of National Affairs, 1989.

Kitch, Edmund W. (ed.). "The Fire of Truth: A Rememberance of Law and Economics at Chicago, 1932–1970." 26 *J. of Law & Economics* 163 (1983).

Klaue, Siegfried, Heinz von Lampe, Kurt Markert, Horst Petry & Klaus Reiniger. *Zur Problematik der Fusionskontrolle*. Frankfurt: Atheneum, 1971.

Klein, Philip A. "American Institutionalism: Premature Death, Permanent Resurrection." 12 *J. of Economic Issues* 251 (1978).

Knauth, Oswald. *Business Practices, Trade Position, and Competition*. New York: Columbia Univ. Press, 1956.

———. *Managerial Enterprise*. New York: W. W. Norton & Co., 1948.

———. "Monopoly Reconsidered." 60 *Political Science Qrly* 563 (1945).

Knight, Frank. *On the History and Method of Economics*. Chicago: Univ. of Chicago Press, 1956.

———. "Immutable Law in Economics: Its Reality and Limitations." 36 *Am. Econ. Rev.* 93 (1946).

———. *Risk, Uncertainty and Profit*. 1921, 1957. New York: Augustus M. Kelley, 1964 repr.

Koback, James. "Three Approaches to the Bureaucratic Dilemma: The Administration and Enforcement of the Antitrust Laws of the United States, France, and the Common Market." 23 *Ala. L. Rev.* 43 (1970).

Kolko, Gabriel. *Railroads and Regulation, 1877–1916*. Princeton, N.J.: Princeton Univ. Press, 1965; New York: W. W. Norton & Co., 1970.

Koopmans, Tjalling. *Scientific Papers of Tjalling C. Koopmans*. Berlin: Springer-Verlag, 1970.

———. *Three Essays on the State of Economic Science*. New York: McGraw-Hill, 1957.

Korah, Valentine. *Competition Law of Britain and the Common Market*. 3d ed. The Hague: Martinus Nijhoff, 1982.

———. "Interpretation and Application of Article 86 of the Treaty of Rome:

Abuse of a Dominant Position within the Common Market." 53 *Notre Dame Lawyer* 768 (1978).
———. "Istituto Chemioterapico Italiano S.P.A. and International Solvents Corporation v. Commission of the European Communities." 11 *Common Market L. Rev.* 248 (1974).
Kristol, Irving. *Two Cheers for Capitalism*. New York: Basic Books, 1978.
Landreth, Harry. *History of Economic Theory: Scope, Method and Content*. Boston: Houghton Mifflin, 1976.
Lanzillotti, Robert. "Pricing Objectives in Large Companies." 48 *Am. Econ. Rev.* 921 (1958); Comments thereon in 49 ibid. 669.
Lavey, Warren & Dennis Carlton. "Economic Goals and Remedies of the AT&T Modified Judgment." 71 *Georgetown L. J.* 1497 (1983).
Lee, Frederic. "The Marginalist Controversy and the Demise of Full Cost Pricing." 18 *J. of Economic Issues* 1107 (1984).
———. "Whatever Happened to the Full Cost Pricing Principle (USA)?" in Wiles, Peter, & Routh, Guy (eds.). *Economics in Disarray*: 233. New York: Basil Blackwell, 1984.
Lekachman, Robert. *Economists at Bay*. New York: McGraw-Hill, 1976.
Le Rossignol, James E. *Monopolies Past and Present*. New York: T. Y. Crowell & Co., 1901.
Leontief, Wassily. "Theoretical Assumptions and Nonobserved Facts." 61 *Am. Econ. Rev.* 1 (1971).
Letwin, William. "Congress and the Sherman Antitrust Law: 1887–1890." 23 *Univ. of Chicago L. Rev.* 221 (1956).
———. "The English Common Law Concerning Monopolies." 21 *Univ. of Chicago L. Rev.* 355 (1954).
———. *Law and Economic Policy in America*. New York: Random House, 1965.
———. "The Origins of Antitrust Policy." 64 *J. of Pol. Econ.* 156 (1956).
———. *The Origins of Scientific Economics*. London: Methuen, 1963.
Levi, Edward. "Aaron Director and the Study of Law and Economics." 9 *J. of Law & Economics* 3 (1966).
Lichtenstein, Peter. Book review: Routh, Guy. "The Origin of Economic Ideas." 12 *J. of Economic Issues* 201 (1978).
Liebhafsky, Herbert H. *The Nature of Price Theory*. Rev. ed. Homewood, Ill.: Dorsey Press, 1968.
———. "Price Theory as Jurisprudence: Law and Economics, Chicago Style." 10 *J. of Economic Issues* 23 (1975).
Lipsey, R. G. & Lancaster, K. "The General Theory of the Second Best." *Review of Economic Studies* 24, No. 1:11 (1956).
Lipsey, Richard G. & Steiner, Peter. *Economics*. 4th ed. New York: Harper & Row, 1975.
Lipstein, Kurt. "Conflict of Laws before International Tribunals." 27 *Transactions of the Grotius Society* 142 (1942).
Lloyd, Henry D. "Lords of Industry." 138 *North American Rev.* 535 (June, 1884).
———. "Story of a Great Monopoly." 47 *Atlantic Monthly* 317 (March, 1881).
———. *Wealth against Commonwealth*. New York: Harper & Bros., 1894.
Locklin, David. *Economics of Transportation*. 7th ed. Homewood, Ill.: Richard D. Irwin, 1972.

Lovejoy, Wallace & Paul Homan. *Economic Aspects of Oil Conservation Regulation*. Baltimore: Johns Hopkins Univ. Press, 1967.

MacAvoy, Paul W. *The Crisis of the Regulatory Commissions*. New York: W. W. Norton & Co., 1970.

MacAvoy, Paul W. & Kenneth Robinson. "Winning by Losing: The AT&T Settlement and Its Impact on Telecommunications." 1 *Yale Journal on Regulation* 1 (1983).

Macdonald, I. A. "The Restrictive Practices Court: A Lawyer's View" 17 *Oxford Economic Papers, N.S.* 354 (1965).

Machlup, Fritz. "Marginal Analysis and Empirical Research." 36 *Am. Econ. Rev.* 519 (1946), reprinted in part in Backman, Jules. *Price Practices and Price Policies*: 132. New York: Ronald Press, 1953.

———. "Theories of the Firm: Marginalist, Behavioral and Managerial." 57 *Am. Econ. Rev.* 1 (1967).

———. *The Political Economy of Monopoly*. Baltimore: Johns Hopkins Univ. Press, 1952.

Malthus, Thomas Robert. *Definitions in Political Economy*. 1827. New York: Augustus M. Kelley, 1971 repr.

———. *Principles of Political Economy with a View to Their Practical Application*. 2d ed. 1836. Boston: Wells & Lilly; New York: Augustus M. Kelley, 1964 repr.

Marshall, Alfred. *Principles of Economics*. 9th ed. 1910. London: Macmillan and Co. 1961.

———. "Water as an Element of National Wealth." (1879), reprinted in Pigou, A. C. (ed.). *Memorials of Alfred Marshall*: 134. New York: Augustus M. Kelley, 1966 repr.

McAllister, Breck. "Where the Effect May Be to Substantially Lessen Competition or Tend to Create a Monopoly." *ABA Section of Antitrust Law* 124 (1953).

McCloskey, Donald N. *The Rhetoric of Economics*. Madison: Univ. of Wisconsin Press, 1985.

McGee, John. (See Goldschmid 1974: 102.)

McKinney, John. "Frank H. Knight and Chicago Libertarianism." 9 *J. of Economic Issues* 777 (1975).

McNulty, Paul. "Economic Theory and the Meaning of Competition." 75 *Qtrly J. of Political Economy* 639 (1968).

———. "A Note on the History of Perfect Competition." 75 *J. of Pol. Econ.* 395 (1967).

Manke, Richard. *Squeaking By: U.S. Energy Policy since the Embargo*. New York: Columbia Univ. Press, 1976.

Massell, Mark. *Competition and Monopoly*. Washington, D.C.: The Brookings Institution, 1962; Garden City, N.Y.: Doubleday, Anchor Books, 1964 repr. (without footnotes).

Mayhew, Anne. "A Reappraisal of the Causes of Farm Protest in the United States, 1870–1900." 32 *J. of Economic History* 464 (1972).

Means, Gardner. *The Corporate Revolution in America*. New York: Crowell-Collier, 1962.

Meek, Ronald. "The Case of the French Physiocrats," in Eagly, Robert (ed.)

Events, Ideology and Economic Theory. Detroit: Wayne State Univ. Press, 1968.

Melody, William. "The Marginal Utility of Marginal Analysis in Public Policy Formulation." 8 *J. of Economic Issues* 287 (1974).

Meltzer, Bernard. "Aaron Director: A Personal Appreciation." 9 *J. of Law & Economics* 5 (1966).

Mill, John Stuart. *Principles of Political Economy with Some of Their Applications to Social Philosophy*. 1848, collected works. Toronto: Univ. of Toronto Press, 1963.

Miller, James C., III. "Interview." 53 *Antitrust L. J.* 5 (1984).

Mishan, Ezra. "The Folklore of the Market: An Inquiry into the Economic Doctrines of the Chicago School." 9 *J. of Economic Issues* 681 (1975).

Mitchell, Wesley. *The Backward Art of Spending Money*. New York: McGraw-Hill, 1937.

Peppin, John C. "Price Fixing Agreements under the Sherman Antitrust Law," 28 *Calif. L. Rev.* 297 and 667 (1940).

———. "The Prospects of Economics." Ibid., 344.

Montague, Gilbert. *The Rise and Progress of the Standard Oil Company*. New York: Harper & Bros., 1904; New York: Arno Press, 1973 repr.

Moody, John. *The Truth about the Trusts*. 1904. New York: Greenwood Press, 1968 repr.

Morison, Samuel E. & Commager, Henry S. *The Growth of the American Republic*. New York: Oxford University Press, 1950.

Morrow, Glenn. "Adam Smith: Moralist and Philosopher," in Clark, John M., Douglas, Paul, Jacob Hollander, Glenn Morrow, Melchior Palyi, and Jacob Viner. *Adam Smith, 1776–1926*. 1926. New York: Augustus M. Kelley, 1966 repr.

Mosley, Leonard. *Power Play: Oil in the Middle East*. New York: Random House, 1973.

Myers, M. L. "Adam Smith's Concept of Equilibrium." 10 *J. of Economic Issues* 560 (1976).

Myrdal, Gunnar. "Institutional Economics." 12 *J. of Economic Issues* 771 (1978).

Nader, Ralph, et al. *The Closed Enterprise System*. New York: Grossman Publishers, 1972.

National Bureau of Economic Research. *Cost Behavior and Price Policy*. New York: 1943.

Neal Report 1968. (See White House Task Force 1969.)

Neale, A. D. *The Antitrust Laws of the U.S.A.* 2d ed. Cambridge: Cambridge Univ. Press, 1970.

Neild, Robert. "The Wider World and Economic Methodology," in Wiles, Peter & Routh, Guy (eds.). *Economics in Disarray*: 37. New York: Basil Blackwell, 1984.

Nevins, Allan. *The Emergence of Modern America, 1865–1878*. New York: Macmillan, 1927.

———. *Study in Power: John D. Rockefeller, Industrialist and Philanthropist*. 2 vols. New York: Charles Scribner's Sons, 1953.

Nordin, J. A. "The Marginal Cost Controversy: A Reply." 14 *Economica* 134 (1947).

O'Brien, Denis P. *Whither Economics?* Univ. of Durham, Britain: Titus Wilson & Son, 1974.

Oppenheim, S. C. *Cases on Federal Antitrust Laws*. St. Paul: West Publishing Co., 1948.

———. "Federal Antitrust Legislation: Guideposts to a Revised National Antitrust Policy." 50 *Mich. L. Rev.* 1139 (1952).

Oser, Jacob & William Blanchfield. *The Evolution of Economic Thought*. 3d ed. New York: Harcourt Brace Jovanovich, 1975.

Paglin, Morton. *Malthus and Lauderdale*. 1961. Clifton, N.J.: Augustus M. Kelley, 1973 repr.

———. (ed.). Malthus, *Principles, supra*.

Pareto, Vilfredo. *Manual of Political Economy*. 1927 ed. New York: Augusts M. Kelley, 1971 repr.

Parsons, Donald & Edward Ray. "The United States Steel Consolidation: The Creation of Market Control." 18 *J. of Law & Economics* 181 (1975).

Pelzman, Sam. "The Effects of Automobile Safety Regulation." 83 *J. of Political Economy* 677 (1975).

———. *Regulation of Automobile Safety*. Washington, D.C.: The American Enterprise Institute for Policy Research, Evaluative Studies 26, 1975.

Peppin, John C. "Price Fixing Agreements under the Sherman Antitrust Law." 28 *Calif. L. Rev.* 297 and 667 (1940).

Peters, G. M. "Is the Third Time the Charm? A Comparison of the Government's Major Antitrust Settlements with AT&T This Century," 15 *Seton Hall L. Rev.* 252 (1985).

Petr, Jerry. "An Assault on the Citadel: Is a Constructive Synthesis Possible?" 18 *J. of Economic Issues* 589 (1984).

Pigou, A. C. "Empty Economic Boxes: A Reply." 32 *The Economic Journal* 458 (1922), repr. in Stigler, George, & Boulding, Kenneth (eds.). *Readings in Price Theory*: 131. Homewood, Ill.: Richard D. Irwin, 1952.

———. (ed.). *Memorials of Alfred Marshall*. 1925. New York: Augustus M. Kelley, 1966.

Polanyi, Karl. *The Great Transformation*. Boston: Beacon Books, 1944, 1957 repr.

———. *The Livelihood of Man*. New York: Academic Press, 1977; Book review. 15 *J. of Economic Issues* 229 (1981).

Pollack, Norman. *The Populist Response to Industrial America*. Cambridge, Mass.: Harvard Univ. Press, 1962.

Posner, Richard. *Antitrust Law*. Chicago: Univ. of Chicago Press, 1976.

———. "The Chicago School of Antitrust Analysis." 127 *Univ. of Pa. L. Rev.* 925 (1979).

———. *Economic Analysis of Law*. Boston: Little, Brown, 1977.

———. "A Movement Called Law and Economics Sways Legal Circles." *Wall Street Journal* 8/4/86: 1.

Pratten, Clifford. "The Manufacture of Pins." XVIII *J. of Economic Literature* 93–96 (1988).

Pribram, Karl. *A History of Economic Reasoning*. Baltimore: Johns Hopkins Univ. Press, 1983.

Quirk, James & Sapsonik, Rubin. *Introduction to General Equilibrium Theory and Welfare Economics*. New York: McGraw-Hill, 1968.

Rahl, James. "Common Market and European Antitrust Systems: An Overview." 40 *Antitrust L. J.* 765 (1971).

———. "Competition and Antitrust in American Economic Policy: Are There Useful Lessons for Europe?" 8 *Common Market L. Rev.* 284 (1971).

Raisch, Peter, Arno Solter, Wolfgang Kartte. *Fusionskontrolle-Für und Wider*. Stuttgart: Verlag W. Kohlhammer, 1970.

Rakowski, James. "The Theory of the Second Best and the Competitive Equilibrium Model." 14 *J. of Economic Issues* 197 (1980).

Ramrath, Stephan. *Die Überragende Marktstellung als Merkmal der Fusionskontrolle.* Köln: Carl Heymanns Verlag, 1978.

Recktenwald, Horst Klaus. *Adam Smith, Sein Leben und Sein Werk.* München: C. H. Becksche Verlagsbuchhandlung, 1976.

Reder, Melvin. "Chicago Economics: Permanence and Change." 20 *J. of Economic Literature* 1 (1982).

Report of the Attorney General's National Committee to Study the Antitrust Laws. Washington, D.C.: G.P.O., 1955.

Report to the President and the Attorney General of the National Commission for the Review of Antitrust Laws and Procedures. BNA Special Supplement No. 897, Jan. 2, 1979.

Reisman, D. A. *Adam Smith's Sociological Economics.* New York: Barnes & Noble (Div. of Harper and Row), London: Croom Helm Condon, 1976.

Rhinelander, Laurens. "The British Antitrust Laws." 40 *Antitrust L. J.* 827 (1971).

Ricardo, David. *Notes on Malthus' Principles of Political Economy.* Baltimore: Johns Hopkins Univ. Press, 1928.

———. *Principles of Political Economy and Taxation.* 3d ed. 1821. Homewood, Ill.: Richard D. Irwin, 1963.

Richardson, G. B. "The Theory of Restrictive Trade Practices." 17 *Oxford Economic Papers* 432 (1965).

Riesenfeld, Stefan. "The Protection of Competition." in Stein, Eric & Nicholson, Thomas. *American Enterprise in the Common Market: A Legal Profile.* vol. 2: 197. Ann Arbor: Univ. of Michigan Press, 1960.

Riesenkampff, Alexander. "The 1980 Amendment and Other Recent Developments in German Antitrust Law." 15 *The International Lawyer* 615 (1981).

Riesenkampff, Alexander & Joachaim Gres. *Law against Restraints of Competition.* Cologne: Verlag Dr. Otto Schmidt, 1977.

———. *Law against Restraints of Competition with 1980 Amendments.* Cologne: Verlag Dr. Otto Schmidt, 1980.

Ripley, William. *Trusts, Pools and Corporations.* Rev. ed. Boston: Ginn & Co., 1916.

Robbins, Lionel. *An Essay on the Nature and Significance of Economic Science.* London: Macmillan & Co., 1935 (rev. ed.).

———. *The Evolution of Modern Economic Theory and Other Papers on the History of Economic Thought.* London: Macmillan & Co., 1970.

Robertson, Dennis. "Those Empty Boxes," *The Economic Journal*, vol. xxxiv. 16 (1924); American Economic Ass'n. *Readings in Price Theory.* 145 (repr. 1952).

Robertson, Ross. *History of the American Economy.* 3d ed. New York: Harcourt Brace & World, 1973.

Robinson, Joan. *Contributions to Modern Economics.* Oxford: Basil Blackwell, 1978.

———. *The Economics of Imperfect Competition*. 2d ed. New York: St. Martin's Press, 1969.
———. *Economic Heresies*. New York: Basic Books, 1971.
———. *Exercises in Economic Analysis*. London: Macmillan & Co., 1960.
———. *What Are the Questions?* New York: M. E. Sharpe, 1981.
Robinson, Joan & John Eatwell. *An Introduction to Modern Economics*. Rev. ed. London: McGraw-Hill, 1974.
Robinson, Romney. "The Theory of Imperfect Markets Reconsidered." 12 *J. of Economic Issues* 871 (1978).
Rockefeller, John D. *Random Reminiscences of Men and Events*. 1909. New York: Arno Press, 1973.
Rogin, Leo. *The Meaning and Validity of Economic Theory*. Freeport, N.Y.: Books for Libraries Press, 1971.
Rotwein, Eugene. "Mathematical Economics: The Empirical View and an Appeal for Pluralism," in Krupp S. R. (ed.). *The Structure of Economic Science*: 102. Englewood Cliffs, N.J.: Prentice-Hall, 1966.
Rout, Lawrence. "Every Six Months, Certain Students Feel Rotten at the Core." *Wall Street Journal* 7/25/79: 1.
Routh, Guy. *The Origin of Economic Ideas*. New York: Vintage Books, 1977.
Rowe, Frederick M. "The Decline of Antitrust and the Delusions of Models: The Faustian Pact of Law and Economics." 72 *Geo. L. J.* 1511 (1984).
Rowe, J.W.F. *Markets and Men*. New York: Macmillan; Cambridge: Cambridge Univ. Press, 1936.
Rule, 57 *Antitrust L. J.* 257 (1988).
St. Clair, Oswald. *A Key to Ricardo*. New York: Augustus M. Kelley, 1957, 1965 repr.
Samspon, Anthony. *The Seven Sisters*. New York: Viking Press, 1975.
Samuels, Warren & Allen Schmid (eds.). *Law and Economics: An Institutional Perspective*. Boston: Martinus Nijhoff, 1981.
Samuelson, Paul. "Economic Theory and Mathematics—An Appraisal." in Stiglitz, Joseph E. (ed.). *The Collected Scientific Works of Paul A. Samuelson*. vol. 2: 1751. Cambridge, Mass.: M.I.T. Press, 1967.
———. *Economics*. 11th ed. Cambridge, Mass.: M.I.T. Press, 1980 ed.; 1976 ed.
———. "The Monopolistic Competition Revolution," in Stiglitz, *infra*, vol. 3: 131 (1967).
Satzky, Von Horst. "Neuregelung reiner Exportkartelle: Kritik am Regierungsentwurf einer 4, GWB-Novelle." *Betriebs-berater* 139 (1979).
Scherer, Frederick M. *Industrial Market Structure and Economic Performance*. 2d ed. Boston: Houghton Mifflin, 1980.
Schumpeter, Joseph A. *Business Cycles*. New York: McGraw-Hill, 1939; 1964 ed. (1 vol. abridged).
———. *Capitalism, Socialism and Democracy*. 3d ed. 1942. New York: Harper & Row, 1950.
———. *History of Economic Analysis*. New York: Oxford Univ. Press, 1954.
———. *Theory of Economic Development: An Inquiry into Profits, Capital, Credit, Interest and the Business Cycle*. Cambridge, Mass.: Harvard Univ. Press, 1912, 1934, 1935.
———. *Ten Great Economists*. New York: Oxford Univ. Press, 1951.

Schwartz, Bernard (ed.). *The Economic Regulation of Business and Industry*. vol. 1. New York: Chelsea House Publishers, 1973.
Schwartz, Louis. " 'Justice' and other Non-Economic Goals of Antitrust, " 127 *U. Pa. L. Rev.* 1076 (1979).
Seager, Henry & Charles Gulick. *Trust and Corporation Problems*. New York: Harper & Bros., 1929; repr. ed., 1973.
Shawcross, Lord. "Luncheon Address." 40 *Antitrust L. J.* 1007 (1971).
Shepard, Lawrence. "Cartelization of the California-Arizona Orange Industry, 1934–1981." 29 *J. of Law & Economics* 83 (1986).
Shepherd, William. *The Treatment of Market Power: Antitrust, Regulation, and Public Enterprise*. New York: Columbia Univ. Press, 1975.
Sherman, John. *John Sherman's Recollections of Forty Years in the House, Senate and Cabinet: An Autobiography*. Chicago: Werner Co., 1895.
Sherrard, Alfred. "Advertising, Product Variation, and the Limits of Economics." 59 *J. of Political Economy* 126 (1951).
Sherrill, Robert. *The Oil Follies of 1970–1980*. Garden City, N.Y.: Anchor Press/ Doubleday, 1983.
Simon, Herbert. *Administrative Behavior: A Study of Decision Making in Administrative Organization*. 3d ed. New York: Free Press, 1976.
Skinner, Andrew & Thomas Wilson (eds.). *Essays on Adam Smith*. Oxford: Clarendon Press, 1975.
Singer, Eugene. *Antitrust Economics: Selected Legal Cases and Economic Models*. Englewood Cliffs, N.J.: Prentice-Hall, 1968.
———. "Industrial Organization: Price Models and Public Policy." 60 *Am. Econ. Rev. (Pt. 2)* 90 (1970).
Smith, Adam. *An Inquiry into the Nature and Causes of the Wealth of Nations*. 1776. Chicago: Univ. of Chicago Press, 1976 repr.
———. *The Theory of Moral Sentiments*. 1759. Rapheal, D. D. & Macfie, A. L. (eds.). Oxford: Clarendon Press, 1976 repr.
Solo, Robert. "Neoclassical Economics in Perspective." 9 *J. of Economics Issues* 627 (1975).
Sosnick, Stephen. "A Critique of Concepts of Workable Competition." 72 *Qtrly J. of Economics* 380 (1958).
Spiegal, Henry. *The Growth of Economic Thought*. Rev. ed. Durham, N.C.: Duke Univ. Press, 1983.
Sraffa, Piero (ed.). *The Works and Correspondence of David Ricardo*. Cambridge: Cambridge Univ. Press for the Royal Economic Society, 1951, 1952.
———. "The Development of Utility Theory." 50 *J. of Pol. Econ.* 307 (1950).
———. "The Laws of Returns under Competitive Conditions." 36 *Economic Journal* 535 (1926).
Stahl, Klaus. "Missbrauchsaufsicht über marktbeherrschende Unternehmen." *WuW* 1980: 451 (1980).
Stanfield, J. R. "The Institutional Economics of Karl Polanyi." 14 *J. of Economic Issues* 593 (1980).
Steiner, Peter. *Mergers: Motives, Effects, Policies*. Ann Arbor: Univ. of Michigan Press, 1975, 1977.
Steppacher, Rolf, Brigirte Zogg-Walz & Herman Hartfeldt (eds.). *Economics in Institutional Perspective*. Lexington, Mass.: D.C. Heath & Co., 1977.

Stigler, George. "The Case against Big Business." *Fortune* 5/52: 123.
———. *The Citizen and the State*. Chicago: Univ. of Chicago Press, 1975.
———. "Comment on Workable Competition." 46 *Am. Econ. Rev. (Proceedings)* 505 (1956).
———. "The Development of Utility Theory," LVIII, *The Journal of Political Economy*, 373 (1950).
———. "Discussion." 53 *Am. Econ. Rev. (Proceedings)* 24 (1963).
———. *Essays in the History of Economics*. Chicago: Univ. of Chicago Press, 1965.
———. "The Economies of Scale." 1 *J. of Law & Economics* 54 (1958).
———. *Five Lectures on Economic Problems*. Freeport, N.Y.: Books for Libraries Press, 1949, 1969 repr.
———. "The Goals of Antitrust Policy." 57 *Am. Econ. Rev. (Proceedings)* 242 (1967): 65 *Columbia L. Rev.* 363 (1965).
———. "The Goals of Economic Policy." *J. of Law & Economics* 283 (1975).
———. "The Influence of Events and Policies on Economic Theory." 50 *Am. Econ. Rev. (Proceedings)* 36 (1960).
———. "Legislative Intent and the Policy of the Sherman Act." 9 *J. of Law and Economics* 7 (1966).
———. "Marshall's Principles after Guillebaud." 70 *J. of Pol. Econ.* 282 (1962).
———. "The Mathematical Method in Economics." in *Five Lectures on Economic Problems*: 37. Freeport, N.Y.: Books for Libraries Press, 1949, 1969 repr.
———. *The Organization of Industry*. Homewood, Ill.: Richard D. Irwin; Nobleton, Ontario: Irwin Dorsed, 1968.
———. "Perfect Competition Historically Contemplated." LVX *J. of Pol. Econ.* 1 (1957), reprinted in his *Essays in the History of Economics, supra*.
———. "The Politics of Political Economists." 73 *Qtrly J. of Economics* 522 (1959), reprinted in his *Essays in the History of Economics, supra*.
———. "Ricardo and the 93% Labor Theory of Value." 48 *Am. Econ. Rev.* 357 (1958).
———. *The Theory of Competitive Price*. 2d ed. New York: Macmillan, 1946.
———. *The Theory of Price*. 3d ed. New York: Macmillan, 1966.
Stigler, George & Boulding, Kenneth (eds.). *Readings in Price Theory*. Homewood, Ill.: Richard D. Irwin, 1952.
Stiglitz, G. (ed.). *The Collected Scientific Papers of Paul A. Samuelson*. 4 vols. Cambridge, Mass.: M.I.T. Press, 1966–1967.
Stocking, George W. *The Oil Industry and the Competitive System: A Study in Waste*. Boston: Houghton Mifflin, 1925.
Stocking, George W. & Watkins, Myron W. *Monopoly & Free Enterprise*. New York: Twentieth Century Fund, 1951.
Stone, Alan. *Economic Regulation and the Public Interest: The Federal Trade Commission in Theory and Practice*. Ithaca, N.Y.: Cornell Univ. Press, 1977.
Sullivan, Lawrence. Book review of Handler, Milton, and others. "Trade Regulation, Cases and Materials." 75 *Columbia L. Rev.* 1214 (1974).
Sutherland, A. "Economics in the Restrictive Practices Court. 17 *Oxford Economic Papers* 385 (1965).
Taft, William H. *The Anti-Trust Act and the Supreme Court*. New York: Harper & Bros., 1914.

Tarbell, Ida. *The History of the Standard Oil Company*. New York: W. W. Norton & Co., 1904; 1966 ed.
Taussig, Frank. *The Tariff History of the United States*. New York: Putnam, 1931.
Tawney, Richard H. *The Agricultural Problem in the Sixteenth Century*. 1912. New York: Harper & Row, 1967 repr.
Temple Lang, John. "Abuse of Dominant Positions in European Community Law, Present and Future: Some Aspects," in Hawk, Barry (ed.). *1978 Fordham Corporate Law Institute*: 25. New York: Matthew Bender, 1979.
———. "Community Antitrust Law and Government Measures Relating to Public and Privileged Enterprises: Article 90 EEC Treaty," in Hawk, Barry (ed.). *1984 Fordham Corporate Law Institute*: 543. New York: Matthew Bender, 1985.
———. "Monopolisation and the Definition of 'Abuse' of a Dominant Position under Article 86 EEC Treaty." 16 *Common Market L. Rev.* 345 (1979).
———. "Some Aspects of Abuse of Dominant Positions in European Community Antitrust Law." 3 *Fordham Int'l. L. Forum* 1 (1979).
Thirlby, G. F. "The Marginal Cost Controversy: A Note on Mr. Coase's Model." 14 *Economica* 48 (1947).
Thomson, Herbert. "Adam Smith's Philosophy of Science." 79 *Qtrly J. of Economics* 212 (1965).
Thorelli, Hans. *The Federal Antitrust Policy*. Baltimore: Johns Hopkins Univ. Press, 1955.
Thurow, Lester C. *Dangerous Currents*. New York: Random House, 1983.
Timberg, Sigmund. "Equitable Relief under the Sherman Act." *Univ. of Illinois L. Forum* 629 (1950).
———. "An International Antitrust Convention: A Proposal to Harmonize Conflicting National Policies towards Multi-National Corporations." 8 *J. of Int'l L. & Econ.* 157 (1973).
Toepke, Utz. *EEC Competition Law*. New York: John Wiley, 1982.
Tollison, Robert (ed.). *The Political Economy of Antitrust: Principal Paper by William Baxter*. Lexington, Mass.: Lexington Books, D. C. Heath & Co., 1980.
Tussing, Arlon & Connie Barlow. *The Natural Gas Industry: Evolution, Structure and Economics*. Cambridge, Mass.: Ballinger Publishing Co., 1984.
U.S. Industrial Commission. *Report on Trusts and Industrial Combinations*. Washington, D.C.: G.P.O., 1901.
Viner, Jacob. *Dumping: A Problem in International Trade*. 1923. New York: Augustus M. Kelley, 1966. repr.
———. "The Utility Concept in Value Theory and Its Critics." 33 *J. of Political Economy* 369 (1925).
von Kalinowski, Julian. *World Law of Competition Overview*. New York: Matthew Bender, 1986.
———. *World Law of Competition*. vol. B4 United Kingdom; vol. B5 Federal Republic of Germany. New York: Matthew Bender, 1987.
Von Neuman, John & Oskar Morgenstern. *Theory of Games and Economic Behavior*. Princeton, N.J.: Princeton Univ. Press, 1953.
Wagner, Susan. *The Federal Trade Commission*. New York: Praeger, 1971.
Walker, Albert. "The 'Unreasonable' Obiter Dicta of Chief Justice White in the Standard Oil Case: A Critical Review." *Moody's Magazine* 6/1911: 395–400.

Walker, Donald. "Clarence Ayres's Critique of Orthodox Economic Theory." 14 *J. of Economic Issues* 649 (1980).
Walras, Leon. *Elements of Pure Economics*. 1874. Trans. 1954. Philadelphia: Orion Editions, 1969 repr.
Ward, Benjamin. *What's Wrong with Economics?* New York: Basic Books, 1972.
Watkins, Myron. *Oil: Stabilization or Conservation?* New York: Harper & Row, 1937.
Watson, Donald. *Price Theory in Action*. 2d ed. New York: Houghton Mifflin, 1969.
———. *Price Theory and Its Uses*. New York: Houghton Mifflin, 1963.
Weiss, Leonard. "The Structure-Conduct-Performance Paradigm and Antitrust." 127 *Univ. of Pa. L. Rev.* 1104 (1979).
West, E. G. *Adam Smith: The Man and His Works*. New Rochelle, N.Y.: Arlington House, 1969; Indianapolis: Liberty Press, 1976.
———. "The Burdens of Monopoly: Classical versus Neoclassical." 44 *Southern Economic Journal* 829 (1978).
Weston, J. F. "Pricing Behavior of Large Firms." 10 *Western Economic J.* 1 (1972).
Whately, Richard. *Introductory Lectures on Political Economy*. 2d ed. 1832. London: Augustus M. Kelley, 1966 repr.
White House Task Force on Antitrust Policy: Report. CCH Trade Regulation Reporter Supp. to No. 415, May 26, 1969.
Wilberforce, Richard, Alan Campbell & Neil Ellis. *Law of Restrictive Trade Practices and Monopolies*. 2d ed. London: Sweet & Maxwell, 1966.
Wilbur, Charles & Robert Harrison. "The Methodological Basis of Institutional Economics: Pattern, Model, Storytelling, and Holism." 12 *J. of Economic Issues* 61 (1978).
Wiles, Peter, John D. *Price Cost and Output*. Oxford: Basil Blackwell, 1961.
Wiles, Peter & Routh, Guy (eds.). *Economics in Disarray*. New York: Basil Blackwell, 1984.
Williams, Philip. *The Emergence of the Theory of the Firm*. London: MacMillan, 1978; New York: St. Martin's Press, 1979.
Williamson, John. "Profit, Growth and Sales Maximization," 33 *Economica* 1 (1966).
Williamson, Oliver. "Introduction, Symposium on Antitrust and Economics." 127 *Univ. of Pa. L. Rev.* 918 (1979).
Wilson, James (ed.). *The Politics of Regulation*. New York: Basic Books, 1980.
Wilson, Thomas & Andrew Skinner. *The Market and the State: Essays in Honor of Adam Smith*. Oxford: Clarendon Press, 1976.
Winter, Sidney. "Satisficing, Selecting, and the Innovating Remnant." 85 *Qtrly J. of Econ.* 237 (1971).
Zimmerman, Erich. *Conservation in the Production of Petroleum*. New Haven, Conn.: Yale Univ. Press, 1957.
Zito, A. S. "Refusals to Deal: The Sherman Antitrust Act and the Right to Customer Selection." 14 *John Marshall L. Rev.* 353 (1981).

CONGRESSIONAL HEARINGS AND REPORTS

Sherman Act.
House Hearings: Committee on Manufactures (1888).

H. Rep. No. 3112, 50th Cong., 1st Sess. (July 30, 1888) and Appendices: Standard Oil; Sugar.
H. Rep. No. 4165, 50th Cong., 2d Sess. (March 2, 1889) and Appendices: Whisky; Cotton Bagging.
S. Rep. No. 829, 1st Sess. (May 1, 1890).
Kintner, Earl, *supra*.
Clayton and Federal Trade Commission Acts.
The numerous reports and debates are collected in Kintner, Earl, *supra*.

GENERAL REFERENCE WORKS

Encyclopedia of American Economic History. New York: Scribner's, 1980.
The Statistical History of the United States. Wattenberg, Ben J., ed. New York: Basic Books, 1976.

Index

ABOUT THE AUTHOR

DUDLEY H. CHAPMAN is an attorney in private practice in Washington, D.C. He has served in a variety of offices in the U.S. government, including the Office of the Counsel to the President, the Antitrust Division of the Department of Justice, and as Assistant Counsel to the 1969–1970 Cabinet Task Force on Oil Import Control.

A graduate of the University of Michigan Law School, where he taught for one year, he practiced law in New York and Brussels before coming to Washington, D.C.

www.ingramcontent.com/pod-product-compliance
Ingram Content Group UK Ltd.
Pitfield, Milton Keynes, MK11 3LW, UK
UKHW020800290926
15470UKWH00003B/876

9 780275 934781